WHY BELIEVE?
ANSWERS TO LIFE'S QUESTIONS

Michael Augros
Michael Barber
Christopher Blum
Tim Gray
Daniel McInerny
John Sehorn

VOLUME 1

Augustine Institute
Greenwood Village, Colorado
2019

Nihil Obstat: Tomas Fuerte, S.T.L*., Censor Librorum*
Imprimatur: Most Reverend Samuel J. Aquila, S.T.L., Archbishop of Denver, Denver, CO USA
February 26, 2019

Copyright © 2019 Augustine Institute. All rights reserved.

With the exception of short excerpts used in articles and critical reviews, no part of this work may be reproduced, transmitted, or stored in any form whatsoever, printed or electronic, without the prior permission of the publisher.

Some scripture verses contained herein are from the Catholic Edition of the Revised Standard Version of the Bible, copyright © 1965, 1966 by the Division of Christian Educators of the National Council of the Churches of Christ in the United States of America. Used by permission. All rights reserved.

English translation of the *Catechism of the Catholic Church* for the United States of America, copyright © 1994, United States Catholic Conference, Inc.—Libreria Editrice Vaticana. English translation of the *Catechism of the Catholic Church*: Modification from the Editio Typica copyright © 1997, United States Catholic Conference, Inc.—Libreria Editrice Vaticana

The Augustine Institute gratefully acknowledges the permission granted by Ignatius Press to adapt selections from two of their titles, both by Michael Augros, for use in chapters 4 through 6: *Who Designed the Designer?* and *The Immortal in You.*

Editors
Christopher Blum, General Editor
Tim Gray, Associate Editor
Daniel McInerny, Associate Editor

Contributing Authors
Michael Augros
Michael Barber
Christopher Blum
Daniel McInerny
John Sehorn

***Why Believe?* Staff**
Kathleen Blum, Editorial Consultant
Jonathan Brand, Editorial Consultant
Ben Dybas, Creative Director
Jane Myers, Graphic Design
Gina Warner, Managing Editor

Augustine Institute
6160 South Syracuse Way, Suite 310
Greenwood Village, CO 80111
Information: 303-937-4420
AugustineInstitute.org
FORMED.org/whybelieve
ISBN: 978-1-7321146-8-5

Printed in Canada

Contents

Chapter 1: Who Do You Say That I Am?   2

Chapter 2: The Drama of a Human Life   18

Chapter 3: Truth and Friendship   40

Chapter 4: More Than Science Can Say   58

Chapter 5: You Are More Than Your Brain   76

Chapter 6: Recognizing God's Existence   96

Chapter 7: Wisdom or the Will to Power?   112

Chapter 8: Creation   130

Chapter 9: Light to the Nations   148

Chapter 10: Jesus and the Fulfillment of the Scriptures   168

Chapter 11: The Crucified Lord of Glory   190

Chapter 12: The Bread of Life   210

Chapter 13: The Body of Christ   228

Chapter 14: He Who Hears You, Hears Me   246

Chapter 15: The Creed   264

CHAPTER 1

Who Do You Say That I Am?

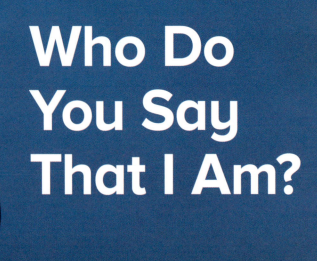

Who Do You Say That I Am?

An interesting episode once took place between Jesus and his disciples as they were walking from one town to another. In those days there were no automobiles, and Jesus did not use a horse or a mule for travel. So it meant good long walks for him and his picked men. These were ideal times for discussion, away from the bustle and distraction of large crowds. On this occasion, Jesus put a question to these close friends and followers. He asked them: "Who do people say that I am?" It was a provocative question. We are told of many things that Jesus said and did, and we can imagine the kind of impression he made, but we lack independent accounts of what people thought of him. Here we can get at least a glimpse of the word on the street. How did people see Jesus?

The disciples gave this answer: "Some say John the Baptist, others say Elijah, and others Jeremiah or one of the prophets." Their answer is what we might more or less have predicted. It meant on the one hand that people saw Jesus as someone very special. Elijah was a legendary prophet from the distant past who had worked miracles and had single-handedly battled pagan priests. Jeremiah was a great prophet who had sustained Israel during the difficult years of its exile and the destruction of the Temple. John the Baptist was a well-known figure, someone everyone had heard of and respected, and who had recently been martyred, a modern hero. To be compared to such noteworthy people was something out of the ordinary. It was not, however, surprising that people who had heard Jesus speak and witnessed the way he lived should have associated him with one of the prophets, since he looked and spoke like a prophet. In fact, the answer given two thousand years ago by the proverbial man on the street is pretty much the same answer that many people still give if they are asked about Jesus. He was a good man, a remarkable personality, and a great religious leader: one of a select category of spiritual giants.

Now when Jesus came into the district of Caesarea Philippi, he asked his disciples, "Who do men say that the Son of man is?" And they said, "Some say John the Baptist, others say Elijah, and others Jeremiah or one of the prophets." He said to them, "But who do you say that I am?" Simon Peter replied, "You are the Christ, the Son of the living God." And Jesus answered him, "Blessed are you, Simon Bar-Jona! For flesh and blood has not revealed this to you, but my Father who is in heaven. And I tell you, you are Peter, and on this rock I will build my Church, and the gates of Hades shall not prevail against it. I will give you the keys of the kingdom of heaven, and whatever you bind on earth shall be bound in heaven, and whatever you loose on earth shall be loosed in heaven."

Matthew 16:13–19

Yet Jesus did not stop there. Having heard the disciples' answers to the first question, he went on to ask another: "But who do you say that I am?" There is something subtle but important implied in this question. If Jesus had been satisfied that the first answer had hit the mark, he would not have needed to ask a second question. If he had thought: "Good; they have seen me truly, they understand me," he would have been content to let the matter rest. But he was evidently not satisfied with the answer. In effect, he said to his disciples: "Yes, I know what people in general are saying about me; but they see me only from a distance. They do not really know me. But you have been living with me day by day, listening to me, seeing how I live, growing in friendship with me. You know me much better. Are you content with that answer, or do you have something else to say? Who do you say that I am?"

Here Peter took the lead and responded with an unlikely answer. He said to Jesus: "You are the Christ, the Son of the Living God." We have so often heard Jesus described this way that we are no longer surprised by the declaration, so it can help to take a step back and consider carefully what Peter was saying. The first half of his answer was significant but not necessarily shocking. God had promised Israel that he would send a chosen person, descended from the kingly line of David, who would re-establish the kingdom of Israel and fulfill the promises God had made to their ancestors. The title "Christ" is the Greek word for the Hebrew "Messiah," which means "the anointed one." Peter was identifying Jesus as that promised person: "You are the Messiah." Important as this was, it was not at all outrageous. After all, someone was going to be the Messiah. Many Jews had thought that John the Baptist was the Messiah, and he had needed to tell them clearly that he was not. And there had been others claiming to be the Messiah who had led rebellions against the Romans. So, to think that Jesus was the promised Messiah was certainly plausible.

4   CHAPTER 1

Guido Reni, Christ Handing Saint Peter the Keys to Heaven, *c. 1624–6, oil on canvas, Louvre Museum, Paris, France.*

It was the second part of Peter's answer that was so astounding: "You are the Son of the Living God." To get a sense of the immensity of this claim, we can look at what some of the Jewish leaders thought of it. John's Gospel says that "this was why the Jews sought all the more to kill [Jesus], because he not only broke the Sabbath but also called God his Father, making himself equal with God" (Jn 5:18). Later, when the High Priests were bringing Jesus captive before Pontius Pilate to be condemned, they raised a similar complaint. Pilate was reluctant to do anything against Jesus because he did not see that any crime had been committed. The High Priests then levied this charge: "We have a law, and by that law he ought to die, because he has made himself the Son of God" (Jn 19:7). The Jewish authorities would not have condemned a man to death merely for claiming to be the Messiah. Claiming to be the Son of God was different. Why?

The key to understanding the Jewish position can be found in the concern that Jesus was "making himself equal with God." When Peter called Jesus the Son of God, he was not using that phrase in the general sort of way that could apply to anyone. There is a sense in which every person is a child of God, since God is everyone's creator and loves each of us. But Peter was insisting on something much more dramatic. He was claiming that Jesus was God himself in human form, that the eternal and immortal God was fully present in this man whom they had come to know. We can appreciate, then, why some among the Jews found the claim to be mind-boggling and unacceptable, and thought that Jesus was either entirely deluded or very dangerous.

How did Jesus respond to Peter's answer? In so many words, he said: "You are exactly right. I am the unique and eternal Son of God." What he actually said was, "Blessed are you, Simon Bar-Jona! For flesh and blood has not revealed this to you, but my Father who is in heaven" (Mt 16:17). The disciples had something of a history of getting things muddled; but this time, with some help from the Father, Peter answered rightly. Jesus then told Peter that this special gift of insight was to be the foundation of his service to the Church: "I tell you, you are Peter, and on this rock I will build my church, and the gates of Hades shall not prevail against it. I will give you the keys of the kingdom of heaven, and whatever you bind on earth shall be bound in heaven, and whatever you loose on earth shall be loosed in heaven" (Mt 16:18–19).

Niccolo Circignani, Christ the Redeemer in Glory with the Heavenly Host, *Fresco, Basilica di Santi Giovanni e Paolo, Rome, Italy.*

The question Jesus put to his disciples on the road that day is the same question faced by everyone: who do we say that Jesus is? The answer to that question will determine much about how we live, what we think important, and how we understand our own identity. If we answer the way the crowds did, that Jesus was a good man and an important religious leader, then Jesus will take his place among any number of such spiritual leaders and philosophers, and we can pay attention to him or not as the inclination takes us. But what if Jesus really is who he said he was? What if he really was the Divine Son of God walking among us in human form? What if he is the one through whom the whole world was created, and who has entered his creation for reasons of the utmost seriousness? What if he is the one who made us, who understands us completely and entirely, who has a plan and a destiny for us, and who has important things to say to us about who we are and how we should live? If that is the case, our whole attitude will be very different.

Every truth—if it really is truth—presents itself as universal, even if it is not the whole truth. If something is true, then it must be true for all people and at all times. Beyond this universality, however, people seek an absolute which might give to all their searching a meaning and an answer—something ultimate, which might serve as the ground of all things. In other words, they seek a final explanation, a supreme value, which refers to nothing beyond itself and which puts an end to all questioning. Hypotheses may fascinate, but they do not satisfy. Whether we admit it or not, there comes for everyone the moment when personal existence must be anchored to a truth recognized as final, a truth which confers a certitude no longer open to doubt.

St. John Paul II, *Fides et Ratio,* 27

Christians are people who have come to answer this question the way Peter did. They have come to believe that Jesus' astounding and thrilling claim is actually true: that he is the Christ, the Son of God. If they are right, if Jesus is who Christians say he is, then nothing that has ever happened or ever can happen is remotely as important as the appearance of God in human form. But if Jesus is not who Christians say he is, then, well, there is not much point in paying attention to him. If he is not the Son of God, he was at best confused and self-deluded, and at worst a charlatan, and we would be wasting our time on him.

So again, the question is posed: who do we say Jesus is? Answering that question is the point of this book.

Christians are people who have come to answer this question the way Peter did. They have come to believe that Jesus' astounding and thrilling claim is actually true: that he is the Christ, the Son of God.

Who Do You Say That I Am?   **7**

What is Faith?

Everyone knows that Christianity involves faith; it deals with things people believe. For example, the Apostles' Creed begins, "I believe in God, the Father Almighty." And Christians often use phrases like: "You gotta have faith." So, it is important as we begin our study together that we are clear about what we mean by faith. What is it, what are its defining marks, and what is the role it plays in understanding what is true about God and the world?

Human Faith

It may sound surprising, but faith is one of the main ways we come to know things. We all exercise faith every day, in many different ways. Without it we can hardly negotiate life. This rule applies not only to spiritual or religious people, but to everyone. Just how does it work?

There is a kind of knowledge that comes to us through our senses: things we see and hear, things that are tangibly present to us. We learn at an early age to trust our senses, even though they sometimes get things wrong. When we say that we know something is true, it often means that we have encountered it with our senses. I saw it; I heard it; I touched it. Seeing is believing. The experimental sciences like chemistry or geology are founded upon this kind of knowledge. There is another kind of knowledge that comes to us through the use of the laws of reason. We know that 2 + 2 = 4, or that a certain animal cannot be, at the same time, both a dog and not a dog, because the rules of thinking demand it. This sort of knowledge is the basis of subjects like mathematics and logic. So far so good. But these two ways of knowing are not sufficient for us to make our way through life. There are all kinds of things that we need to know the truth of, even though we do not encounter them with our senses or cannot logically prove them. Let us take some examples. When you buy food at a supermarket or a restaurant, you have no way to prove that the food is not poisoned, or that the people who run the business are not out to harm you. You need to count on their good will and their competence. When you step onto an airplane, you need to trust that the pilot is neither a hijacker nor a drunk. There is no way to prove it, and you cannot put it to an experimental test. Nonetheless, in each case, you have good grounds for believing. Your own previous experience, along with that of countless others, the existence of protocols and quality controls, perhaps your personal knowledge of the people involved, will give you the confidence you need to act upon what you believe. In other words, you are exercising faith.

A little thought will make clear that much, even most, of what we know and take for granted comes to us through the exercise of faith. This is true even of matters that might be experimentally verified. How many of us have ever been to the Fiji Islands? Yet we all know they are to be found in the South Pacific, because we have exercised faith in the people who have conveyed this information to us. Almost everything we learn in school, from science to history to geography, we take on faith. Even when we cannot immediately prove the truth of what we are learning, we still believe it, partly because it seems plausible and partly because we trust the people who are teaching us. The converse is also true: we tend not to think something is true when it seems highly implausible, or when our source has been shown to be untrustworthy. If you read in a reputable news source that the Queen of England is living in Buckingham Palace, you will likely believe it. It seems plausible, and the source is reliable. If you read in a questionable publication that Elvis is living on the dark side of the moon, you are unlikely to believe it. It seems implausible, to say the least, and the source is untrustworthy. In the two cases, the grounds for your belief differ. This kind of exercise of faith, of testing the grounds of what is presented to us and either believing or not on the basis of our assessment, is a daily human activity. We all do it, all the time.

Almost everything we learn in school, from science to history to geography, we take on faith.

Who Do You Say That I Am? 9

There are some matters—among the most important in life—that can never be simply proven by logic or experiment, and yet that we need to know. The most common example is our assessment of someone else's character. If we were to ask, how do we know that our parents really love us or that our friends are not secretly trying to take advantage of us? How can we be sure that we are not like the Baudelaire children, facing a crafty Count Olaf who only is pretending to care for us so that he can get his hands on our inheritance? The answer is, we exercise faith. We examine the grounds for trusting or mistrusting the character of those around us, and we either give or withdraw our trust on that basis.

Resolve to believe nothing, and you must prove your proofs and analyze your elements, sinking further and further, and finding in the lowest depth a lower deep, till you come to the broad bosom of skepticism. Life is for action. If we insist on proofs for everything, we shall never come to action: to act you must assume, and that assumption is faith.

Blessed John Henry Newman (1801–1890), "The Tamworth Reading Room" (1841)

This type of knowledge through faith is vitally important. Life presents us with a series of tasks and challenges, most of which require cooperation in order to be met with success. To cooperate with another person means that we need to trust him or her, and the weightier and riskier the endeavor, the more important that trust becomes. If we are picking sides for a soccer game, the level of trust required is pretty minimal. But what if we are choosing a spouse or considering someone as a partner in a business venture? Much of our happiness or success depends upon our assessment of the person's character. This is the drama at the heart of many works of great literature, from *Pride and Prejudice* and *War and Peace* to *The Lord of the Rings* and *The Odyssey*. One reason for the drama is that it is never a simple matter to arrive at a true assessment: our senses alone will not enable us to see into the depths of another person's soul. In the end, we must believe that the evidence we have about another's character gives us grounds for entrusting our happiness to this person, or else, unconvinced, for refusing to commit our trust.

Divine Faith

Faith, then, in its everyday, human exercise, involves things that we need to know, but that we cannot grasp by our senses or by the rules of logic alone. Christian faith, faith in God, works the same way. For example, in matters of human faith, we trust a person with a good reputation, someone known to be trustworthy. So also with divine faith. God has a good reputation; he has been spoken of as trustworthy by millions of people over thousands of years. Again: we put our human faith in people with a proven track record of helping others. So also with Christian faith: God has been a great benefactor of the human race, and multitudes of people have found him to be a constant source of help and goodness. Finally, we place human faith in people who are competent or powerful enough to help us. God certainly qualifies in those departments.

Another and even more important similarity between human and Christian faith is the way the act of faith opens the door to a meaningful relationship. When Frodo and the other frightened hobbits at the Prancing Pony put their trust in the mysterious ranger called Strider, they embarked on a great friendship and a series of adventures. Whenever we put our faith in another person, the possibility of a meaningful friendship and an adventurous partnership arises. We do not know at the outset where that adventure might take us or what the journey ahead will reveal about the character of our new friend. It is one of life's mysterious joys to find out. The benefits of this kind of faith can be enormous and life-changing. Whether it is a young Padawan who trusts her Jedi master, or the Karate Kid confiding himself to Mr. Miyagi or Mr. Han, the one who finds a trustworthy teacher or a faithful friend has discovered a treasure. We take a step of faith like this every time we begin another chapter of our lives and every time we entrust ourselves to another person.

In faith, Christ is not simply the one in whom we believe, the supreme manifestation of God's love; he is also the one with whom we are united precisely in order to believe. Faith does not merely gaze at Jesus, but sees things as Jesus himself sees them, with his own eyes: it is a participation in his way of seeing. In many areas in our lives we trust others who know more than we do. We trust the architect who builds our home, the pharmacist who gives us medicine for healing, the lawyer who defends us in court. We also need someone trustworthy and knowledgeable where God is concerned. Jesus, the Son of God, is the one who makes God known to us (cf. Jn 1:18). Christ's life, his way of knowing the Father and living in complete and constant relationship with him, opens up new and inviting vistas for human experience.

Francis, *Lumen Fidei*, 18.

So it is with Christian faith, only with more momentous consequences. The act of faith in God opens up the door to a relationship with him. It invites us into a profound friendship with the one who made us, with the one who beckons us forward into the great adventure he intends us to share with him. The Letter to the Hebrews states that faith is "the assurance of things hoped for" and "the conviction of things not seen" (Heb 11:1). Christian faith claims that God, who is eminently trustworthy, has desired to be in deep friendship with us and, in the context of that relationship of trust, has shown us things of paramount importance that we could not have known otherwise. The confidence that Christians have in God's goodness and their trust in his friendship provide the grounds for their conviction about "things not seen."

The act of faith in God opens up the door to a relationship with him.

Charles Poërson, Saint Peter Preaching in Jerusalem, 1642, Oil on canvas, Los Angeles County Museum of Art, Los Angeles, California, USA.

The Christian Task of Apologetics

The book is the text for an introductory course in apologetics. "Apologetics" means a defense, and its use by Christians goes back to St. Peter himself: "Always be prepared to make a defense [*apologia* in Greek] to any one who calls you to account for the hope that is in you, yet do it with gentleness and reverence" (1 Pet 3:15). This verse gives us important clues concerning the business of apologetics. The first is to see the proper context for engaging in apologetics. He did not say: "Defend your faith to everyone you meet, no matter who they are or what they are interested in." He supposed that people would be struck by the attractive quality of hope in Christians—the hope of blessings from a good God, the hope of healing, the hope of forgiveness of sins, the hope of eternal life—and that they would want to understand the basis of that hope. It is as if someone were to say: "We appreciate all these things that you are so confidently hopeful about, and we understand that they are good. Who would not hope for such things? But what grounds do you have for thinking them to be true?"

Making a defense in this case does not mean trying to prove the truth of the faith beyond any possible doubt. It does not mean jumping into a fierce argument and coming up with a way to win it. It does not mean scoring off other peoples' points of view. When St. Peter said that the defense should be done "with gentleness and reverence," this is partly what he meant. If someone were to ask us why we had a special affection for a close friend who had stood by us in a dark time, we would be eager to speak of our friend's fine qualities, to recount all he had done for us, and to recommend his friendship as good and beneficial. But we would not want to force the matter. So it is with Christian apologetics. Christians eagerly respond to those who inquire about their hope by saying: "You wish to know why we believe what we believe about God, what his friendship has meant for us, what we have learned from him, and why we are so happy about it all? We will gladly tell you. But it is for you to determine what to do about it."

Christians eagerly respond to those who inquire about their hope by saying: "You wish to know why we believe what we believe about God, what his friendship has meant for us, what we have learned from him, and why we are so happy about it all? We will gladly tell you."

The Point of This Book

The two volumes of *Why Believe?* have been written in the spirit of St. Peter's recommendation. They have been assembled by a team of Catholic scholars and educators—some of them converts, others life-long Catholics—who bring their different academic specializations and backgrounds to a joint venture. We want to help the serious inquirer appreciate the coherence, beauty, and nobility of the Catholic faith, and to see that faith for what it is: God's invitation to eternal life with him and with the whole company of heaven.

We live at a time when all kinds of voices are offering answers to life's most important questions. Rival gospels abound, each with its own set of promises and propositions. At the same time, questions about the Christian faith come from many quarters. In responding to this complex situation, the authors share a perspective summarized in 1989 by Pope Benedict XVI, then Joseph Cardinal Ratzinger: "We can give a meaningful answer to the questions raised [about the Christian faith] only if we do not permit ourselves to be drawn into the battle over details and are able instead to express the logic of the faith in its integrity, the good sense and reasonableness of its view of reality and life." This means that not all the possible issues and questions our time is posing will find their way into *Why Believe?* Nor should they, for the aim of *Why Believe?* is to help its readers achieve a synthetic understanding of the Catholic faith that will give them the resources to answer on their own many questions beyond the ones treated here.

The plan of *Why Believe?* is as follows. We begin in a philosophical mode, that is, by reflecting on our common experience as human beings. In chapters 2 and 3, we will consider our choices and our relationships as they relate to our Ultimate Good or happiness. In chapters 4 through 6, we will turn our attention to nature, asking whether our knowledge of the world around us enables us to conclude that we are different from the beasts and that God exists. In chapters 7 and 8, we will address two common opinions that are opposed to Christian faith: the claim that truth cannot be attained by human beings, and the notion that Darwin's theory of evolution contradicts the Bible's account of creation. The second half of our first volume turns to the properly theological, that is, to questions that can be answered only with the help of divine revelation. Chapters 9 through 14 offer a sustained examination of the question of revelation itself, but especially of Jesus as the fulfillment of the prophecies of the Old Testament, as the definitive revelation of God's love, and as the founder, bridegroom, and head of the Church. This volume's concluding chapter looks at the significance of the Creed recited at each Sunday Mass.

The second volume of *Why Believe?* treats the faith as a guide to a good life on earth that culminates in eternal life with God in heaven. After an initial chapter on God's mercy and our need for it, we will consider the varying and often confusing modern messages about the meaning of life and happiness. We will then carefully examine the view of the human person presupposed and confirmed by the Gospel. Along the way, we will explore such topics as the relation of body and soul, of emotions and reason, human sexuality, family life, the virtues, grace, and law. The final chapters of *Why Believe?* continue the examination of the Christian life with an inquiry into the Church, the offer of salvation that she makes to us, and her sacraments and the life of charity. We end by examining suffering, death, and eternal life, before turning to a final chapter on mission and discipleship. The goal of all this study and reflection is to grow in the knowledge and love of God.

To the Reader

We can envision, as you begin this book, that you might find yourself in one of three positions with regard to faith. You might consider yourself to be a serious Christian who has discovered the truth of God's love in Christ and is attempting to live by what you believe. Or you might have been brought up in the faith, baptized and even confirmed, but you are unsure what to make of it and how you stand toward it. Finally, you might have either never really known much about Christianity or the Catholic faith, or have distanced yourself from it; perhaps you do not consider yourself to be a Christian at all. This book is for you, whatever your current attitudes are toward Christ and the Church. At the very least, it will help you to grow in sympathy for others as you understand more clearly the nature and the claims of this faith that has been professed by so many and various people—young and old, rich and poor, men and women, educated and simple, from every culture in the world over the course of centuries—and has led many of them to leave everything behind in its pursuit, even to go gladly to their deaths in its defense. At best, it will be the discovery of the great adventure of your life. Our thoughts and our prayers are with you, as we make our defense for the great hope within us, and as we give our answer to that all-important question posed by Jesus: "Who do you say that I am?"

Review Questions

1. What was the significance of St. Peter's confession that Jesus is "the Son of the living God" (Mt 16:16)?

2. What is human faith? Why is it essential for everyday life?

3. How is Christian or divine faith similar to human faith?

4. What is the task of apologetics?

5. Why did St. Peter insist that the defense of the faith be accomplished with gentleness (1 Pet 3:15)?

6. What is the best context for the Christian believer's engagement in apologetics?

7. What do you think of St. Pope John Paul II's claim that "there comes for everyone the moment when personal existence must be anchored to a truth recognized as final, a truth which confers a certitude no longer open to doubt"? How would you argue in support of that claim against someone who sought to oppose it?

Put Out Into the Deep

For a beautiful meditation on faith in Christ, the encyclical letter *Lumen Fidei*, drafted by Benedict XVI and brought to completion and published by Pope Francis, would be a fitting complement to this chapter. The encyclical offers a guided tour of the discussion of the virtue of faith found in the *Catechism of the Catholic Church*, 142–184.

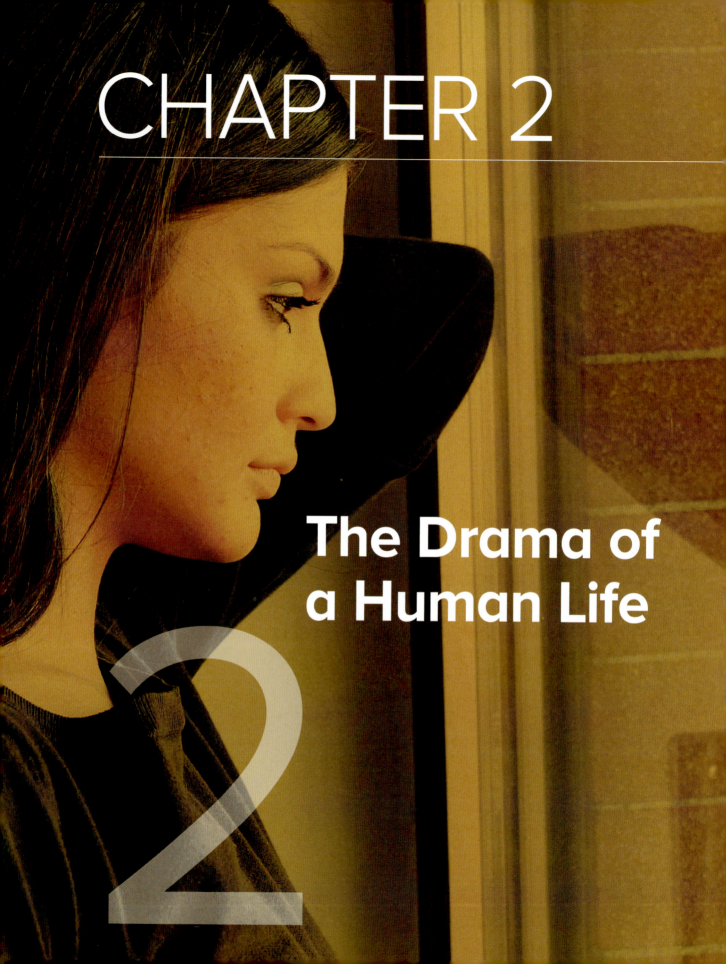

CHAPTER 2

The Drama of a Human Life

Their journey has been long, and they have lost more than one friend on the way. And now, the two hobbits, Frodo Baggins and Samwise Gamgee, led by the devious Gollum, find themselves climbing the seemingly endless Stairs of Cirith Ungol on the edge of Mordor. Their quest is to carry the One Ring to the only place where it can be destroyed: the volcanic fires of Mount Doom. When they volunteered for this quest, neither Frodo nor Sam could have envisioned how demanding the journey would be. The stairway they are on winds around a mountain, and with still far to climb they pause for rest in a dark crevice in the mountain rock. They eat and drink what they believe might be their last meal together, and as they rest Samwise becomes reflective:

> And we shouldn't be here at all, if we'd known more about it before we started. But I suppose it's often that way. The brave things in the old tales and songs, Mr. Frodo: adventures, as I used to call them. I used to think that they were things the wonderful folk in the stories went out and looked for, because they wanted them, because they were exciting and life was a bit dull....But that's not the way of it with the tales that really mattered, or the ones that stay in the mind. Folks seem to have been just landed in them, usually—their paths were laid that way....But I expect they had lots of chances, like us, of turning back, only they didn't....I wonder what sort of a tale we've fallen into?

The Drama of a Human Life

In this passage from J. R. R. Tolkien's *The Lord of the Rings*, Sam Gamgee initiates a fascinating train of thought: he begins to realize that the journey he and Frodo are on is comparable to the adventures he knows from the old tales and songs. Like the characters in those tales, Sam and Frodo have just "landed" in their adventure. Frodo, after all, did not ask for the One Ring, and he certainly did not ask for Sauron, lord of Mordor, to come looking for it. The two hobbits, Sam notices, like the characters in the stories they love, have also had chances to turn back. Yet they have struggled on, for they know that only by the destruction of the Ring can the world they have known and the people they have loved be saved. As they rest on the stairs, Sam and Frodo see their lives as a story, with its ending still unknown. Will it be a comedy, a story of happy fulfillment, or will it be a tragedy, a story of failure, death, and destruction?

We too may wonder what sort of a tale we have fallen into. Admittedly, we do not have a One Ring to destroy, but we are in the middle of our own adventures, adventures that we have in many ways just landed in, with chances of our own of giving up, and with the outcome of our stories still very much up in the air.

In this chapter, our aim is to understand how our lives—not this or that episode but our entire lives—take the form of a story, and how seeing our lives as stories helps us to find our place in the overarching story of the cosmos and achieve the happiness for which we long.

Objection: Life is No Story

Before we get started, however, we must face the objection that our lives do not much resemble the stories we love. Stories, after all, are artificial things constructed by novelists and screenwriters for our entertainment. Stories are precisely what life is not. Think about life for a moment: the alarm sounds, we get up, get dressed, swallow breakfast, head out to school or work, trudge through the day, go to practice, do homework, then get to bed for a few hours' sleep before we get up and do it all over again. That is life: repetitiveness and tedium and fatigue broken up by momentary bursts of fun. Life seems like anything but the exciting adventures we read about in novels or see at the movies. In fact, we may think that if our life is a movie, then we should like to have our money back.

20   CHAPTER 2

Think about life for a moment: the alarm sounds, we get up, get dressed, swallow breakfast, head out to school or work, trudge through the day, go to practice, do homework, then get to bed for a few hours' sleep before we get up and do it all over again.

There is certainly a point to this objection. A human life, if somehow written down or captured on film in its entirety, would indeed be far too long and full of inessential detail to capture our interest. When we read a biography of a famous person, much is left out, and thank goodness. Authors or screenwriters typically do not tell us what their subjects had for lunch every Wednesday afternoon, unless those Wednesday lunches are somehow relevant to the theme of the story they want to tell. Indeed, there is the rub. Biographies in book or script form are highly selective in just the way life is not. Some biopics, like Steven Spielberg's *Lincoln* and *The Post*, do not try to tell the entire life story of their subject. They focus on a defining episode of the subject's life, hoping to reveal the essential quality of the person. And this, so goes the objection, is precisely what makes stories different from human life. Whether based on real-life people or ones wholly imaginary, stories are made-up things, little mechanisms of selected and carefully-arranged detail about interesting people that somehow bring us delight.

What is a Story?

But wait. If stories involve selected and carefully-arranged detail about real or imagined people or even anthropomorphized creatures, then they must have some connection to human experience. If stories did not have anything to do with our lives, then their characters and conflicts and themes would fail to hold our attention. What, then, is the connection between stories and human life?

To answer this question, it would help to know what novelists and playwrights and screenwriters do when they create stories.

Begin by thinking of your favorite novel, short story, or movie. What is the most essential ingredient in the story? The most essential ingredient is a protagonist in passionate, even desperate, pursuit of a goal. What is a protagonist? While the usual definition of protagonist is the chief actor or main character of a story, the ancient Greek roots of this word reveal something more interesting. In ancient Greek, "protagonist" literally means "first competitor." The word, then, implies that a story essentially is a challenge, a trial, in which a character is put to the test. And what is the contest all about? Whether the protagonist will succeed in attaining the goal.

The Greek roots of the word protagonist also imply that another necessary ingredient of stories, besides the protagonist and his or her goal, is conflict.

This means that if a piece of writing does not feature a protagonist in pursuit of a goal, then it is not a story. It may be a character sketch, a piece of colorful description, an anecdote, even a joke. But it will not be a story.

The Greek roots of the word protagonist also imply that another necessary ingredient of stories, besides the protagonist and his or her goal, is conflict. Imagine if in *Star Wars* there were no Empire trying to stop the Rebellion from bringing freedom to the galaxy. Imagine if in *The Hunger Games* Katniss Everdeen did not have to deal with twenty-three other competitors fighting for survival. The principle is absolute: no conflict, no story.

A definition of story has begun to emerge. We might state it this way:

> *A story is an ordered sequence of events, with a beginning, a middle, and an end, in which a protagonist pursues a goal and, after a series of progressive complications (that is, conflicts), either succeeds or fails in attaining the goal, by his or her own efforts, not by chance.*

This definition further clarifies that conflict in a story must be progressive. In other words, circumstances for the protagonist must always get worse, until a final conflict (the climax) which decides the issue of the protagonist's pursuit of the goal once and for all. Important to notice in this definition, too, is that the protagonist's success or failure at achieving the goal must come about by his or her own choices, not by chance or luck. If ten minutes from the end of the original *Star Wars*, the Death Star had been destroyed by a chance meteor crashing through space, rather than by Luke Skywalker's heroic efforts, we would have finished the movie feeling let down, if not furious. We would have thought that we had not been given the story we had been promised.

The Drama of a Human Life

Life as Quest for the Ultimate Good

Does this definition of story apply to our own lives? Only if we can identify in our lives a protagonist, a "first competitor," in search of a goal.

It may seem hardly worth stating that we are the protagonists of our lives. But throughout history there have been those who have claimed that our lives are controlled, not by our choices, but instead by the gods, by fate, by material necessity, or by chance. Good drama, however, whether on stage, screen, the page, or in the events of our lives, assumes the free choices of the protagonist. When we delight in Jason Bourne outwitting his pursuers by some ingenious device or getaway, we are only admiring in Bourne what we admire in ourselves: the ability to deliberate among various options, judge which one of the options is best, and then choose and act upon that judgment.

As a protagonist, Jason Bourne has an identifiable goal: to survive long enough to discover who made him into an assassin. But when we consider our own lives, we may be hard-pressed to find such a clear, overriding goal. It is not that we lack goals. The issue, rather, is that we have so many of them. A typical day will find us in pursuit of a good grade on a test, tasty food for lunch, victory in a game, a chat with a friend, and sufficient hours of sleep. And these are only a few of the goals we pursue in a typical day. Does this mean that we are the protagonists of many stories, as many stories as we have goals?

That is one possibility. But consider another one. Notice that in everything we pursue—a grade, food, victory, friendship, sleep—we are pursuing something that is good. And what do we mean by "good"? We mean something that brings to perfection one of our human capabilities. The good grade is a sign that we have advanced in knowledge; nutritious food helps to maintain health; a chat with a friend helps to perfect our capability as a social being. In everything we do we are pursuing some good. And in light of this fact, the ancient Greek philosopher Aristotle (384–322 B.C.) made the following surprising argument. He said that if there were not some overarching good to our lives, some Best or Highest or Ultimate Good, then we would have no reason to pursue any good whatsoever. This is a powerful argument. Aristotle's point is that if there were not an Ultimate Good that served as the resting place of our desire, then our desire would not be motivated to search for any good at all, because desire for goodness, by definition, is not a quest for some partial good, but for that which will totally and completely satisfy our desire for goodness—which means that if the good in front of us does not bring ultimate satisfaction, then we will keep on looking until we find such a good. As long as we are seeking any good at all, then, we are implicitly seeking an Ultimate Good.

Clearly, it would matter a great deal to the plot-line of our lives if we could find out what this good is. Seeing it, we would be in possession of the goal for our strivings. We would better understand ourselves and the shape of the story we are living. How do we go about discovering it?

Aristotle said that if there were not some overarching good to our lives, some Best or Highest or Ultimate Good, then we would have no reason to pursue any good whatsoever.

The Drama of a Human Life

The Usual Suspects

As it happens, there is a name for this Ultimate Good, one that we all know and use frequently. Ask people for the simplest, most straightforward description of what they want most out of life, and you will quickly be told what it is: happiness.

Our culture is obsessed with the question of happiness. Yet at the same time, we human beings are notorious for disagreeing about what truly makes us happy. Some seek happiness in pleasure. Some seek it in family life. Some seek it in a successful career. Many seek it in some combination of these three.

In ancient and medieval philosophy and theology, it was customary for thinkers to begin inquiring into the nature of happiness by examining a list of the most popular candidates, what we might call the usual suspects. On this list were such goods as wealth, pleasure, honor, fame, and power.

There are reasons why the items on this list are so perennially popular. Each one of these goods makes a powerful claim for being the source of human happiness. How can we be happy if we have no wealth and sink into the depths of poverty? Pleasure, also, seems to be essential to the good life. Eating, drinking, sexual activity, even the comfortable feel of a favorite piece of clothing: these are real goods that bring to perfection some part of what it means to be human. Who, moreover, expects to be happy without possessing honor or a good reputation? And who does not think that utter powerlessness seriously diminishes our satisfaction with life?

And yet, there also seems to be something dangerous in taking any of these items for our Ultimate Good. Each one, while possessing some aspect of goodness, seems to undermine itself when taken for the highest and best good, as if it cannot bear the weight of the responsibility. Take wealth. We know that the Ultimate Good must be a good that is truly ultimate, that is, the final resting place of our desire, our total and complete satisfaction. If something is our complete satisfaction, it cannot be a means to some other good that is more desirable. Yet this is just what wealth is: a means to the possession of other goods that we consider more valuable. We do not value dollar bills and coins for their own sake, rather for their power to purchase the things we need and want.

26   CHAPTER 2

A consideration of the other goods usually suspected to be the source of happiness reveals similar fatal flaws. In one way or another, each fails to meet one or more of the basic requirements of human happiness. What are those requirements? Well, whatever else it is, happiness would seem to be:

- A good that we value for its own sake, that is, never as a means for the sake of some more valuable good;

- A good that is specific to our nature as embodied rational souls with a supernatural destiny (that is, not a good, like pleasure, that can also be enjoyed by lower animals);

- A good that, to a certain extent, we are able to achieve on our own (that is, independently of the good opinion of others, as is necessary with the goods of honor and reputation).

Before we go further in trying to identify the good that meets these requirements, let us consider two more candidates for happiness, candidates that for many today are even more attractive than those we have considered so far.

The Drama of a Human Life

The Grandeur and Poverty of Eros

In F. Scott Fitzgerald's novel, *The Great Gatsby*, the protagonist Jimmy Gatz arranges his entire existence so as to capture the heart of the woman of his youthful dreams, the now-married Daisy Buchanan. In doing so, he takes as his Ultimate Good a romantic relationship, but a romantic relationship conceived of in a particular way.

In order to win back Daisy, Gatz sets his sights on amassing enormous wealth, because it was his lack of money that had been the cause of his losing Daisy some years before. He thinks that his great wealth—ostentatiously displayed in his Long Island mansion, spectacular car, and outrageous parties—and the phony persona of "Jay Gatsby" will impress Daisy enough so that she will leave her husband and reunite with him. Gatsby's happiness, it should be clear, is not wealth itself. His wealth is only the means by which he hopes to impress Daisy. Neither is pleasure his ultimate goal. No doubt his desperate desire to win Daisy back involves physical passion, but Gatsby does not create his gaudy world merely for pleasure. For Gatsby, Daisy has assumed a stature far beyond that of an attractive physical object; indeed, she has become a kind of goddess for him. She is the Beloved for whom he, her slave, is willing to do or sacrifice anything. Thus Gatsby makes his money by illegally trafficking in liquor, and he covers up a crime in order to protect Daisy from the law.

In The Great Gatsby, *Jimmy Gatz arranges his entire existence to capture the heart of a woman. His happiness is not wealth itself. His wealth is only the means by which he hopes to impress her.*

28 CHAPTER 2

This romantic worshipping of another human being we will call, following the great Christian apologist C.S. Lewis (1898–1963), Eros, after the ancient Greek goddess of love. The word Eros nicely captures both the erotic, sexual aspect of a desire like Gatsby's, as well as the quasi-religious devotion he has for Daisy. For Gatsby, and for many in our culture, Eros is happiness in its highest and best sense.

Think, for example, of the lyrics of the songs on your favorite playlist. It is likely you will find some, perhaps many, that are singing in the voice of Eros. The slave (whether male or female) is either celebrating, pining for, or anticipating the attentions of the Beloved. In all such popular songs, the Beloved is a kind of deity the service of whom is the all-consuming passion of the lover. Eros, to be clear, goes far beyond plain romantic love. In Jane Austen's *Pride and Prejudice*, Elizabeth Bennet and Fitzwilliam Darcy fall in love and eventually marry, but their love, situated within the life of virtue, is far different from that of Eros. For in Eros the lover dreams of finding someone to worship, and, ideally, be worshipped by in return, and does not care what moral cost must be paid in the pursuit.

In Eros the lover dreams of finding someone to worship, and, ideally, be worshipped by in return, and does not care what moral cost must be paid in the pursuit.

As C.S. Lewis observes, the dream of Eros cannot help but turn into a nightmare. Why? Because no flawed human being can sustain being placed on such a pedestal. When one is consumed by Eros, the Beloved is without blemish or fault of any kind. The Beloved can do no wrong. Yet eventually, and inevitably, the real human being shows up with all his shortcomings, and the worshipful servant then is left with disillusionment and even vengeful resentment. In the life of Eros, what begins as a divinity often ends up as a demon from hell. Can you call to mind the lyrics of a popular love song in which the lover is revealed in full vindictive mode?

The Drama of a Human Life

Finding the Real You

In his well-known 2005 commencement address at Stanford University, Apple co-founder Steve Jobs made the following exhortation to the graduates:

> Your time is limited, so don't waste it living someone else's life. Don't be trapped by dogma, which is living with the results of other people's thinking. Don't let the noise of others' opinions drown out your own inner voice, heart, and intuition. They somehow already know what you truly want to become.

Who is not, at least to some extent, attracted to this ideal? Many if not most Americans, especially, seem to take living with this kind of authenticity as the deepest satisfaction available to human beings.

But there is also a serious limitation to the ideal. For who is to say what is the true, the genuine, life for a person? If it is her own inner voice, then it seems that she would be the sole judge of truth for her life. Such a person would not only be the protagonist of her life, she would be its creator as well. What, then, would stop her from creating a life that is selfish, or self-destructive, or harmful to the good of others?

For who is to say what is the true, the genuine, life for a person? If it is her own inner voice, then it seems that she would be the sole judge of truth for her life.

Many defenders of the ideal of authenticity, however, would reasonably claim that no authentic human life can be lived in selfish, self-destructive, or harmful ways. They would argue that we are made to live in healthy relationship with ourselves and with others. For who would want a life without physical, emotional, and spiritual growth, without friendship, community, and love?

The problem is that different people give different accounts of what it means to enjoy emotional and spiritual health. Steve Jobs claimed that it demands the rejection of dogma in the name of authenticity. A Catholic believer, however, would argue that authenticity is rooted in reality and that the truths about God and humanity taught by the Catholic faith—the Church's dogmas—are reality's bedrock. So, many would claim that sex outside of marriage is an authentic expression of love, whereas Catholics would point to the widespread suffering occasioned by promiscuity as a sign that this view is unrealistic. Who then decides? If it all comes down to individual preference, then the ideal of authenticity is nothing more than a kind of power, an assertion of one's own vision of the best life against that of others. And if that is our situation, what prospect do we have of enjoying the goods of cooperation, friendship, and love?

The Plot Outline of Our Lives

We can now add two more requirements to those we have discovered so far. Because both Eros and the ideal of authenticity fail in delivering ultimate satisfaction, we can discern that whatever else happiness is, it is:

- A good that is so perfect that it can never disappoint us;

- A good that allows us to live the life we are meant to live but which is more than merely our personal preference or the result of our cultural formation.

These requirements, added to the three we have already noted, give us a first sketch, call it a plot outline, for the story of our lives. Yet it is too incomplete to guide us. We still need to know what good could possibly meet all of these requirements? What good allows us to experience real happiness?

The Catholic Church has long followed the lead of ancient philosophy in calling rational activity, or living the truth, the life of virtue.

Acting Like a Human Being

Recall that one of the requirements of happiness is that it must have something to do with our nature as rational animals. To paraphrase a thought of Aristotle, acting rationally is the function of human beings; it is what we are made to do. And when we act as we are made to do, this activity satisfies all the conditions of happiness we have listed. Acting rationally (1) is activity most of all pursued for its own sake and not as a means to something else; (2) puts us in control of our lives as much as that is possible; (3) never disappoints us; and, finally, (4) assures us of living the authentic life we are meant to live.

Put generally as acting rationally, however, happiness does not sound terribly exciting. But it is exciting, once we take a closer look at what acting rationally really means.

To live according to one's rational nature means to live in the truth, and we human beings live in the truth in two fundamental ways: first, when we use our minds to grasp and behold truth, and second, when we put the truth into action. We live in the truth in the first way whenever we think deeply (as we are doing now) about what it means to live a human life; whenever we read a work of great literature and are swept away by the truths embodied by the characters and their conflicts; whenever we think about whether a certain act is just or not; whenever we grasp a principle of mechanical or chemical engineering; whenever we learn how to take and edit digital photographs; in other words, whenever we use our minds to gain access to the reality around us.

We also live in the truth whenever we put the truth into action by doing good deeds and forming our moral character. When we take that principle of mechanical engineering and use it to build a structure that will serve our community; when we take that principle of justice and struggle to see it embodied in public policy; when we take our knowledge of digital photography and go out and shoot a beautiful movie: these are all ways in which we put the truth into action in our lives and so achieve a measure of happiness.

We live in the truth whenever we put the truth into action by doing good deeds and forming our moral character.

The Catholic Church has long followed the lead of ancient philosophy in calling rational activity, or living the truth, the life of virtue. Our English word virtue ultimately stems from an ancient Greek word meaning "excellence." To be virtuous is to bring to excellence, that is, to perfection, one or another aspect of our rational nature. Happiness, in short, simply is virtuous activity.

The Drama of a Human Life

But hold on, you may be thinking. What happened to love in all this? Happiness understood as "rational activity" or "living the truth" or "the virtuous life" still sounds too brainy to be the source of ultimate satisfaction.

Be not afraid. Love is right there in rational activity. As long as we understand that love is not essentially emotion but an act of the will—which is to say an act of the appetite of reason—then we can understand that to live in the truth means to love and find joy both in the discovery and beholding of the truth and in the putting of that truth into action. Love and truth always come bound up together. This is a theme we will be exploring further in our next chapter.

The Degrees of Happiness

For now, let us return to the thought of our lives as a story. We are in position at last to see the full dramatic arc of a human life. It is, as perhaps all stories are, a quest, a search for happiness understood as living the truth in love. God is the ultimate author of this story, not us.

A human life well-lived is a quest that leads to ever more perfect degrees of happiness. The more we live according to truth and love, the more purified and satisfying our happiness becomes. The first degree of happiness is experienced when we live the virtues in regard to practical affairs: in our friendships, our studies, our marriages, our parenting, our business enterprises, our political action. Although our daily bread in this life is the happiness we find in practical affairs, a deeper experience of happiness is available to us when with admiration and love we gaze upon the truths revealed to us by God. This contemplative happiness is

A human life well-lived is a quest that leads to ever more perfect degrees of happiness.

more perfect because it is not essentially a function of the body but of the intellect, and thus is free from the things that come to be and pass away. Contemplation in this life, however, as the act of an embodied being, must always be fitful. Perfect contemplation, and thus perfect happiness, can only be experienced in the next life, in that perfect union with Truth and Love in which we behold God face to face.

"We look not to the things that are seen but to the things that are unseen; for the things that are seen are transient, but the things that are unseen are eternal" (2 Cor 4:18).

Our Personal Chapters

In the passage from Tolkien's *The Lord of the Rings* with which we began, Sam Gamgee realizes that the magical star-glass given to Frodo by the Lady Galadriel contains some of the light of the great jewel, the Silmaril, that is told of in one of the old tales of the hero Beren. "Why, to think of it," says Sam, "we're in the same tale still!"

So far, we have been considering the main contours of the story in which every human being has a role: the quest for happiness, that virtuous life in truth and love, that leads to perfect union with God in Heaven. But Sam Gamgee's insight must also be our own: our individual stories are only chapters in the overarching story of God's providential history of the world. We are living in the same tale that goes back to the very foundation of the cosmos, carrying in the magical star-glass of our hearts the light that shines forth from the face of God.

Our personal chapter, however, will contain much that is unrepeatable, special to our own adventure. Our individual story will include the mission, the primary vocation, that God has invited us to follow. It will include our family, our childhood and adolescence, our relationships with our siblings and friends and co-workers, our education, our employment, our successes, defeats, and sins as well as acts of faith, hope, and charity. We will be the hero or heroine of our own chapter, but only a bit player in someone else's. Our closest friends and loved ones will know much of our story, but only God will plumb all the secret treasures of our hearts as we venture toward him.

To return to a point made at the outset, it may seem that much of what goes on in our lives is not relevant even to our personal stories: waiting for the bus, looking for car keys, the snack we enjoy before bedtime. But the opposite is in fact the case. Every human action that we perform, no matter how small, can be an act of virtue, and thus be an important part of our ever-deeper experience of happiness.

God, infinitely perfect and blessed in himself, in a plan of sheer goodness freely created man to make him share in his own blessed life....To accomplish this, when the fullness of time had come, God sent his Son as Redeemer and Savior. In his Son and through him, he invites men to become, in the Holy Spirit, his adopted children and thus heirs of his blessed life.

Catechism of the Catholic Church, 1

Death the Antagonist

As we saw in examining the essential elements of story, there is no such thing as a story without conflict. And all conflict in human life stems from the ultimate antagonist in our quest for happiness: death.

An antagonist is a person or force in a story that works against the protagonist's efforts: Iago to Othello, Voldemort to Harry Potter. And that antagonism is exactly what the phenomenon of death is, especially when we remember that St. Paul said that "the wages of sin is death" (Rom 6:23). Death is the consequence of our disobedience of God's commands. It is the penalty for refusing to play our part in the story God is writing with the cooperation of our choices, and instead endeavoring to write an alternate story in which we decide what the dramatic arc will be.

You have made us for yourself, and our hearts are restless until they rest in you.

St. Augustine, *Confessions* I.1

Every human protagonist has to do battle with death, both the little deaths that oppose us every day—such as ignorance, weakness, fatigue, lack of resources, lack of friends, political injustice—and that bodily death that confronts us at the climax of our lives, when it is ultimately decided whether or not we will stay true to our rational nature and the grace that God has given us.

From the point of view of faith, however, we do not do battle with death on our own. In fact, in the deepest sense the battle with death has already been fought and won by our Savior. Our task is to join our combat with his on the cross in order to give our struggle an ultimate value that can never be defeated. Even in the face of death, the believer in Christ can always hope in the Resurrection and thereby know that his or her life will always, no matter the hardships endured, turn out in the end to be what the Italian poet Dante Alighieri (1265–1321) called a divine comedy.

Questing with Friends

As Frodo and Samwise in *The Lord of the Rings* continue to reflect upon their lives as story, they begin to play with the idea of themselves as characters and of people reading about their adventures in the future. "And people will say," says Sam, "'Let's hear about Frodo and the Ring!'" To which Frodo responds: "But you've left out one of the chief characters: Samwise the stouthearted. 'I want to hear more about Sam, dad.... Frodo wouldn't have got far without Sam, would he, dad?'"

At more than one point in our discussion of the narrative structure of human life, we have touched on the importance of friendship. In speaking of death, we identified the lack of friends as one of the little deaths that mar our happiness. We also recognized that happiness in this life means, in part, living the virtues in friendship with others, and that the perfect happiness of Heaven is a union, a friendship, with God himself. It is impossible for us to imagine a happy life not accompanied by friends. Just as Frodo needed Sam, so we need our friends to help us in our quest for the Highest and Best Good.

For this reason, we must move from this discussion of happiness and virtue to a discussion, in our next chapter, of the nature of friendship and its relation to happiness. In deepening our understanding of what true friendship is, we will deepen our understanding of what it means to live the truth in love.

Review Questions

1. What is the objection that immediately presents itself to the claim that our lives take the form of stories?

2. What is story? Explain the definition offered within the chapter.

3. What is Aristotle's argument for the necessity of an Ultimate Good?

4. What must the characteristics of happiness be if it is to be our Ultimate Good?

5. Why are wealth, Eros, and authenticity each self-defeating if taken as our ultimate end?

6. What does it mean to live according to reason?

7. What is the significance of death within the storyline of our lives?

Put Out Into the Deep

If you have not yet experienced the delight of reading *The Lord of the Rings*, waste no time in finding a copy. If you have, we recommend a short story by J.R.R. Tolkien called "Leaf by Niggle," an imaginative tale of the kind only Tolkien could write that touches on the way seemingly ordinary aspects of life are transformed into great beauty and significance when seen from a true and ultimate perspective.

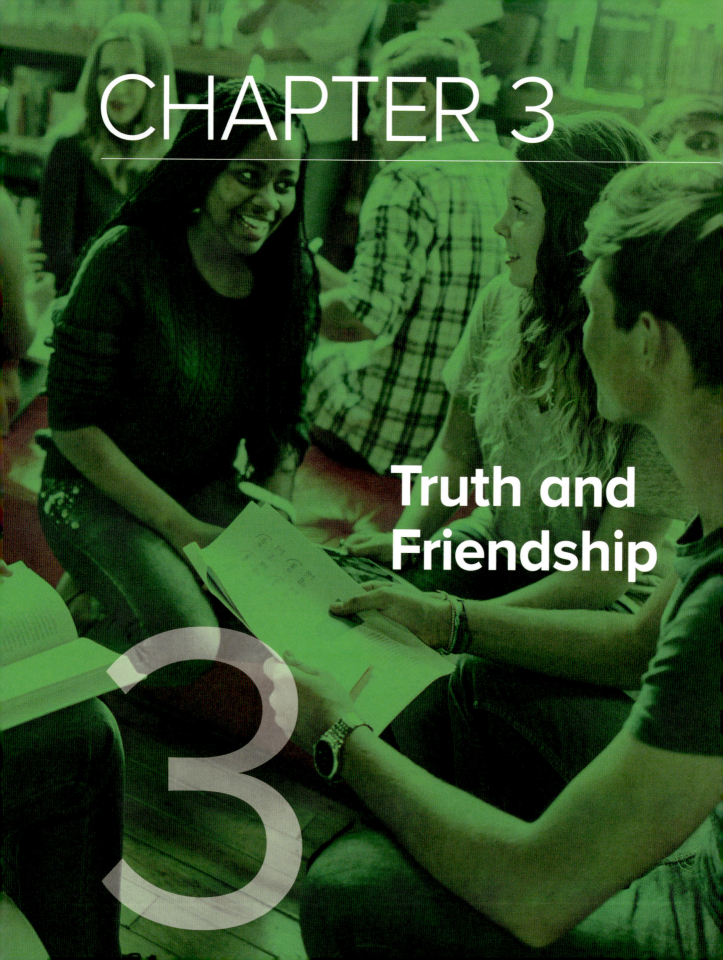

CHAPTER 3

Truth and Friendship

Most of you are reading this chapter during your high school years, and so the chances are that your life is full of the concerns of friendship. The reason is that this is the one period of life in which you will be part of an institution filled with hundreds, perhaps even thousands, of people exactly your own age who have remarkably similar backgrounds and experiences. In the classroom, on the athletic field, in clubs and other activities, you are daily engaged with large numbers of people pretty much just like yourself, and so it is natural that several if not many of these people will be among those you call friends.

But you are immersed in friendships today for another reason, and that is the easy availability of digital social media platforms that connect you to people, platforms for which the young have an undeniable affinity. A 2015 Pew Research Center study on internet use by teens came up with the following conclusions:

- 57% of teens claim to have made at least one new friend online, with 64% of these claiming to have met at least one new friend on a social media platform;

- 88% of teens claim to stay in touch with friends via text messaging at least occasionally, with 55% claiming to do so every day.

With good reason, then, Pope Francis has said that digital technology offers us "immense possibilities for encounter and solidarity" that are "truly good" and may be seen as "a gift from God."

The Holy Father's praise for social media, however, also came with an important observation, that "communication is ultimately a human rather than a technological achievement." We need to remember that there is a dark side to the pursuit of friendship through social media. The same 2015 Pew Research Center study found that 68% of teens claimed to have experienced negative interactions on social media platforms, and 26% claimed to have fought with a friend online. These statistics may not seem so surprising. Even before the advent of digital technology, adolescents doubtless experienced plenty of strife, including fights and break-ups. But more recent evidence regarding teen use of social media paints a darker picture still. A September 2017 article in the *Atlantic Monthly* by psychologist Jean Twenge, "Have Smartphones Destroyed a Generation?," argues that in 2012 a dramatic, unprecedented change began to occur in

Truth and Friendship   41

the behavior of adolescents. Why 2012? Because that was the year the number of Americans owning a smartphone surpassed the 50% mark.

The generation born between 1995 and 2012 is more saturated in digital technology than any earlier generation. Twenge cites as one example a 2017 survey of 5,000 American teens which discovered that 75% owned an iPhone. But it is not simply that your generation—the generation now beginning to be called the iGen—is using more digital technology than ever before. The problem, Twenge argues, is that the ubiquitous and excessive use of digital technology, in particular text messaging and social media platforms via the smartphone, distorts the meaning of friendship and negatively impacts teens' mental health. According to Twenge's research, today's teens go out less, date less, work for pay less, sleep less, and get their driver's licenses later than the Millennials and Generation Xers who preceded them. Happily, they also engage in less sexual activity, which has resulted in a drop in the teen pregnancy rate. But not so happy is the fact that instead of socializing with their friends out in "real life," teens today are more likely to be found behind the closed door of their bedrooms engaging in a social life through their smartphones. And this new habit is plainly hurting today's adolescents. Twenge cites a study which concluded that teens who spend more than the average amount of time on screen activities are more likely to be unhappy, while those who spend more time than average on non-screen activities are more likely to be happy. Increasingly, teens who spend large amounts of time pursuing their social lives through their smartphones are reporting how lonely and depressed they feel.

In considering the adolescent pursuit of friendship in contemporary American culture, we discover a startling paradox. Even as today's teens spend more and more time on devices designed to connect them to friends, they are in fact experiencing more and more loneliness and depression. There are many reasons for this contradictory situation, some of which have to do with dangers inherent to digital space. But the main reason for the paradox is that all of us, and not only adolescents, are living in a society that has lost sight of the real meaning of friendship. The aim of this chapter is to help rediscover what the true meaning of friendship is and how friendship contributes to our search for a happy life. Along the way we will see how friendship pursued primarily through social media tends to undermine itself.

Kinds of Love and Kinds of Friendship

Human beings are naturally social animals. There is no disputing it. Without having to be instructed or specially motivated we gravitate toward other human beings, seeking to converse with them, understand them, play with them, even allowing some to become intimate companions with us on our way through life. These last we call our friends. There can be many reasons why a certain individual does not have friends. Sometimes the fault belongs to others who fail to be friendly to him or her; sometimes the wound is self-inflicted. However the situation may come about, an individual without friends is like a plant without sufficient sunlight and nourishing soil. The nature within the lonely person lacks the appropriate conditions in which to flourish.

> O LORD, who shall sojourn in your tent? Who shall dwell on your holy mountain? He who walks blamelessly, and does what is right, and speaks truth from his heart; who does not slander with his tongue, and does no evil to his friend.
>
> Psalm 15:1–3

In his *Nicomachean Ethics*, Aristotle said that no one would choose to live without friends, even if he or she were able to possess all other goods. Obviously, friendship has some very close connection to happiness. But what is it? If happiness, as we discovered in chapter 2, is living the truth in love, or in other words, living the virtues, then we need to know how friendship fits with this definition. Is friendship one of the virtues, even the highest virtue? Is it a kind of love, and if so, then how does it differ from other kinds of love? And what is friendship's particular relationship to truth?

Let us begin to explore these questions by seeing what connection there is between friendship and love. Aristotle distinguished between three kinds of love, but we must be careful not to understand his use of "love" here as meaning exclusively romantic love. He meant something more like our word "desire," which can be directed as much at a good cup of coffee as at a human being. Aristotle said that we love, or desire, three types of things:

- useful things,
- pleasurable things,
- and those intrinsically good things which genuinely perfect us as human beings.

In speaking about "love," Aristotle means something more like our word "desire," which can be directed as much at a good cup of coffee as at a human being.

Each one of these objects of love can manifest itself in one of two ways. Usefulness can manifest itself in individual useful items, like a laptop or a car, but it can also manifest itself in relationships between persons. If someone takes her car to the shop because she needs new brakes and she is not able to install the brakes herself, that person and the mechanic are establishing a useful relationship with one another: the car-owner makes use of the mechanic's expertise and the mechanic makes use of the car-owner's need in order to earn some money. This useful relationship is a good thing, a "lovable" thing in the generic sense we are using of that word, and Aristotle even goes so far as to call such a relationship a friendship.

Pause for a moment and realize how much life is full of such relationships. A carpool, a driver's ed course, a summer job, a training course in CPR: these are all useful partnerships without which daily life would be impossible. "Still," you may ask, "isn't it a little much to call these relationships friendships? Most of the time when I take my car to the mechanic I don't even learn the mechanic's name!"

No one is saying that useful friendship is the highest and best kind of friendship, but insofar as it is a human relationship based upon a mutual love of the useful, we can call it, somewhat loosely, a friendship. Aristotle, in fact, qualified his affirmation of useful friendships by calling them "accidental" friendships. By accidental he did not mean that they occur by unhappy chance. Rather, he meant that they do not possess what is essential to friendship. This distinction tells us two things that are very important. First, it tells us that simply being in a partnership with someone, even one in which a great deal of time is spent in the company of the other person, is not what is essential to true friendship. A student might spend months working with a peer math tutor, for example, but if the tutor is no more to the student than a means of getting an A in a math class and ultimately into a good college, then something essential to friendship is missing. Out of a kind of social pressure the student and the tutor might even become connected with one another on social media, but this all by itself does not magically turn their useful partnership into a genuine friendship; it simply paints a veneer of closeness around a relationship that is not especially close at all.

A second important thing we learn from Aristotle's calling useful friendships only accidental is that self-interest is not of the essence of true friendship. In accidental friendships, we are more concerned with ourselves than with the other person. Someone taking her car to the mechanic is certainly happy to give the mechanic a chance to earn a living, but as soon as the mechanic does something seriously to impair his usefulness to the car-owner—by overcharging or proving himself inept—then the partnership typically ends. Concern for the mechanic's livelihood extends only so far as his usefulness to the car-owner, because the car-owner's self-interest is primary. Whatever else true friendship is, therefore, it must be a partnership based on something other than usefulness. It is not self-interested but rather concerned with the goods held in common by the two friends. Can partnerships based on the love of pleasure fulfill these criteria and thus qualify themselves as true friendships?

Friendships Founded on Pleasure

Consider some examples of what present themselves as friendships based upon pleasure. Joe enjoys sitting next to Jim in chemistry class because Jim's doodles of the teacher make the time pass quickly. A couple meets at a party and develops a romantic relationship involving sexual intimacy. (A Christian, to be sure, does not view as friendly a relationship that involves breaking the commandments; we acknowledge, however, that many today will use the word friendship to describe just such a liaison.) Here we have partnerships, and although in each there is a kind of using of the other, the point is the attainment of some pleasure. Such relationships may seem like true friendships. The mutuality involved in each, the shared activity, appears to be more substantial than that between the car-owner and the mechanic. Joe enjoys hanging out with Jim in a way he would not with his mechanic. Similarly, the romantic partners enjoy one another's company in a closeness we do not seek in useful friendships. Each of these partnerships seems more personal and more valuable for its own sake than the useful friendships considered earlier. Can we not call them true friendships?

Aristotle's position is clear: pleasurable friendships are just as accidental as useful friendships, because the point of the partnership is the pleasure the relationship gives, not the good of the other person. Pleasurable friendships, in other words, are self-interested, and the proof of this, so Aristotle argued, is that as soon as the pleasure disappears, such friendships rapidly dissolve.

Truth and Friendship   47

Behold, how good and pleasant it is when brothers dwell in unity! It is like the precious oil upon the head, running down upon the beard, upon the beard of Aaron, running down on the collar of his robes!

Psalm 133:1–2

If because of a failing grade Jim stops making wise cracks in class and concentrates on his notetaking, then Joe is going to look elsewhere for entertainment. And when a casual sexual partner starts demanding of the other partner something more than physical pleasure, that often spells the end of the relationship. Friendship might continue in either case, but if so it will be based on something more than pleasure.

Pleasurable friendships, like useful friendships, fail to meet the most important criterion of a true friendship: in these relationships the partners are not interested in the other for the other's own sake, but for their own self-interest. Aristotle claimed that friendships among young people are typically of this pleasurable kind, because the young are guided by their feelings, and when feelings are our only guide we tend to be self-interested.

Take a survey, now, of your own friendships. How many are focused exclusively on the enjoyment you get out of it? In making this survey do not think that having some pleasurable friendships is inherently wrong. It may not be a good idea for Joe to tune out of the chemistry lecture in order to joke around with Jim in the back of the room, but there is nothing wrong with the two boys enjoying some laughs at lunchtime. Their friendship might not go any deeper than that, but that does not constitute a moral failing on their part.

The snare of self-interest, however, is subtle and deceptive. Sometimes what we take to be a real friendship is merely some scheme of self-interest in disguise. A romantic relationship might begin with what feels to both partners like total focus on the other for the other's own sake. But then one partner starts acting unexpectedly. Interest in the relationship flags, and one or both partners are left with a broken heart. In many such break-ups, especially among the immature, what the hurt partner grieves is not so much the loss of the beloved but the pleasurable feelings that were once enjoyed in the presence of the beloved. But even in those romantic relationships defined by the Eros we talked about in chapter 2, when the lover takes the beloved as a kind of idol, it is really the clawing need to worship and be worshipped by another that characterizes the relationship, rather than attention to the other's good.

Today's social media platforms often help to mask the accidental nature of pleasurable friendships. While it may be possible for real friendship to find expression through social media, these platforms provide the illusion that those whom we "friend" or "follow" online are people about whom we care for their own sakes. There is often no significant communication of any kind between those connected via social networks, but only a mutual staring through the windows of one another's lives as we peer at one another's streams. But even when we do actually communicate with friends on social networks, it is often the dopamine rush that motivates the conversation rather than concern for the good of our friends. Dopamine is a neurochemical released in the brain whenever we experience a sense of gratification. And when we experience effortless gratification, such as when we interact online, we quickly become addicted to the rush of dopamine. The pleasures of social media, combined with its easy and constant accessibility, help to create real dopamine addictions. This is the reason why, as Twenge observes, many teens today sleep with their smartphones in bed with them or at least very close by. It also explains why social media is for many the last thing checked before going to sleep at night and the first thing checked upon waking. For many people, and not only the young, social media serves more like a drug or security blanket than it does a venue of real human interaction. What is wanted is the buzz of expressing oneself, of knowing what is happening, of not feeling like one is being left out, or at least of being jolted out of boredom. Yet the paradoxical result for many social media users is precisely that they do feel left out, that their lives do not measure up to the ones they are viewing online, and this, all too often, leads to loneliness and depression.

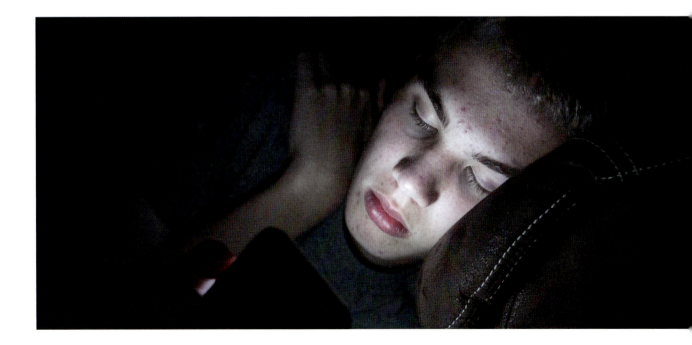

True Friends

Essential to true friendship is concern for the friend for the friend's own sake. In befriending someone beyond usefulness and pleasure we strive foremost for the other's good, not our own. And what does this mean, to want the good of the other? Keep in mind what we have learned about the meaning of good. The good is that which perfects, which fulfills, human nature. So, in wanting the good of our friends we want that which will perfect or fulfill them. We want their highest and best good. We want our friends to be happy.

Remember, too, that third type of love we distinguished at the outset: our love for those intrinsically good things which genuinely perfect us as human beings. Put briefly, this is the love of happiness or the life of virtue. Now, we can pursue the life of virtue independently of others, just as we can pursue something useful or pleasurable independently of others. But we can also pursue the virtuous life in partnership with a friend. What would such a pursuit look like?

In order to make the answer to this question as concrete as possible, let us take a look at virtuous friendship in the context of a story. It makes sense to do so, for as we learned in chapter 2, each of our lives takes the form of a story. But what is a story that gives us a clear picture of virtuous friendship? A popular one is Jane Austen's masterpiece *Pride and Prejudice*.

Jane Austen (1775–1817) was an English clergyman's daughter, whose otherwise quiet life in the country was enlivened by belonging to a large and energetic family with a wide acquaintance and gregarious habits. Based upon this rich human experience, she wrote six novels—including Sense & Sensibility *(1811),* Pride & Prejudice *(1813), and* Emma *(1815)—universally acknowledged as classics.*

The Friendship of Elizabeth Bennet and Fitzwilliam Darcy

Pride and Prejudice is a paradigm of romantic comedy. Set in England during the early years of the nineteenth century, the novel revolves around two young people, the witty and vivacious Elizabeth Bennet and the taciturn Fitzwilliam Darcy, who meet at a dance and immediately put one another off. Each possesses a certain pride as well as prejudice that finds the other repellant. Elizabeth believes that the prodigiously wealthy Darcy is a conceited snob, and Darcy thinks that Elizabeth, though attractive, is too low on the social scale to be a serious object of his attentions.

But as they keep meeting one another, Darcy cannot help but become more attracted to Elizabeth. Finally, he succumbs to his feelings and proposes marriage. Elizabeth rebuffs him, however, as it is clear in his proposal that he believes Elizabeth and her family to be beneath him.

Yet this is only the halfway point in the novel. In the second half of the story, events transpire that give Elizabeth a deeper understanding of Darcy's character. She learns from trustworthy sources that Darcy is a kind, generous, upright man, and that he was absolutely right in his assessment of the moral shortcomings of the dissolute George Wickham, whom Elizabeth had liked and defended. Unfortunately, she finds out the truth about Wickham the hard way, when Wickham runs off with her youngest sister Lydia—just as Elizabeth was beginning to think that all might not be over between herself and Darcy. Given the social scandal of Wickham's and Lydia's living together before marriage, Elizabeth fears that not only will her family's reputation be irreparably damaged, but also that Darcy will never want to speak to her again.

Then Elizabeth and her family receive unexpected news: Wickham's considerable debts have been paid and he and Lydia have been married in London. Who put up the money? And who persuaded them to marry? After a little investigating Elizabeth discovers that it was Darcy who went and found the couple's hideaway, paid Wickham's debts, and saw to it that Wickham made an honest woman of Lydia. When Elizabeth reveals to Darcy that she knows the secret of his generosity, Darcy responds that, while he wanted to help the Bennet family, his principal reason for acting as he did was his love for Elizabeth. This declaration paves the way in the climactic scene for a second proposal, and the comedy ends, as comedies should, with a happy marriage.

Both Elizabeth and Darcy undergo a moral transformation on their way to the altar. The characteristics of pride and prejudice each manifested at the beginning of the story are replaced at the end by burgeoning virtues of humility and that right practical judgment traditionally known as prudence. But what is most interesting about

Truth and Friendship   **51**

their respective character arcs is that Elizabeth and Darcy serve as one another's catalyst of change. It is Elizabeth's refusal of Darcy's first proposal—in particular her stinging rebuke that Darcy had failed to act in a gentlemanlike manner—that rouses Darcy from his conceited slumber, reminding him that only a virtuous man who places himself at the service of others deserves to win the heart of a woman like Elizabeth. And it is Darcy's letter to Elizabeth after this failed proposal, a letter in which he defends himself against Elizabeth's charge that he had mistreated Wickham by revealing the true story of Wickham's philandering and profligate ways, that opens Elizabeth's eyes to her own pride and lack of judgment. Each corrects the other, and while the corrections when first delivered were no doubt fueled by a bit of resentment, Elizabeth and Darcy's growing love for one another dissolves the resentment and allows the truth of the corrections to be received with humility and result in greater self-knowledge.

What we have in *Pride and Prejudice* is a love story, but it is not any old love story. Because the story of Elizabeth and Darcy is a story of growth in virtue, it escapes the trap of Eros that dooms, for example, Gatsby's pursuit of Daisy in Fitzgerald's novel. Elizabeth and Darcy have no interest in making idols of one another. Their passion is real, but they do not confuse that passion with the virtue that is essential to the happy life. And what allows them to escape that confusion is the fact that they learn how to be friends before they learn how to be married lovers. True friendship, we have learned, is seeking the genuine good of the other and not caving in to selfish interest. This is the lesson that Elizabeth and Darcy learn. Their pride and prejudice were like weeds growing out of an excessive focus on self. But when they humbly accepted critiques of their characters, each began to look for ways to be of service to the other's welfare, and the happy ending soon followed.

Because the story of Elizabeth and Darcy is a story of growth in virtue, it escapes the trap of Eros that dooms, for example, Gatsby's pursuit of Daisy in Fitzgerald's novel.

Friendship as Living the Truth in Love

We have defined virtue as living the truth in love. Friendship is one manifestation of virtue: it is the way virtue is lived out in selfless partnership with another. When Elizabeth Bennet and Fitzwilliam Darcy put aside their pride and prejudice and start putting the good of the other above self, they are exercising virtues of humility, generosity, and patience cooperatively.

Note well that virtue is living the truth in love. And so friendship, living the virtues in selfless partnership, is founded upon truth. Elizabeth and Darcy become friends and eventually spouses because each tells the truth about the other. Darcy was even more eager to propose to Elizabeth a second time because he knew that, as someone willing and able to tell him hard truths about himself, she was a far more valuable spouse than he had originally thought. Friendships in which the friends fail to tell the truth to one another cannot really be friendships. It is a question whether even useful or pleasurable friendships could exist for very long without the habit of truth-telling.

We might think that virtuous friendship sometimes demands keeping a vital truth from our friend. Joe might think it an act of generosity, for example, to spare Jim pain by not telling him that he is seriously ill. Or Joe, upon hearing Jenny disparaging Jim, might decide not to share this with Jim, once again to spare him pain. In the latter case, Jim is not owed the knowledge of what Jenny said, and is probably better off without it. In the former, however, while not absolutely obliged to tell Jim of his illness, there is a certain debt of friendship Joe owes to Jim when it comes to the most pressing issues in his life. Because Joe and Jim share a close friendship founded upon virtue, it is natural and good for Joe to share the news of a serious illness with his friend, though, if Jim is himself suffering from ill-health or some other serious misfortune, it might be wiser for Joe to refrain from doing so, at least for a time.

Friendship as a Common Good

Truth is a common good. This means it is a good that is neither exclusively mine nor exclusively yours, but ours. Think about a simple truth of addition: 2+2 = 4. The truth of this equation is not something that either of us possesses privately. Granted, the circumstances in which you learned this truth—perhaps it was Mrs. Jones's first grade math class—are particular to you, but the truth itself is in no way particular to you and your circumstances. 2 + 2 = 4 no matter who taught it to you, where you learned it, when you learned it, how you learned it, or even how well you remember it. This simple equation rises above the particularity of matter entirely. We need certain brain synapses to fire in order to think it, but the truth is not itself brain activity. All truth transcends the material. It belongs to the life of the intellect, which—as we will be exploring in detail in the chapters that follow—is part of our spiritual life as human beings.

As a common good, furthermore, truth is not diminished when it is shared. When it comes to a pizza, one person's portion decreases the more the pizza is shared with others. The same with other material things. But common goods like truth only come into being in partnerships and community, and so not only are they not diminished when they are shared, they actually increase in value. While it may be possible for a person beyond the age of reason to grasp simple truths of arithmetic without the aid of a teacher, most learning requires a teacher. And any teacher's knowledge, moreover, depends upon an entire tradition of teachers and learners who over time have built up a store of knowledge and methods of inquiry. No member of this community of inquirers possesses the truth as a private possession; the truth belongs to all of them together. Truth's very possession, in fact, depends upon the intellectual work of the community as a whole and increases the more the community works together to search for it.

From all this we can see why friendship and truth go so perfectly together. Virtuous friendship requires a foundation in truth, and the pursuit of truth requires virtuous friendship for its very being. As grounded in the love of truth, friendship itself is a common good. A friendship is neither mine nor yours but ours. It is a gift we hold in common, not diminished when it is shared but increased in the life friends spend together.

Sometimes our concern for the truth can put us in conflict with our friends. When young, Aristotle spent nearly twenty years as a student in Plato's Academy in Athens. But as he grew older, some of Aristotle's key philosophical ideas diverged from those of his master. Eventually, Aristotle left the Academy and founded his own school. In the Nicomachean Ethics *he explained his motivation to do so: when it comes to the truth and to one's friends, reverence is due to the truth first. The point of this statement is not that Aristotle wanted to become enemies with Plato because they had a philosophical disagreement. Rather, Aristotle meant that nothing, not even our goodwill toward close friends, should come between us and the highest of goods: truth.*

A Counter-Revolution

Our culture is getting lonelier and lonelier. Studies show the number of Americans reporting having no close friends has been rising, with "zero" now being a common response from people asked how many confidantes they have. Other research, meanwhile, has shown the negative impact loneliness has on mental and physical health, and that friendships safeguard health as much as quitting smoking and much more even than exercise.

There are many reasons for the increase of loneliness in our culture, but one of them surely is that we have lost the sense of what friendship really is and how it contributes to genuine happiness. Everyone has an instinctual sense that friends contribute greatly to happiness, but too many expect useful and pleasurable friendships to deliver the kind of satisfaction that only a virtuous friendship can provide. Because of their immersion in social media, today's teens have a particular challenge in keeping these distinctions straight. Certainly, social media can be a useful supplement to friendship. But social media also tempts its users to focus on pleasure, superficial connections, and comparison to, rather than service of, others. A counter-revolution to the digital revolution is now necessary, a revolution in which the participants put down their devices and take to the streets to begin the happy task of forging friendships rooted in a common love for truth.

Sanctify them in the truth; your word is truth. As you sent me into the world, so I have sent them into the world. And for their sake I consecrate myself, that they also may be consecrated in truth.

John 17:17–19

Review Questions

1. How would you describe your use of social media? Do you think social media enhances your friendships? Are there ways it inhibits true connection with your friends?

2. How do you see the use of social media leading to loneliness and depression?

3. Are you able to distinguish in your own life useful, pleasurable, and virtuous friendships?

4. What virtues do you see in play in your own friendships?

5. Can you think of an occasion when a friend helped you to grow in virtue? How did the friend approach the situation? How did you first react? What role did truth play in your growth?

6. In speaking of truth as a common good, Aristotle describes the virtuous friend as "another self." What do you make of that description? Do you count your best friends as "other selves?"

7. Do you agree that one of the keys to happiness is to have strong friendships anchored in a common love for truth? If so, then what practical steps can be taken to gain such friendships?

Put Out Into the Deep

If you have not read Jane Austen's *Pride and Prejudice*, a treasure awaits you. This is not "chick lit." Men and women enjoy it equally. And, despite its spoilers, the summary above will not have ruined the experience. The rich characters and the ironic, at times laugh-out-loud humor are sufficient to keep even the repeat reader satisfied time and time again. Highly recommended also is C.S. Lewis's *The Four Loves*, part of which focuses on the love that is friendship and offers valuable lessons in how to recognize it.

CHAPTER 4

More Than Science Can Say

4

We are heirs to a vast inheritance of truth bequeathed to us by generations of discoverers, and our lives have been marvelously enriched by the technological inventions of recent centuries. We are so awed by this accumulated learning that it can be hard to distinguish between what we know from our own experience and what we have been taught in classrooms and museums, or by books, websites, and documentaries. Tragically, many have forgotten that the quest for scientific understanding reposes upon a confidence in the intelligibility of the world that is rooted in our everyday experience and confirmed by the Jewish and Christian revelation that God gives order and beauty to creation. Some even claim that science overturns belief in God and defines what we can know about the world. It is of great importance for our examination of the claims of the Christian faith, therefore, to say something about the scope and the limits of science.

Modern science can say countless true things about the world and about you: about what sort of creature you are, how you and your parts work, where you came from. But the very success of modern science can tempt us to believe that its questions are the only questions, its answers the only answers, and that there is no more to say about you or the natural world than what it can say. Since the infancy of modern science, certain thinkers and writers have succumbed to this temptation and taken it upon themselves to tell us that science is simply the whole truth about us. The late historian of science William Provine, for example, said:

> Modern science directly implies that the world is organized strictly in accordance with mechanistic principles. There are no purposive principles whatsoever in nature. There are no gods and no designing forces that are rationally detectable. . . . Modern science directly implies that there are no inherent moral or ethical laws, no absolute guiding principles for human society. . . . When I die I shall rot and that is the end of me. There is no hope of life everlasting. . . . There is no ultimate meaning for humans.

If you do not differ from your nearest primate relatives in any sharp and significant way, it would be ridiculous to believe that a divine being (if such a being exists) would take any special interest in you.

There are plenty of people around today saying the same sorts of things. You do not have to read obscure books or journals to find them. You can just go to college (as long as it is not a particularly religious college). Or you can simply read the news. In an article in the *New York Times*, University of Washington psychology professor David Barash described how he kicks off every school year by giving his students what he calls "the Talk." The Talk is about how evolution and religion do not mix. The first clash comes with the existence of a divine being, as one might expect. Living things do not require a supernatural creator, he explains to his students, since life, though "wonderfully complex," is an "entirely mechanical phenomenon." Barash goes on to say that "no literally supernatural trait has ever been found in Homo sapiens; we are perfectly good animals, natural as can be and indistinguishable from the rest of the living world at the level of structure as well as physiological mechanism."

So the message is not new, but it is not going away either. And it is newly aggressive, pervasive, and persuasive. It is also rather bleak in outlook. According to it, you are in no way exceptional or spiritual. You are purely mortal, and just an animal—indeed, just a machine, no more than a temporary association of molecules that will one day disband in order to become other things. Great consequences attend this view of human nature. If you are thoroughly mortal, you will never possess perfect happiness or be reunited with lost loved ones. If you do not differ from your nearest primate relatives in any sharp and significant way, it would be ridiculous to believe that a divine being (if such a being exists) would take any special interest in you.

One possible recourse for those with religious beliefs running contrary to this stark message is to call into question the science upon which it is supposedly based. Evolution draws a good deal of fire, for example, both because its central tenets conflict with certain interpretations of Genesis and because it is not yet a fully worked-out science.

We will not take that approach, nor will we criticize it.

This chapter will simply explore another kind of response entirely to the idea that you are nothing but what modern science can say you are. Whatever deficiencies do or do not plague the current orthodoxies of evolutionary biology, a much broader and less noticed error underlies the thinking of those who would reduce you to your molecules. The error is the assumption that if you were somehow exceptional, if there were something immortal or spiritual in you, then modern biology would tell us all about it. But that is unreasonable. If you have an immortal soul, should you expect it to show up as a white spot somewhere on an X-ray or on a picture produced by an MRI scan? Should the trait of immortality be encoded somewhere in your genome? Of course not. Yet such are the tools and terms of biology. And they are quite excellent for their purposes, too. Only, they do not function very well as detectors of immortality or finders of souls, whether such things exist or not. To the degree that biology restricts itself to terminology that is fully reducible to that of chemistry and physics, its methods will be ill-suited to discovering whether you have a soul and what its nature might be.

All the data, vocabulary, principles, and methods of modern science, deep and far-reaching as these may be, are yet too narrow to include everything we can know about ourselves and the world of nature. Arriving at this conclusion with perfect clarity would require many books, and would even constitute an entire education in its own right. Considerably less time and effort is required in order to get some real sense that there is more to us and to nature than modern science can ever say. To catch a glimpse of that truth will be the purpose of this chapter and the two to follow; we will begin with three brief indications of it.

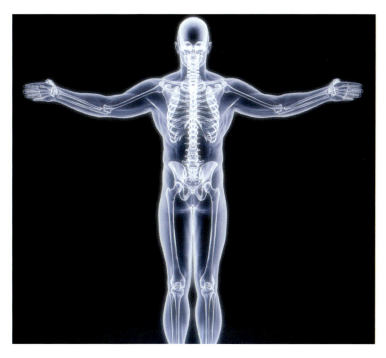

If you have an immortal soul, should you expect it to show up as a white spot somewhere on an X-ray or on a picture produced by an MRI scan?

More Than Science Can Say   61

More Than a Perfectly Good Animal

First, the idea that you stand at some unremarkable point along a continuum of animals, like a particular shade of gray somewhere between black and white, might not clash with any facts about the fossil record or your DNA, but it clashes pretty violently with any ordinary experience of you. The difference between chimp DNA and your DNA is relatively slight, and therefore wildly disproportional to the difference between chimp intelligence and yours. Imagine spending the rest of your days entirely in the company of chimps, never to see another human being as long as you live, and you will perceive the vast gulf separating human from chimp, even if you are unable to articulate the nature of that difference. When Hamlet wanted to express his disappointment in humanity, contrasting the greatness of what a human being can and should be with what human beings all too often are, he delivered his famous "What a piece of work is a man!" speech. Now imagine it slightly altered:

> *What a piece of work is a chimpanzee! how noble in reason! how infinite in faculty! in form and moving how express and admirable! in action how like an angel! in apprehension how like a god! the beauty of the world! the paragon of animals!*

If this lofty description strikes you as somehow true of human beings, but as a staggering impropriety in the case of chimps, then it simply cannot be the whole truth about us that we are no more than "perfectly good animals." Nor is this a display of egotism or species pride. It is an honest response to significant differences separating us from the other members of Animalia. Nor again is Shakespeare playing on our religious beliefs; he is appealing to an ordinary grasp of what a human being is. If modern science is blind to any radical differences between us and the beasts, that is not because there is no such difference, but because mainstream science, due to certain limitations in its methods and purposes, misses it.

A second indication that biology, chemistry, and physics cannot paint the complete picture of you comes right out of the words of those who say the opposite. If we say that you are made of atoms, or that you have and use a brain that obeys the laws of physics and chemistry, or that you are an animal, we will agree with what science says about you; but we will in no way be forced to deny that you are also something more—for example, that you are a being capable of moral choices, good and bad. If we go a step further and say that you are nothing but atoms, or that your actions are the products of nothing more than the laws of physics and chemistry, or that you are merely an animal, we are no longer just agreeing with what science says; we are adding negative claims besides, ones that science cannot in any way prove. More than that, once we add this "nothing but" to every positive thing that science says about you, we will be forced to draw some awkward conclusions about you—for instance, that you are not a moral entity. Right and wrong, just and unjust, and other such terms will become quite meaningless, or else names for illusions. Some materialist thinkers have tried to save morality by deriving it from natural impulses in us that natural selection supposedly fine-tuned to the benefit of our species.

Science cannot force us to deny that we are capable of moral choices.

But why should we obey these commandments of natural selection? And what would it mean for us to obey if we have no free will anyway? Provine and many others like him are much more clear-sighted. If you are nothing but an animal, or nothing but a collection of atoms, and certainly if you have no free will, there will be no objective measure or meaning to human goodness and wickedness. That is the true consequence, not of the scientist's, but of the materialist's picture of you. And that consequence is patently absurd. No one truly believes this doctrine, although many think they believe it, since it follows from other things they do believe. Who, besides rapists (and not even all

More Than Science Can Say　63

of them), believes that rape, in plain truth, is neither better nor worse than any other human behavior? When it comes to living their lives, materialists wish to act uprightly, expect to be treated fairly, and hope to see punished those who do injustices to them and their loved ones. They get righteously indignant about things. They think (or think they think) in one world, and live (and really think) in another one entirely. This intellectual schizophrenia is a symptom of a bad theory, the theory that you are nothing but molecules, nothing but neurons, nothing but an animal. It is reminiscent of the Greek philosopher Zeno's supposed refutations of the existence of motion, which were extremely clever, and yet even he could not have believed motion did not exist when he needed to go to the bathroom.

An indication that you are not just an animal is the very fact that you wonder or worry about whether you are just an animal.

A third indication that you are not just an animal is the very fact that you wonder or worry about whether you are just an animal. What other animal does that? There is at least that clear and significant difference between you and the rest of the species in the kingdom. You are also capable of grasping infinity in some way, since you can see that there is no such thing as a greatest number, and you can wonder whether the universe is finite or infinite in size. Unless we think animals contemplate the infinite, we must think that the human mind differs from the animal mind in some way as the infinite does from the finite. How this capacity of your mind could differ from animal intelligence merely in degree would be very difficult to say. Intellectually, you seem to be not only bigger and brighter than any other kind of animal, but superior to all of them put together, and in another class entirely.

Philosophy is like Breathing

In order to understand better these kinds of truths about ourselves, what methods ought we to employ? While the methods of modern science are indispensable for approaching many questions about ourselves, the methods of philosophy are more relevant to questions about our essential differences from animals and machines, about our moral nature, and about the possibility of our possessing immortal souls. Now in many circles, philosophy has a bad name. Sometimes it is roundly deserved. Some of the worst nonsense in the world is the sort of philosophy that would have you lose sleep over whether everyone you know is really a zombie, or frighten you with the thought that you might really be just a brain in a vat and that your memories are phony implants, or get you all in a frenzy about other such absurdities that no one, not even any of their inventors, really believes. Sound philosophy has nothing of that flavor. Instead, genuine philosophy takes it as a principle to be applied without apology that people other than yourself exist, and that you really know this, and that other people know this too, and that anyone who tries to call this sort of thing into doubt is playing a silly mind game.

What distinguishes the philosophical approach from the scientific one? To the extent that they are distinct, philosophy exploits the data of our ordinary experience, while science exploits extraordinary forms of experience (technically-assisted observations and the like). It is possible to trust ordinary experience to answer questions it cannot answer or to reach a precision it cannot reach. But trusting ordinary experience in that naive manner is only philosophy or science poorly done. Modern science, as much as philosophy, must rely on the data of ordinary experience, and the difference between science and philosophy in that regard is that science uses other forms of experience in addition, whereas philosophy takes full advantage of the data of ordinary experience.

More Than Science Can Say

When it comes to questions about our immortality or lack thereof and God's existence, it is desirable for all of us to know the truth of such matters for ourselves, so far as that is possible.

If you agree with this assessment of things, and even if you disagree, then you are already engaging in philosophy yourself. Philosophy is like thinking and breathing: not something that we can do or not do if we like, but something that we must do, and must do either badly or well. We are all of us philosophers, like it or not. Even those who pretend to despise philosophy have their reasons (that is, their philosophical principles) for doing so. The least educated persons, the most unreflective, still think about and entertain definite views or hopes concerning life after death or the absence thereof, having as much invested in such questions as any learned professor.

We will approach the great questions about you, then, as philosophers—certainly not as players of mind games on the one hand, nor again as neuroscientists or particle physicists or biochemists on the other, but as careful thinkers going forward from facts about you already known to you at least implicitly, facts that no one really doubts, and that no one can deny without undermining all the sciences and descending into flights of fancy.

Why employ philosophy and not modern science? Why not approach these questions about ourselves through the lens of particle physics or neuroscience or some such discipline? Why forgo the use of such formidable knowledge?

Certainly not because of anything wrong with physics, neuroscience, or biochemistry. Plenty of authors, properly trained and credentialed in those great disciplines, are already applying those disciplines to ask and answer certain questions about you. But in order to answer the questions about ourselves and the world that relate most directly to the Christian faith, it is both possible and desirable to overcome two limitations of modern science. The first limitation is that these sciences reason from only some of the facts about you, while ignoring others that are extremely useful for answering our present questions. This limitation will become evident in a moment.

Their second limitation is that such sciences require outsiders to take many matters on faith. Descriptions of the structure of your DNA or the topography of your brain necessarily rest on the work of specialists, not purely on data readily accessible to everyone. When it comes to questions about our immortality or lack thereof and God's existence, it is desirable for all of us to know the truth of such matters for ourselves, so far as that is possible. Medicine, biology, chemistry, and physics all have much to contribute to our search for truth. Perhaps, when pursued without adding "nothing but" to their assertions, these disciplines have something to say in answer to the big questions we will be asking here. Be that as it may, it turns out those big questions are already answerable, even definitively, quite apart from the methods of modern science.

This modern concept of reason is based on a synthesis between Platonism (Cartesianism) and empiricism, a synthesis confirmed by the success of technology. On the one hand it presupposes the mathematical structure of matter, its intrinsic rationality, which makes it possible to understand how matter works and use it efficiently: this basic premise is, so to speak, the Platonic element in the modern understanding of nature. On the other hand, there is nature's capacity to be exploited for our purposes, and here only the possibility of verification or falsification through experimentation can yield decisive certainty. . . . If science as a whole is this and this alone, then it is man himself who ends up being reduced, for the specifically human questions about our origin and destiny, the questions raised by religion and ethics, then have no place within the purview of collective reason as defined by "science," so understood, and must thus be relegated to the realm of the subjective. The subject then decides, on the basis of his experiences, what he considers tenable in matters of religion, and the subjective "conscience" becomes the sole arbiter of what is ethical. In this way, though, ethics and religion lose their power to create a community and become a completely personal matter. This is a dangerous state of affairs for humanity, as we see from the disturbing pathologies of religion and reason which necessarily erupt when reason is so reduced that questions of religion and ethics no longer concern it.

Benedict XVI, "Faith, Reason, and the University: Memories and Reflections" (*The Regensburg Address*), September 12, 2006

Your Insider's View

We suggested just a moment ago that there are certain types of ordinary experience of you that modern science makes little use of, but philosophy explores as far as it can. Let us consider an example. There are two distinct views of you. One of these is yours alone. We can call this your insider's view. You can feel your hands from within them; other people cannot do that. Other people can feel your hands only from the outside, as when they shake your hand. You can also feel what your hands feel like from the outside, when you use one hand to touch the other. This other view of you, the one available not only to you but also to outsiders, is the public view of you. We might also call it the outsider's view, as long as we realize that it is to a certain extent available to you as well, and not only to outsiders. You can see what your hands look like in much the same way that any other person can see your hands. You cannot, however, see the back of your neck the way an outsider can. Even if you can to some extent perceive yourself as others do, you cannot always do it as well or completely as others can, and so it makes sense to call the second view of you the outsider's view. The scientific approach to human nature begins mainly from observations of human beings made from the outside, whereas the philosophical approach also uses observations we can all make of our own activities from within.

There are two distinct views of you. One of those is yours alone. We can call this your insider's view.

Whether you are playing the piano, mowing the lawn, delivering a speech, or watching TV, there will be both an outsider's way of viewing you and also your own insider's view of yourself performing the same activities. Wherever there is both a third-person and first-person experience of you, the two agree considerably. And this agreement gives rise to a question. Does their agreement mean that they are simply redundant? Or does one view of you say things about you that the other does not?

The outsider's view of you clearly says many things about you that your insider's view does not. How many cells are there in your body? Why do you need to breathe? Does your blood circulate, or does it just slosh back and forth in your veins? Your insider's view has nothing to say in answer to such questions. Just from your experience of being you, from that first-person perception of yourself that no one else can share, you are not aware that you have cells at all, let alone how many or what kinds. What elements are you made of? How does your body break down food? Where are your childhood memories stored? Your mere experience of being you will tell you none of these things, no matter how carefully you analyze it. Once we begin to take a serious look at you from the outside, however, these questions now become answerable, particularly when we assist and enhance the outsider's view of you with special equipment. You yourself can see that your blood or skin is made up of cells by looking at a sample under a microscope. This is not your insider's view at work, however, but the public view of you that any number of other people can share.

The outsider's view of you affords important information about you that is not to be had any other way. It is an irreplaceable source of many important truths about you. That side of your self-experience is indispensable.

That answers half the question. What about your insider's view? Does it have things to say about you that the outsider's view of you cannot say? The answer is not as obvious here as it is in the case of the outside view of you. At first your insider's view seems to be nothing more than your own personal take on things that are accessible also from the outside alone. Of course, what you dreamed about last night is not something an outsider can figure out (or not yet) without you telling them. Then again, what you dreamed about last night or what song is stuck in your head are idiosyncrasies of yours. Such facts about ourselves are of little interest to others, and are not particularly revealing about what it means to be human. If personal peculiarities are all that is exclusively available by means of the insider's view, then we could and should ignore it in the pursuit of serious knowledge about what you are, since human nature is not a peculiarity of yours, but something you share in common with others.

The outsider's view of you affords important information about you that is not to be had any other way. It is an irreplaceable source of many important truths about you.

from **St. John Paul II's encyclical** *Faith & Reason* (1998)

Men and women have at their disposal an array of resources for generating greater knowledge of truth so that their lives may be ever more human. Among these is philosophy, which is directly concerned with asking the question of life's meaning and sketching an answer to it. Philosophy emerges, then, as one of noblest of human tasks. According to its Greek etymology, the term philosophy means "love of wisdom." Born and nurtured when the human being first asked questions about the reason for things and their purpose, philosophy shows in different modes and forms that the desire for truth is part of human nature itself. It is an innate property of human reason to ask why things are as they are, even though the answers which gradually emerge are set within a horizon which reveals how the different human cultures are complementary....

Nonetheless, it is true that a single term conceals a variety of meanings. Hence the need for a preliminary clarification. Driven by the desire to discover the ultimate truth of existence, human beings seek to acquire those universal elements of knowledge which enable them to understand themselves better and to advance in their own self-realization. These fundamental elements of knowledge spring from the wonder awakened in them by the contemplation of creation: human beings are astonished to discover themselves as part of the world, in a relationship with others like them, all sharing a common destiny. Here begins, then, the journey which will lead them to discover ever new frontiers of knowledge. Without wonder, men and women would lapse into deadening routine and little by little would become incapable of a life which is genuinely personal....

Although times change and knowledge increases, it is possible to discern a core of philosophical insight within the history of thought as a whole. Consider, for example, the principles of non-contradiction, finality and causality, as well as the concept of the person as a free and intelligent subject, with the capacity to know God, truth, and goodness. Consider as well certain fundamental moral norms which are shared by all. These are among the indications that, beyond different schools of thought, there exists a body of knowledge which may be judged a kind of spiritual heritage of humanity. It is as if we had come upon an implicit philosophy, as a result of which all feel that they possess these principles, albeit in a general and unreflective way. Precisely because it is shared in some measure by all, this knowledge should serve as a kind of reference-point for the different philosophical schools. Once reason successfully intuits and formulates the first universal principles of being and correctly draws from them conclusions which are coherent both logically and ethically, then it may be called right reason or, as the ancients called it, orthós logos, recta ratio.

On her part, the Church cannot but set great value upon reason's drive to attain goals which render people's lives ever more worthy. She sees in philosophy the way to come to know fundamental truths about human life. At the same time, the Church considers philosophy an indispensable help for a deeper understanding of faith and for communicating the truth of the Gospel to those who do not yet know it.

Your insider's view brings much more to the table than your idiosyncrasies, however. It also grants you your only access to certain crucial pieces of information about what kind of being you are. We should expect this to be the case. What are you, after all? A human being. That means, among other things, that you are alive, that you have a number of senses, and that you can think. All these things go on inside you: living, sensing, thinking. The outsider's view provides indispensable information about your outside. By the same token, your insider's view should provide indispensable information about your inside, your inner life.

Your insider's view brings much more to the table than your idiosyncrasies; it also grants you your only access to certain crucial pieces of information about what kind of being you are.

What questions about you does your insider's view help to answer that cannot be answered from the outsider's view of you alone? An exhaustive list of such questions would be long. But we can consider some examples. For instance, suppose for a moment that you have never had any experience of seeing. You were born completely blind and have always been in that condition. You have never seen a glimmer of light, a movement, a color, or a shape. You are, however, a neuroscientist, and your specialty is the neuroscience of vision. You know the physics of light and color as well as anyone in the world. You understand in exquisite detail all the electrical and chemical mechanisms from the photoreceptors in the eye to the regions of the brain that are active when people see. Do you now understand what seeing is? Do you know what people mean by the word see? Do you know what people mean by the word blue?

When people say that the sky is blue, they do not mean anything about wavelengths and frequencies, or neurons and synapses. They are naming a quality they immediately perceive, not the result of a measuring process or an instance of a scientific principle or a piece of organic equipment by which their seeing takes place.

When people say that the sky is blue, they do not mean anything about wavelengths and frequencies, or neurons and synapses. Those thoughts generally do not occur to them at all. They are naming a quality they immediately perceive, not the result of a measuring process or an instance of a scientific principle or a piece of organic equipment by which their seeing takes place. Blue names none of those things, but just an immediately perceived quality. And this immediately perceived quality is entirely left out of the objective science of color. What we call seeing is likewise a certain activity we are immediately aware of in ourselves when we perform it, and it is just this thing we are immediately aware of that is entirely left out of the objective, outsider's description of what is happening in the eyes and brain of a seeing person.

Here we have an example of how the two views of you somehow agree, but speak very different languages; neither language is reducible to the other, although they correspond. When you see that the sky is blue, certain things are going on in your brain. When you see that the grass is green, other things are going on in your brain. When you look back at the sky, the same things that were going on in your brain before are going on again. There is a more or less definite correlation between what you experience when you see and those things simultaneously going on in your brain that can be described even by those who have never seen anything. The two go together, your act of seeing and the objective correlatives of that act that simultaneously take place in you. But we cannot reduce one to the other, even if they are somehow mutually dependent. No amount of description of chemical and electrical events in your eyes and brain could ever contain what seeing means to those of us who have experienced it, or convey it to those who have never experienced it. That meaning comes only from the direct experience of seeing, which takes place only in the insider's view, in the view of the one doing the seeing.

More Than Science Can Say

Your insider's view is therefore an original and irreplaceable source of your knowledge of what it means to see, hear, taste, smell, feel, imagine, remember, understand, desire, fear, or love. The only direct access you have to these kinds of internal activities is your insider's view. You quite rightly attribute the same kinds of activities to others when you see the outward signs of them. When you do, you remain continually dependent on your only direct experience of such things—namely, within yourself—in order to know what you mean by their names. We tend to believe that we simply see that people see, without any implicit reference to our own seeing. Really, though, we never directly perceive any act of seeing but our own. In others, we see their eyes and their facial expressions and their movements, things quite different from an act of seeing, although capable of indicating the presence of such an act to those who have experienced it directly, and who are in fact experiencing it directly in themselves even while they are looking at others. In this way, it is the easiest and most natural thing in the world for us to supplement our outsider's view of others with information gleaned from our insider's view of ourselves, since others (at any rate other human beings) are indeed other selves. Our insight into outsiders, into other people and animals, obviously depends on our outsider's view of things. But it also depends on our insider's view, and the dependence is subtle enough that we easily overlook it.

From this quick sketch, we can already see that the two views of you are in fact complementary, each saying certain things about you that the other does not, or not so clearly. That is the beginning of appreciating the difference of method between science and philosophy. Now that we have some sense of how philosophy works, we can go on to see how its special methods can help answer some of the great questions about you and the natural world.

The insider and the outsider views of you are in fact complimentary, each saying certain things about you that the other does not.

Review Questions

1. Spokespersons for modern science sometimes claim that science suffices to explain all of reality. What are some of the immediate implications of this claim?

2. What is the erroneous but typically unspoken assumption that modern science makes about human nature?

3. What are some indications that human beings are essentially different in kind from chimpanzees, and not related to them by mere differences of degree?

4. Why is it unhelpful when scientists and interpreters of science add the phrase "nothing but" to their explanations?

5. Explain the difference between the outsider's view of you and your insider's view with respect to the sense of sight and the experience of seeing.

6. What is philosophy? What would it mean to say that human beings are in some sense naturally or inevitably philosophers?

Put Out Into the Deep

If you are especially interested in the relationship between modern experimental science, on the one hand, and philosophy, theology, and our moral convictions on the other, a classic work you may enjoy is *The Abolition of Man* by C. S. Lewis. Originally published in 1943, this lively book—really an essay—is a thoughtful argument that scientific knowledge is rightly valued when it is located within the context of a whole human life oriented towards wisdom.

CHAPTER 5

You Are More Than Your Brain

Now that we have a rough sense of how philosophy works, we will put it to use and see how we can discover some of the fundamental ways in which we differ from other animals and from machines. The things that set us apart all have to do with our minds. Regardless of the degree to which we possess human intelligence (indeed, even if some of us cannot exercise it at all due to some impediment in our brains), we are the kind of being that possesses that special type of intelligence, and it most of all distinguishes us from other kinds of living things. Dogs can smell many things better than you can, and eagles can see many things better than you can. But you can outthink all dogs and eagles put together—so much so, that you might feel insulted if someone tried to praise you by saying you are smarter than any dog he had ever met. If we humans have a peculiar excellence, it lies in thinking and in the other acts that go with thinking and follow from it, such as deliberating, choosing, planning, and the like. What we will discover is that our minds are in fact nonmaterial, nonbodily powers that are not properties of our bodies as our sense powers are.

The first step toward making that discovery will be to distinguish our intellects from our imaginations. The second step will be to learn the difference between images, which are the products of our imaginations, and universals, which are the special concern of our intellects. The third step will be to see why our intellect's power to grasp universals means it cannot be a function of the brain. The fourth step will be to explain why we need brains in order to use our intellects, even though our intellects are not our brains or powers of our brains.

Intellect and Imagination

Is your mind (or intellect) the same thing as your imagination, just another name for it? Or are they two distinct mental powers? Are mind and imagination like vision and eyesight: two names for the same thing? Or are they like vision and hearing, two distinct powers? Or are they instead related as the general to the specific, as sense power and vision? Probably most people would suspect that mind and imagination are two different powers, but they would struggle to say just how they differ.

Intellect and imagination are somehow distinct powers, even if we also use their names interchangeably at times. This is especially clear in the case of things that you can think about but cannot imagine. If some things are thinkable but not imaginable, then thinking and imagining cannot be the same, and the power of thinking must be different from the power of imagining. So:

Imagine a square inscribed in a circle. (Not too hard.)

Now imagine a regular octagon inscribed in there. (Tougher.)

Now imagine a regular thirty-billion-sided polygon inscribed in the same circle.

This last request is impossible to fulfill. The polygon itself is not impossible, but it is impossible for you to form an image of it that is distinct from the circle in which it is to be inscribed. Forming an image of a thirty-billion-sided polygon that is distinct from a circle goes well beyond the power of your imagination. Yet you readily understand that such a polygon is possible, and that it is distinct from the circle in which it is inscribed. The polygon has angles in it, the circle does not. You accurately understand the difference even though you cannot accurately picture it.

78   CHAPTER 5

There is yet another difference, one that is more profound, between intellect and imagination. Your imagination is concerned only with individual things, while your intellect can grasp universals. To see what this means, we should begin from a little-noticed difference that we can observe among the countless truths you are capable of understanding. One type of truth is impossible for you to know without checking into it—you must use your sense powers to examine the subject that the statement is about before you can see for yourself that it is true. That done, you will know the truth of the statement. Checking is both necessary and sufficient in such a case. We might style this kind of truth a checkable truth.

For example, suppose someone places a carton of unopened and undated milk in front of you, and asks you whether the milk has gone sour. You do not yet know but can certainly find out. The best way to find out is not to run off and hide in a closet somewhere and think quietly to yourself about the meaning of the statement "That milk has gone sour." Examine that statement all you like, turn it over in your mind a thousand times in the darkness of the closet, and you still will not be able to tell whether it is true. The answer does not lie in the statement itself, but in the milk carton. Plainly, you must open the carton and give the milk a whiff. From the comfort of your closet, you might guess that the milk has gone sour, and even guess correctly. But you cannot know that you are right. And as many times as you guess correctly about such a question, you will also guess incorrectly. You cannot know the truth of the matter until you have checked into it with your senses. Whatever the truth is about the milk, it is a checkable truth.

Just like using your sense of smell to check whether milk is sour or not, some truths are impossible for you to know without checking into it—you must use your sense powers to examine the subject that the statement is about before you can see for yourself that it is true.

Is it necessary to speak of checkable truths as though they were something special? Are not all truths checkable—that is, impossible for us to know until we can check them and fully known to us once we have checked them (when that is possible)? Is it ever possible, in other words, to know that something is true about a bunch of things we have never personally checked?

It is possible. Behold the marvelous power of your intellect: it enables you to know (and not merely guess) the truth about all kinds of things you have never specifically checked. Impossible-sounding, perhaps. True nonetheless. Consider the statement "Every bachelor is unmarried." Is it true? Of course it is. And you know it. And you are not merely guessing. And you can know this is true from the seclusion of any broom closet in the world, without meeting every bachelor personally in order to shore up your conviction about this general statement. This is not a checkable truth, then. It is neither possible nor necessary to check its subject, every bachelor, in order to become sure of its truth.

We might style this kind of truth a conceptual truth. You can tell it is true even with your eyes closed or from inside a closet. To know such a truth we do depend on prior sense experience, of course, and on the present use of our memory and imagination, not just our intellect. Probably none of us would ever have thought up the idea of bachelorhood (or anything else) had we never experienced any sensory contact with the world. Nonetheless, once we have formed the concepts and brought them to mind, we can see the truth of the statement without having to check every bachelor, and indeed it is impossible to check that by sensory inspection (there are simply too many possible bachelors). In calling such a truth a conceptual one, we do not mean that we can come to know it independently of any sense experience whatever or that it is a truth about mere concepts. On the contrary, it is a truth about things—bachelors—but its truth is something we can see without having to consult all the individual instances, once we have formed certain concepts about them.

Not every conceptual truth is the sort that attributes a part of a definition to its subject. If some number of apples is equal to some number of oranges, then you know that double the number of apples is equal to double the number of oranges.

Not every conceptual truth is the sort that attributes a part of a definition to its subject (as unmarried is part of the definition of bachelor). Consider this case: "Every square contains less area than the circle that passes through its four corners." If you know what a square is, and what a circle is, and what area is, you cannot fail to see the truth of this statement. You can know the truth of that statement without having to check all individual squares. This truth is therefore not a checkable one, but is instead of the conceptual variety. And yet the predicate does not merely tell us what square means, but instead describes a property that must belong to every square.

Here is another example: "The doubles of equal things are also equal." This, too, is verifiable without checking all individual cases. If some number of apples is equal to some number of oranges, then you know that double the number of apples is equal to double the number of oranges without ever needing to see the apples or oranges in question.

Nontrivial conceptual truths exist outside mathematics as well. For example, "There is truth" is itself such a truth. (It could never be true that "there is no truth," since that statement itself would then be a truth.) Again, "Nothing acts on itself without some distinction between what is acting and what is being acted on," as a person who is scratching himself must be distinguishable into the part doing the scratching and the part being scratched. And here is an intelligible truth about causes: "If something is inclined of itself to be or behave a certain way, but it is not being or behaving that way, then there is an outside cause influencing it."

Examples like these convince us that there are all kinds of conceptual truths out there and that you come equipped with the ability to know them. You are therefore the owner of an intriguing power: the power to know something with certainty about an infinity of things (certain individual bachelors, squares, numbers, causes, and so forth) you have never seen.

Universals

Whence comes this strange power of yours to know, with perfect certainty and infallible accuracy, certain properties that belong to every particular square or to every particular "thing that is acting on itself "? Where do you get your knowledge about cases you have never seen before? How do you do this?

The secret lies in your power to grasp and isolate a certain kind of sameness in things. Earlier we saw certain differences your intellect picks up but your imagination misses, such as the difference between "circle" and "thirty-billion-sided regular polygon." But your intellect picks up on more than subtle differences in things. It can also grasp the pure sameness in things in a way that your imagination cannot.

You Are More Than Your Brain   81

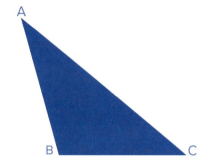

You must be able to grasp something common to all possible triangles, for example, or else you could never be sure that "every triangle can have a circle drawn through its three points," or that "no triangle is a square." Any triangle you encounter in your sense experience will necessarily include the things common to all triangles, but it will also combine these commonalities with other things peculiar to its own individual case. Consider, for example, the triangle ABC here on this page. Whatever is common to all triangles must of course belong to it—it has three straight sides, three corners, and contains an area, for instance. But it also presents certain features found only in some triangles, such as its specific area and the particular ratio of its sides and its special shade of blue. Besides these things, it also has other properties all its own, and which it shares with no other triangle in the universe, such as the place it occupies on this page.

Imagine for a moment that you could not form any idea of triangle ABC that isolated the features it held in common with all other triangles, but instead every notion you had of it, just like ABC itself, necessarily included its idiosyncrasies, such as its color and its unique location. Suppose you were similarly limited regarding all other triangles, and all other things. Then all your ideas would be of individual things in all their individuality, and so all your names would have to be proper nouns. If you could form verbs at all, they would be proper verbs, each one expressing only a single individual action performed in a unique time and place in history, in all its individuality. You could not speak, in fact—or not in the usual sense of the word. Much less could you ever know the truth that "every triangle has three sides" or the more sophisticated truth that "every triangle can be circumscribed by a circle."

Imagine for a moment that you could not form any idea of triangle ABC that isolated the features it held in common with all other triangles, but instead every notion you had of it, just like ABC itself, necessarily included its idiosyncrasies, such as its color and its unique location.

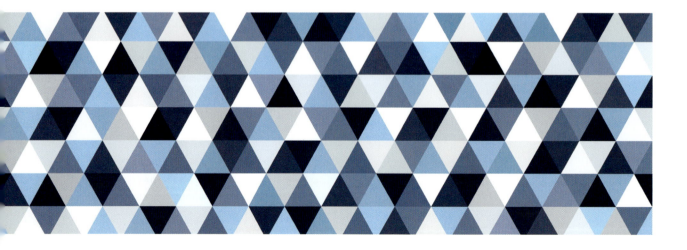

82   CHAPTER 5

Of course you do know such things, and you can speak in common nouns and verbs. Therefore, you form notions of things that are not bound up with their individual peculiarities. You can form notions of things that include only those features of theirs that they share in common with other similar individuals, notions that leave out the peculiarities of each individual. When you say triangle, for instance, you mean three-sided plane figure, which notion does not include blue (nor does it include not blue), and it does not include "here on this page" (nor does it exclude that). It remains strictly noncommittal about such peculiarities of this or that triangle. A notion like this, isolating the repeatable content common to an infinity of possible particular instances, is called a universal idea, or else just a universal for short.

Once you form a universal idea, you can then inspect it in your mind and see certain things that must belong to it. The idea has a kind of life and comes with inherent laws of its own, and you can discover these after you have formed it in your mind in response to seeing particular instances and noting the commonality in them. Any universal idea can thus tell you certain things about itself. These are the conceptual truths about it. Other questions it will stubbornly refuse to answer. For example, if you inspect the universal idea of what a triangle is, you will find that any two sides taken together must be greater than the third side. But if you are wondering whether any triangle in the world is purple, your universal idea of what a triangle is maintains a strict silence on the question, because it is open to all colors, as well as to being colorless. For all the universal idea of a triangle can tell us, it might be that every triangle in the world is purple, or it might be that none is.

Your mind is full of universal ideas. It is thanks to them that you are sometimes able to know things about an infinity of particulars you have never checked. If you were destitute of all universal notions about triangles, you could not verify any statements about triangles except in the particular cases you had bothered to inspect. As it is, you are sure of many universal truths about triangles and about many other things, due to your native ability to form universal ideas of them.

What power in you is responsible for the formation of universal ideas? If the word intellect names your power to understand truths, and especially conceptual truths, then we must attribute the work of universal-formation to your intellect, since universals are the foundation of your ability to grasp such truths.

Can we also attribute this act to your imagination? Can we, in other words, identify your universal-forming intellect with your image-forming imagination? Let us put the matter to the test. Consider your universal idea of animal. Can you imagine this universal notion? Can you imagine what is common to all animals, and only what is common to them?

Imagine an animal. Does it have any bones? If so, then you have not imagined what is common to all animals, since not all animals have bones. Does it lack bones? If so, then you still have not imagined what is common to all animals, since not all animals lack bones. You cannot form an image of an animal without committing yourself one way or another. The image must be of something bony or else boneless, and again it must be either four-legged or not, have a tail and claws or not, and so on. It must also have some particular color and shape, and yet no color or shape is common to all animals.

You cannot form an image of an animal that is common to all animals. Your universal idea of animal, then, is not an image. Your power of forming universal ideas, your intellect, is another power entirely.

You simply cannot form an image of what is common to all animals. You have no trouble, on the other hand, understanding what is common to all animals, since you understand, for example, that it is common to all animals to be alive, or to have the sense of touch, and a whole bunch of other things. These universal ideas of yours, unlike your images of animals, do not oblige you to include any features that are peculiar only to certain animals.

Your universal idea of animal, then, is not an image. It is not a product of your imagination. Your power of forming universal ideas, your intellect, is another power entirely.

Strange and unimaginable as universal ideas are, the truth demands that we not try to deny their existence and replace them with something more comfortable and manageable. They are a plain fact of human mental life. Your body forms countless chemical substances without requiring you to notice it, and you become aware of them only by paying special attention to the human body at work (mainly by means of an outsider's view). In similar fashion, your intellect forms universal ideas without requiring you to notice it, and so you become aware of them only by paying special attention to your mind (by means of your insider's view). Once we do pay such attention, however, our formation of universal ideas becomes a simple matter of fact.

Your Brain Is not Your Intellect

Universal ideas are what is special about your intellect. It alone knows them. No other power in you can form them. Our next question is whether your intellect is the same as your brain, whether it is some part or function of it. Since your intellect contains universal ideas, the question amounts to asking whether your universal ideas are in your brain.

One way to find out is to take a closer look at your senses and imagination. Do they exhibit any decisive symptoms of being in your body? If so, we can look for those same symptoms in the case of your intellect, and if we find them, we may conclude that your intellect is a power of your brain after all. If not, that will be a powerful sign that your intellect is a nonmaterial power.

A power that belongs to a body part performs different parts of its work in different parts of the body part. The gripping power of your hand works partly in each finger, partly in the thumb, partly in the palm. If a knowing power belongs to a body part, then it will follow this rule. It will do part of its work over here, another part over there, in different portions of some body part. Consequently, the chief symptom of a cognitive power belonging to a body part is that its work will also be distributed in space. It will form cognitive representations that are divisible into spatially distinct parts.

You Are More Than Your Brain   **85**

The meaning of this will become plainer with the following considerations. Whenever we know or perceive things, we produce internal representations of them. We usually do this so effortlessly that it sometimes takes a little reflection to realize that our seeing a tree, for example, involves constructing a visual likeness of it within ourselves. If you go cross-eyed, you see two of everything. Why is that? Surely not because the number of things in the room has suddenly doubled. No, the two appearances of each thing must be due to something going on within you when you are cross-eyed. If you press (gently) near your eyes with your fingers, the whole room appears to jiggle. Unless this gentle pressing with your fingers really causes the whole room to jiggle, it must be instead that you are jiggling something else that resembles the room. This is the visual representation you are producing in yourself when you see, and by means of which you see.

These representations of things that your knowing powers form can tell us a lot about the powers themselves. In particular, when the representations are made up of parts that exhibit spatial relationships to each other, that is because they exist in something made up of spatially distinct parts. In other words, sensory representations are spatially distinct because they exist in different parts of a sense organ.

Whenever we know or percieve things, we produce internal representation of them. For example, seeing a tree involves constructing a visual likeness of it within ourselves.

86   CHAPTER 5

For example, the visual representations of things that you produce in yourself always form a kind of field. They are spread out in a kind of space. The grass occupies this lower portion of your visual field, then a tree stands there above the grass, and the blue sky comes in at the top. Things are above and below each other, to the left and right of each other, in your field of vision. No doubt this spatial arrangement in your vision corresponds in some way to the spatial arrangement of things in reality outside you. Your visual field is nonetheless a work of your vision, something your sense of sight produced within itself, in more or less faithful imitation of those exterior realities. The spatial extension (the spreading out this way and that way) of your visual field is a necessary consequence of its existing in some portion of your brain, since your brain is itself a thing extended in space, having distinct parts and a shape and size. Like a movie screen, your brain must represent things in a way that is spread out in space precisely because it itself is spread out in space.

Your imagination exhibits the same symptom of being something spread out in a part of your body (presumably your brain). In your visual imagination, as much as in your vision itself, the image of the tree stands above that of the grass and beneath that of the sky. Or imagine a square. Now, holding on to that square in your mind, imagine also a circle at the same time. Do the two have any spatial relationships to one another? Yes, necessarily so. Either the square and the circle are outside each other, or one contains the other, or they overlap, for example. And if they are outside each other, then they are either on a level with each other, or one is higher up than the other. And the square is either equal to the circle in area, or else it is larger or smaller. Since your imagination takes up room in your body, residing in some region of your brain, its representations of things must be distributed in the different portions of that region, and so those representations will bear spatial relationships to one another.

Sense powers and imagination are powers of your brain, and they act like it. Each of these cognitive powers forms representations that are divisible into parts bearing spatial relationships to one another. That is the telltale sign that these powers exist in some organ of your body and form their representations of things in it.

You Are More Than Your Brain

A square is a quadrilateral plane figure that is both equilateral and right-angled.

A circle is a plane figure contained by one line such that all the straight lines falling upon it from one point among those lying within the figure are equal to one another.

Euclid, *Elements of Geometry*

Does your intellect also exhibit this symptom of being in some part of your body? Do the representations of things that it forms bear spatial relationships to one another? The representations it forms of things are its universal ideas of them. Think, for example, of what a square is. Now, holding on to that universal idea, think also of what a circle is. Do these two things you are thinking of bear any spatial relationships to one another? Is "what a square is" above or below or to the left of "what a circle is"? A ridiculous question. These things have no "where" to them, and bear to one another no spatial relationships at all. Does "what a square is" contain more area than "what a circle is," or are they equal in area, or is "what a circle is" the bigger of the two? An equally nonsensical question. The universal idea of a circle has no size, just as the definition expressing it mentions no particular size. Consequently, the universal idea of a circle and that of a square can have no relationships of size.

Not even your ideas of spatial relationships have spatial relationships to each other. Are your ideas of parallel and perpendicular parallel to one another? Or perpendicular? Or askew? All nonsense. Or what about the universal truth that "every triangle can be circumscribed by a circle"? Where is that in relation to the truth that "whatever contains a breadbox also contains what is in the breadbox"? Do these two truths about spatial relationships overlap somehow, or is one of them to the left of the other? Does one sit on top of the other or contain the other? Meaningless questions. These truths do not present themselves to your mind as things that have spatial relationships of any kind. They are quite unlike a circle and a square in your imagination.

The one symptom common to all your other cognitive powers, declaring them to be distributed throughout certain parts of your body (or your brain), is noticeably missing in the case of your intellect. The representations it forms are not spatially distinguished from or related to one another.

So, your intellect does not behave like a power that exists in an organ of your body. And that is because it does not. This same result can be shown more exactly and rigorously by means of other arguments of philosophy, but this sketch will do for our purposes.

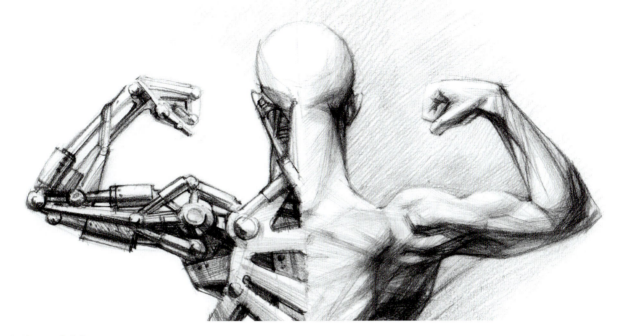

Why We Need Brains for Thinking

And now a lovely corollary falls into our hands: you are something much more than a machine. Our bodies in many ways resemble machines, or rather our machines embody many principles that nature (including human nature) has employed before us. Consequently, we more easily discover the likenesses between ourselves and our machines than the differences.

One general difference is that we know things. However much our sensory and imaginative equipment might resemble a computer program and even operate on similar principles to some extent, the sensory simulations of the world that we produce in our brains differ fundamentally from the images in a computer file or displayed on a computer monitor. A digital file may bear an analogy to certain sounds and images, and by running the right program a computer can reproduce those images on a monitor and the sounds in a speaker and thus play back a movie. But the movie is no more seen or heard (or enjoyed) by the computer than it is seen by a movie screen on which it is projected or heard by the air that vibrates with the sound of it. A computing machine does not take its input or its output to be representations of things, but as far as it is concerned (if it can be said to be concerned) all the things it processes are just its own things, its own internal goings-on, not somehow presentations of other things. A chess program does not say to itself, "Aha! these incoming signals go with a specific chess move that my opponent is making against me." It merely redistributes electrons in accord with the pathways and rules built into it, just as the wiring in your house does not take the currents running through it to be about something else, and the plumbing in your walls does not take the water coursing through it to be of something.

You Are More Than Your Brain

Thanks to imaging techniques such as MRI, it is possible to map the image of something you see to the neurons at the back of your brain.

Regarding input as somehow about something else is irrelevant to the functioning of a computer program. And there is no reason to attribute such an attitude to a computer, except to amuse ourselves.

Our senses are different. When you see a house, you are not devoid of awareness as the wiring in your house is or as a computer program is. Nor do you experience the appearance of the house as something existing purely within yourself or as a bunch of electric input corresponding to nothing. Instead, you experience it as the shape of a thing foreign to yourself, other than yourself—it is not merely a shape, but it is the shape of that house. That is the great glory of seeing, and the whole point of it. That other things somehow in this way get to re-exist in you is precisely the miracle of knowing. There are those who doubt that things outside their minds ever correspond in any way to the images and thoughts they form of them, but we will not here lose time over these poor (and uncommon) people.

Your sense powers already raise you up above the machines. These powers bring outside things into your inner world and leave them recognizable to you as other things, not mere input to be run through an unconsciously performed process whose output is of interest only to someone else.

Still, your sense powers reside in certain organs of your body, and they produce their sensory representations by employing certain properties of matter. Thanks to imaging techniques such as MRI, it is possible to map the image of something you see to the neurons at the back of your brain. However oddly distorted and immersed in utter darkness that image on the brain may be, it is your visual representation to yourself of the visible object. It is also the product of the electrical and chemical activity of your neurons, and it has shape, size, and location.

Universals are another story entirely. There can be no mapping of these on the brain. They do not exist in your brain at all, any more than on a sheet of paper. Certain symbols of universal things, such as your visual images of printed words on a page or imagined words in your mind, can occupy space in your brain. But the universals themselves that these symbols signify must be free of spatial relationships to other things, something impossible to avoid in a brain. Electrical circuitry can do many things, but it cannot form anything free of spatial limitations and individualizing conditions. It is in principle powerless to form a universal idea of anything. You have many things in common with the machines. You nonetheless differ from them categorically and permanently, in kind and not in degree.

The nonmaterial nature of your mind also emphasizes your difference from the other animals. Your intelligence differs from that of the animal as the universal from the particular, since no animal can form a universal thought. But the universal differs from the particular as the infinite does from the finite, since every universal enables its possessor to know things

You are much more than a perfectly good animal, and to call you the best of the animals is a gross understatement. There is something in you that goes entirely beyond what it means to be an animal, since it goes beyond mere bodily existence.

You Are More Than Your Brain

about an infinity of individuals. We can now further conclude that your intellect differs from the mind of an animal as the nonmaterial from the material. This is no mere difference of degree. You are much more than a perfectly good animal, and to call you the best of the animals is a gross understatement. There is something in you that goes entirely beyond what it means to be an animal, since it goes beyond mere bodily existence.

It is important not to confuse this conclusion with the mistaken idea that your intellect does not depend on your brain in order to function. Although your intellect is not your brain or even in your brain, it nevertheless depends on it. A knock on the head affects thinking, even (or especially) thinking about universal truths.

But in what way? There are two possibilities. Your intellect depends on your brain either (1) as the organ in which it exists and as the organ of other cognitive powers supplying it with its materials for thinking or (2) only as the organ of other cognitive powers supplying it with its materials for thinking.

The first of these alternatives is impossible. Your intellect is not a power in your brain or in any bodily organ. It is incorporeal, as we have seen. Accordingly, it does not depend on your brain or on any part of your body as a power depends on an organ to host it. Instead, your intellect is to what goes on in your brain as your sense of sight is to visible objects. Without visible objects, your sense of sight can exist, but it will

Although your intellect is not your brain or even in your brain, it nevertheless depends on it.

Your imagination depends on your brain both for its own power and for other powers that supply it with its objects (you cannot normally imagine qualities without having sensed them first in some way)

have nothing to do. Without your brain, your intellect can exist, but it will have nothing to do. Your intellect depends on your brain because your brain is the organ of other cognitive powers supplying your intellect with its objects—with the raw materials out of which to extract universal content while leaving aside the peculiarities of the individual things represented in sense or imagination.

The dependence is real and very strong. When your sensory activity languishes, your intellectual activity suffers correspondingly. When all your sensing and imagining are shut down, as in a dreamless sleep, all your thinking about universals ceases as well. In relation to your powers of sense and imagination, your intellect is like a judge who relies entirely on witnesses not because they will pass judgment or hand down rulings, but because they alone can supply the matter to which laws may be applied and about which decisions may be rendered. Prevent witnesses from entering the court, and all rulings cease. That is not because witnesses are the ones who hand down rulings. Prevent sensation, imagination, and brain activity, and all your understanding of universal truths must stop. That is not because your senses, imagination, and brain are the things that understand universals.

You Are More Than Your Brain 93

Your senses depend on your brain only for their power, not to supply them with their objects, which they contact directly. Your imagination depends on your brain both for its own power and for other powers that supply it with its objects (you cannot normally imagine qualities without having sensed them first in some way). Your intellect, on the other hand, depends on your brain only for its objects, not for its power. There is an interesting symmetry among your powers.

You are something truly astonishing. And more than a little strange. You have a body, this is not the whole story. You have a nonbodily, nonmaterial side to you as well.

Aquinas on the Incorruptibility of the Soul: A Paraphrase

The souls of the animals do not exist except in union with their bodies, because, lacking reason, the animals do not have any function that transcends the powers of their organs. So, when the body of an animal dies, its soul dies with it. But the human soul does have a power that transcends the power of its organs, and that power is the intellect, which lives in the company of immaterial universal ideas, or forms, which is why Aristotle called the mind "the place of forms." And so, this power whereby we think and choose—the intellect, together with its appetite, the will—exists in itself and endures after the death of the body.

For the full argument, see Summa Theologiae, I, question 75, especially article 6.

94   CHAPTER 5

Review Questions

1. What are the most immediately noticeable differences between the imagination and the intellect?

2. What is a checkable truth? What are some examples of uncheckable truths, that is, truths that cannot and do not need to be checked?

3. What is a universal idea? Use the example of the triangle to explain the concept in your own words.

4. How does the chapter's discussion of universal ideas show that the intellect does not behave like a power that exists in an organ of the body?

5. How does the intellect depend upon the brain?

Put Out Into the Deep

If you find the inquiry of this chapter and the preceding one to be intriguing, then you will greatly appreciate the book from which they were adapted, *The Immortal in You: How Human Nature Is More Than Science Can Say*, by Michael Augros (Ignatius Press, 2017).

CHAPTER 6

Recognizing God's Existence

In the last couple of chapters, we have caught a glimpse of how the methods of philosophy can shed light on human nature. In this chapter we will see how philosophy can provide us with insight into nature in general by revealing it to be the work of a cause that transcends nature entirely. This is the same as proving the existence of a being that deserves to be called God. Philosophy has many ways of going about this, but we will look at only one, the inference to a unique, primary, uncaused cause of all things. Although deducing God's existence in a perfectly rigorous way is difficult, and is one of the last things done in a well-ordered and complete philosophical training, it is possible to obtain worthwhile insight into how such proofs work by looking at one of them in abbreviated form, as we will do here.

Before we begin, let us pause to note that using reason to come to see that God exists is not contrary to faith, but complements it. To be sure, Christian faith is a gift from God and cannot be turned into or replaced by philosophical knowledge. But that does not mean none of the truths connected with God can be known by reason. That God is a Trinity of persons, that one of those persons became man, that we are made children of God and heirs of eternal life by means of baptism: such truths are beyond the power of reason to establish, and we adhere to them entirely by faith, taking them on God's word. But that there exists an eternal God at all was known even to pagan philosophers such as Plato and Aristotle, although they had never heard of Christ or his promises and sacraments. The Bible itself confirms the possibility of the human mind coming to know God's existence by reflection on the world he has made and indeed denies the legitimacy of atheism since the world so clearly announces the existence of its maker to honest rational inquirers:

> *For the wrath of God is revealed from heaven against all ungodliness and wickedness of men who by their wickedness suppress the truth. For what can be known about God is plain to them, because God has shown it to them. Ever since the creation of the world his invisible nature, namely, his eternal power and deity, has been clearly perceived in the things that have been made (Rom 1:18–20).*

Recognizing God's Existence

Although St. Paul's phrase "clearly perceived" suggests sensory knowledge, it is, of course, plain that the knowledge of God that we can attain by the natural light of reason is the conclusion of an argument. In that regard, it is similar to the solution to a math problem: until we have covered the proper mental ground, so to speak, by working through the steps of the problem, we do not know the answer. To those steps we now turn.

For all men who were ignorant of God were foolish by nature; and they were unable from the good things that are seen to know him who exists, nor did they recognize the craftsman while paying heed to his works.

Wisdom 13:1

On Causes

We will begin with this question: what sorts of things need a cause? The most obvious things that require explanation, that depend upon a cause, are things that are inclined to be some way other than the way that they are in fact. If an object is heavy, and thus has a downward tendency, and yet it is not in fact falling down but is instead sitting still in midair, then something is holding it up. Even things that are not inclined to be otherwise than they are still require a cause to be as they are if they exist under one of many alternatives to which they have no particular inclination of their own. For example, although wood is not opposed to being in the form of a desk or a chair, it is also not particularly inclined to be or become a desk or a chair, and so whenever we find wood in such a form, that is due to a cause outside the wood (a maker of desks and chairs).

Now everything in the natural world is open both to existing and to not existing. Those are real alternatives possible to anything we encounter. Not only animals, but even stones and stars, come into existence and pass out of it, and so do tiny particles. Existence is therefore just an alternative to which natural things are open, and not something that absolutely has to belong to them. That means they owe their existence to some sort of cause. Most things, and certainly all familiar things that we can name, depend on one kind of cause or another either to come into existence, or to remain in existence, or both.

Although wood is not opposed to being in the form of a desk or a chair, it is also not particularly inclined to be or become a desk or a chair, and so whenever we find wood in such a form, that is due to a cause outside the wood (a maker of desks and chairs).

Next, let us ask whether everything that exists needs a cause. An illustration or two will help us learn the answer. Suppose you are going to hang a lamp suspended by a chain. The power cord runs through the links, but it is the chain that will support the lamp's weight. The lamp itself will hang from something (the chain), but nothing will be hanging from it. The highest link on the chain might hang from a bit of hardware screwed into an electric box fixed to a ceiling joist, but the ceiling joist is not hanging from anything; instead it is sitting on the supporting walls, which sit on the foundation of your house, which sits on the earth, which does not need to sit on anything at all. To simplify things, we can suppose that the ceiling joist is a steel I-beam with a little hook on it from which the highest link of your chain is to be hung. That way the chain itself is hanging from something (the I-beam) that is not hanging but only sitting on something else. And now let us focus on the things that are hanging and on the things they are hanging from.

Every link in the chain hangs from something else and has something hanging from it. Every link is essentially a middle in that sense. There is something hanging after it, and there is something before it from which it hangs. And nothing could hang from any particular link if that link itself were not hanging from something else. If you unhang a link, you also unhang whatever is hanging from it. Now the lamp is hanging from something (namely, the last link of the chain), but nothing is hanging from it. It is not a middle but rather the end of the line. The I-beam has something hanging from it (namely, the highest link in the chain), but it is not itself hanging from anything, so it is not a middle either, as far as hanging goes, but it is the beginning of the whole hanging business.

We can add as many links as we like, but we will never produce a chain that can hang all by itself and suspend our lamp. That is just the way it is with chains.

Notice that the whole chain, and not just each particular link, is also a middle. There is something after it, hanging from it (namely, the lamp), and there is also something before it, from which it hangs (namely, the I-beam). If the I-beam were to disappear, the chain and the lamp would come crashing down. Is this dependence on the I-beam for the suspension of the chain and the lamp due to the number of links in the chain? Suppose we had started with a ten-link chain. What if we were now to increase the number of links to a hundred? (We could make room for more links either by raising the I-beam or by shrinking the size of the links in the chain.) Nothing is changed. Clearly, we still cannot hang anything from the hundred-link chain unless the hundred-link chain is itself hung from something else, such as the I-beam. We can add as many links as we like, but we will never produce a chain that can hang all by itself and suspend our lamp. That is just the way it is with chains.

Could we do away with the I-beam if we had a chain with an infinity of links in it? We could not. If there is nothing for that whole chain to hang from, it will not hang, and nothing can be hung from it. There is nothing about those links in themselves that makes them want to hang in space. A big chain, even an infinite one, would be much more apt to sit in a big pile than to hang in a straight line in some specific direction. Infinity does not have such a magic power, then, that it can make a chain hang without the chain's hanging from anything.

This pattern of relationships is not unique to hanging things and chains and lamps, of course. We find a similar relationship among moving things such as train engines and cabooses. The caboose is a part of a train of cars that gets pulled (or pushed) by something else but does not itself move any other car in the train. It is the end of the line. The opposite is true of the engine, which pulls another car but is not itself pulled by any car. It is like the I-beam or the earth in the example with the suspended lamp. The engine can be immediately coupled to a caboose, but usually there are cars in between. A boxcar, for instance, gets pulled by a car but also pulls another car. Each boxcar is a middle in that sense, having a puller before it and something it pulls after it.

100   CHAPTER 6

Now, can we do away with the engine and still get the boxcars to move? Plainly, they will move if they are on an incline. But we want them to move not by gravity, which is something other than the train, but of themselves, and in a direction of our choosing, which is what the engine had made possible. Clearly two coupled boxcars will not suffice for that effect. They will just sit on the tracks or move in a direction determined by natural forces and not by an engineer. That is because each of our two boxcars is unable to move anything else except insofar as it is itself being moved by something. Neither one has anything in it to initiate motion. So, each member of our boxcar couple is waiting for the other one to make a move. Neither one of them is a mover or puller by itself. Each is only a would-be mover.

Is this because we do not have enough boxcars? What if we have five hundred boxcars all coupled together? Still no good, of course. They will still just sit there, going nowhere. Really, we have just increased the size of the middle, of the thing that cannot pull anything unless it is pulled by something before it. In fact, we now need a more powerful engine than we initially needed to move our two original boxcars.

What, now, if we have an infinity of boxcars on an infinite track? Will the infinity emancipate them from their dependence on an engine? Will they be able to pull the caboose? Not a bit. Individual boxcars do not pull anything except while they are being pulled by something else. Consequently, a whole train of boxcars also does not pull anything except while it is being pulled by something else, regardless of the size of that train. That is just the way it is with boxcar trains. There is nothing about boxcars, even an infinity of them, that would incline them to move to the left on the tracks instead of to the right. Infinity does not have such a magic power, then, that it can make a train of mere would-be movers move anything.

A boxcar is unable to move anything else except insofar as it is itself being moved by something else. Even an infinite amount of boxcars does not make a train of mere would-be movers move anything.

Recognizing God's Existence

Both the chain and the train are examples of series of causes acting together in order to produce some ultimate effect. Each member of these series receives its ability to be a cause of something from a prior thing. In the interests of brevity, we limited ourselves to two examples. In the interests of making the examples as representative as possible, we chose one example to illustrate causes of rest (the hanging lamp) and the other to illustrate causes of motion (the train). But the point of these examples is of course to exemplify. The general point illustrated by the chain and the train is not at all specific to chains and trains. The lesson of the chain link is that it is impossible for "things hanging from something else" to be all there is. There must also be something from which things hang and which is not itself hanging from anything. The lesson of the boxcar is that it is impossible for "things pulled by something else" to be the only kind of pullers in town. There must also be something by which things are pulled and which is not itself pulled by anything. The more general lesson that one can draw from such illustrations is that it is impossible for "things caused by something else" to be self-explanatory. There must also be something by which things are caused and which is not itself caused by anything. The reason is the same in the particular cases and in the general one: the middle causes, when multiplied, just produce one big, fat middle cause. And it is not possible for a middle cause to be the whole story, since every middle by definition has something before it.

We can now frame a general deduction of the existence of a first cause:

> *If there were caused causes, with no first cause, they would constitute a middle with nothing before it; but it is impossible for there to be a middle with nothing before it.*
>
> *Therefore, there cannot be caused causes with no first cause.*

It follows that there is at least one absolutely first cause.

We now know that there is a first cause—at least one thing in existence that is a cause of the existence and coming-into-existence of other things, but which in turn has no cause for its existence, but simply is. Similarly, it is the cause of other things being causes, it causes them to cause things, but there is no prior cause of its causation. It is able to cause things all by itself.

Why There Is at Most One Absolutely First Cause

Next we must ask how many absolutely first causes there are. Can there be more than one absolutely first cause? The truth is that there is only one such entity, and we can come to this conclusion in the following ways.

First, we can infer that there is just one first cause from the unity of the world of nature. The universe is not just a collection of things that have no relationship to each other. Instead, we find that one part is a necessary condition for or even produces another, as the basic forces of the world produce the simplest atoms, these atoms and gravity produce stars, the stars produce other elements, the elements produce certain compounds, and the compounds are necessary conditions for living things. Living things themselves, even in competing with one another, improve each other, and when some prey on others they hold their numbers in check making possible a healthy and long enduring ecosystem. And living things cooperate as much as, or more than, they compete: plants produce the oxygen and fruits that animals need, and animals produce the fertilizer that plants need, for example. So, the world is a unified order of things. Now things that are in themselves many and diverse, such as all the kinds of things in the natural world, are not unified and one just by being many and diverse. Many and diverse musicians do not constitute one orchestra just because they are many diverse musicians. Hence there is always a cause of the unity and order of things that have somehow come together in one thing,

Things that are in themselves many and diverse, such as all the kinds of things in the natural world, are not unified and one just by being many and diverse.

Recognizing God's Existence   103

if they are in themselves many and diverse. Sometimes what causes many things to become one thing might itself consist of things many and diverse. For example, Congress consists of many members, but it can pass laws that unify the country in various ways. In such cases, however, the many (e.g., the members of Congress) must themselves be somehow united already (e.g., by meeting together and agreeing on one view about what is good for the country) before they can unite other things that are many and diverse (e.g., the different states). In short, whenever those that act to unite other things are themselves many, they succeed only to the extent that they themselves have somehow been unified by a prior cause. Some compelling argument or evidence, for instance, must unify the members of Congress, convincing a sufficient number of them to vote together on some bill. Hence things many and diverse are capable of unifying other things that are many and diverse, but only to the degree that they themselves have already been unified by some prior unifying cause.

Now there is at least one absolutely first cause of all things, as we saw. So, if there were two or more first causes, they could not produce the unity of the natural world except by being united together in some joint effort, and hence through some prior unification of them by some cause. If that cause in turn is also somehow a joint effort, then it will be due to some prior unifying cause again. This sort of thing cannot regress infinitely, but we must come to a first cause of all this unification which is itself in no need of a prior unifying cause, which means it does not consist in many things that have been unified, but simply is one single cause. And since this is the first cause of all the unification and efforts of the other causes after it, it alone is truly an absolutely first cause. Hence the true first cause of things cannot be two or more, but must simply be one.

Sometimes what causes many things to become one thing might itself consist of things many and diverse. Congress consists of many members, but it can pass laws that unify the country in various ways.

When a certain property belongs to a certain subject precisely as such and without any depence on any outside cause at all, then such a property belongs only to that subject in that way and belongs to other things only with dependence on that subjects causal influence. For example, the property of being blue will belong to things (such as a bluebird or frosting on a cake) only because the chemical composition of the color blue is present in both.

Another way to infer that there is only a single absolutely first cause in existence is as follows. When a certain property belongs to a certain subject precisely as such and without any dependence on any outside cause at all, then such a property belongs only to that subject in that way and belongs to other things (if at all) only with dependence on that subject's causal influence. Here are some examples to illustrate that principle: (1) the property of being even belongs to the number two, and is simply an immediate and natural property of it, belonging to two all by itself and not due to evenness belonging to any other number, and consequently the property of being even belongs to other numbers only to the extent that there is something "two" about them, as six is even because it has two equal parts; (2) the property of brightness belongs to a light source just by itself, precisely because it is a light source, and consequently it belongs to other things (such as snow or reflective bodies) only with dependence on a light source; (3) the property of being blue belongs to a certain general type of chemical composition (e.g., some family of compounds with a certain similar structure) precisely because it is the natural property of such a composition, and for no other reason, and consequently being blue will belong to other things (such as a bluebird or the frosting on a cake) only because some version of that chemical composition is present; (4) an end I have in view (e.g., the restoration of my health) is good as such and in itself, and not because of its connection to something else that is good for me, and consequently anything else that is not an end in itself but which is still good for me, will be good for me only because of the goodness of some end—a certain surgery, for example, is good for me, but only because having my health restored is good for me. In general, when a certain property belongs to a certain subject as such and without any dependence on any outside cause at all, then such a property belongs only to that subject in that way, and belongs

Recognizing God's Existence   105

to other things (if at all) only with dependence on that subject. Now if we try to suppose that there are two or more absolutely first causes, A and B, what happens? Because A is an absolutely first cause, in no way dependent on anything else to exist or act, existence and action belong to it as such and due to no other cause whatsoever. But then (by the principle we just finished elaborating) existence and action cannot belong to anything else in that way and must belong to other things (if at all) only through the causal influence of A. That means B, if it is really something other than A, cannot exist or act except with dependence on A. Therefore, B is not really a first cause after all. So, there is no way for the first cause to be more than one.

Three corollaries immediately follow. The most obvious of these is that there is exactly one first cause, which follows thus:

- There is *at most* one first cause (just shown).

- There is *at least* one first cause (shown earlier).

- Therefore, there is *exactly* one first cause.

Just like the engine of the train causes the boxcars to move, all beings derive from the one and only first cause.

The LORD looks down from heaven upon the children of men, to see if there are any that act wisely, that seek after God.

Psalm 14:2

Another corollary is that all other things besides the first cause (whatever it is) have a cause of their being. There can be only one self-existing thing, only one thing that does not in some way owe its existence to an outside cause, as our reasoning has shown. All other things, then, have their existence with dependence on one or more causes. The third corollary is that all things besides the first cause derive their existence from it. Anything other than the first cause has a cause of its being (by our second corollary); if that cause is the first cause, then we are done. If that cause is not the first cause, then that cause in turn has a cause of its being. And this cannot continue endlessly (according to the reasoning at the beginning of this chapter, illustrated by the chains and trains). This sequence must terminate in an absolutely first cause. But there is only one of those. Therefore, all beings derive, whether immediately or through many intermediate causes, from the one and only first cause. All things are like a vast tree, whose leaves sprout from its twigs, whose twigs grow from its branches, whose branches extend from its main limbs, and whose main limbs stem from a single trunk.

The First Cause of Things Is A Mind

It is tempting to conclude that the absolutely first cause of all things is the basic material of the natural world, whether we take that to be energy or something else. After all, every familiar thing depends on the basic material of nature in order to come into existence and to exist, since every natural thing is made of it, and every artificial thing is as well. And the most basic material, whatever it might be, could not be made of anything more basic, and so it is a first cause of some sort. Could the absolutely first cause of all things simply be the most fundamental material in the natural world?

That is impossible for a number of reasons; here we will consider four of them.

First, we just showed above that there cannot be many instances of an absolutely first cause. But if the fundamental material of all things were, say, elementary particles, there could be (indeed are) many instances of such things. The materials in a particular cat are not the same individual materials as the ones in the dog sitting beside it. So, there

Recognizing God's Existence   107

The materials in a cat are not the same individual materials as the dog sitting next to it. Therefore, no material can be first cause of things.

cannot be many instances of an absolutely first cause, but there can be many instances of an absolutely fundamental material or particle, and therefore no fundamental material or particle can be an absolutely first cause of things.

Second, every material is a bodily thing, a thing having dimensions and dimensional parts. The material for a statue, for example, may be a mass of marble, which has a top half and a bottom half, a left half and a right half, and so on, and so it is made up of many distinct parts. Now a thing made up of distinct parts cannot exist without its parts existing together. The cause of the parts existing together, however, cannot simply be the parts themselves, since things that are of themselves distinct are not of themselves united, as the many members of a symphony orchestra are united not simply by the individual existence of each one, but by some additional unity. Nor can the cause of the many parts being together be the whole material they constitute, since that material's own existence is the result of, not the cause of, its parts existing together. Therefore, every bodily thing, everything having dimensions and parts that have size and location, owes the union of its parts (and hence its existence) to something outside itself. But every material is a bodily thing. Hence every material owes its existence to something outside itself. Therefore, no fundamental material can be the absolutely first cause of things.

Third, the first cause of the world of nature is responsible for its order, beauty, and intelligibility. Now a cause that does not tend to produce order, beauty, and intelligibility as such, but only as some sort of side effect, does so only by chance and rarely; someone throwing darts at a wall without aiming at anything in particular, or perhaps while blindfolded, might sometimes produce a pretty or recognizable pattern, or even spell out a word quite by chance. But that will be rare, and the result will not be spectacular. The order, beauty, and intelligibility of the natural world, however, pervades the whole of it in both time and space. Some animals and plants are ugly, but they are relatively rare in comparison with the number of beautiful animals and plants. Mountains and valleys and oceans and rivers are beautiful, as are clouds and stars and the sun and moon. These things are not, then, purely the result of agencies that do not tend to produce them as such. Consequently, the order, beauty, and intelligibility of the world are due to a cause that tends to produce these results as such. But the only cause that can tend to produce order, beauty, and intelligibility as such, and that can do so by itself and without dependence on any prior cause, is a mind. Therefore, the first cause of all things, which independently produces these qualities of the universe, is a mind.

Every productive cause must be equal to or superior to its effects in dignity, nobility, and perfection. The basic reason for this is that nothing can give what it does not somehow possess.
A horse cannot produce more kinds of animals than horses.

Fourth, every productive cause must be equal to or superior to its effects in dignity, nobility, and perfection. The basic reason for this is that nothing can give what it does not somehow possess. A math teacher cannot teach more math than she knows; but any math her students do learn from her must be math that she also knows (although her students' mistakes and the limitations in their understanding will not be found in her). A horse cannot produce more kinds of animals than horses. An argument cannot prove more conclusions than its premises warrant. A worker cannot contribute more energy to a building project than he has in his own body. Much more could be said in explanation of this very general principle. But if we apply it to the present case, we can see that the first cause of the existence of all things must contain in itself in some way all the perfection and nobility that it confers on things in giving them their existence. So, the first cause of things must be alive and intelligent, since it confers these perfections upon some beings. This is yet another reason why the raw materials in nature cannot be the absolutely first cause of things—they do not actually contain in themselves the perfections and dignities of all natural things, since they are not alive or intelligent, as the noblest natural things are. If

Recognizing God's Existence

inanimate material and energy alone produced intelligent beings, they would be conferring an intelligence upon things that they themselves in no way possessed.

The absolutely first and uncaused cause of all things, then, which alone has existence all by itself, and which contains in some superior manner the perfections that it confers on other things, is alive and intelligent. This being is not an it, but is a personal being. And he deserves a special name. That name is God.

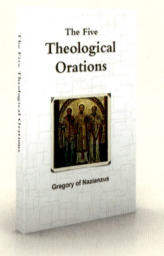

That God, the creative and sustaining cause of all, exists, sight and instinctive law informs us—sight, which lights upon things seen as nobly fixed in their courses, borne along in, so to say, motionless movement; instinctive law, which infers their author through the things seen in their orderliness. How could this universe have had foundation or constitution, unless God gave all things being and sustains them? No one seeing a beautifully elaborated lyre with its harmonious, orderly arrangement, and hearing the lyre's music will fail to form a notion of its craftsman-player, to recur to him in thought though ignorant of him by sight.

St. Gregory Nazianzen (329–390), *Theological Orations*

Review Questions

1. What is a cause, and what sorts of things need causes in order to be?

2. How do the examples of the chain and the boxcars help to appreciate that even an infinite series of caused causes (assuming that such a series could exist) would nevertheless require a first cause?

3. How does our appreciation of the unity and order of nature help us to understand why there must be only one first cause?

4. If existence belongs to the first cause as a property, why must there be only one first cause?

5. Why must the first cause be a mind and not some basic material substance?

6. How does the understanding of God that we gain from this chapter show that God is different from the Force?

Put Out Into the Deep

This chapter was specially adapted for *Why Believe*? by Dr. Michael Augros from another of his books, *Who Designed the Designer? A Rediscovered Path to God's Existence* (Ignatius Press, 2015). The editors highly recommend this book for those of you who wish to learn more about arguments for God's existence, together with Ralph McInerny's introduction to the subject, *Characters in Search of Their Author* (Notre Dame, 2003).

CHAPTER 7

7 Wisdom or the Will to Power?

There is a meme that has been going around the internet in recent years: "The universe doesn't care about you." What would lead someone to conclude that? Well, imagine someone who rejected the arguments put forward in the preceding three chapters. Chapter 4, recall, examined the error in the assumption that if there were something immortal or spiritual in human beings, then modern biology would be able to tell us about it. Chapter 5 challenged the view that thinking is merely brain activity. And chapter 6 argued that nature is the work of a cause that transcends nature entirely, namely God. So someone who rejected these arguments would believe there is nothing immortal or spiritual about human beings, that all thinking is just brain activity, and that God does not exist. The usual name for such a person is "atheist," though a common variant is "materialist." The atheist believes that we cannot look to a divinity to give purpose and meaning to our lives and to the rest of the universe. The atheist, in other words, rejects the notion that purpose and meaning are built into the universe by God or by any other being or principle. Whatever purpose and meaning exist in life is what we human beings decide to put into it. For this reason, the atheist concludes that "The universe doesn't care about you."

A recent Gallup poll concluded that about 10% of Americans say they do not believe in God (though only 3% actually identified as atheists). Another recent study, however, found that something closer to 25% of Americans do not believe in God. Whatever the precise numbers are at present, current trends suggest that you who are teenagers today will live out your futures in a culture where atheism, perhaps even a militant atheism, is an increasingly common outlook.

Wisdom or the Will to Power?

The Christian apologist, therefore, needs to prepare for this cultural battle. The battle is not over this or that Christian doctrine. It is over the very heart of the Gospel and the very heart of the philosophy that undergirds the Gospel. It is a battle over the true story of humanity: whether the author of that story is God, or whether the author of that story is human beings themselves.

To prepare you for this battle is one of the chief goals of this book. At the same time, all Christians need to keep in mind that, while military metaphors have their place, our engagement with the culture needs most of all to be a dialogue in pursuit of truth and undertaken out of love and respect even for those, indeed especially for those, with whom we most vehemently disagree. We cannot change a culture unless first we love the people who belong to it. And one of the key ways in which we can express that love is to try to understand as well as possible the viewpoints of those with whom we disagree, as a necessary first stage in the mutual pursuit of truth.

In this spirit we will in this chapter delve into the stories atheists tell themselves about how human life should be lived. In doing so we will discover what it means to be a protagonist in a universe that "doesn't care about you," and we will discover as well the incoherence and even destructive consequences of the atheist narrative. We will then be in a better position to offer the culture a more coherent and far happier story.

One of the key ways in which we can express love is to try to understand as well as possible the viewpoints of those with whom we disagree, as a necessary first stage in the mutual pursuit of truth.

The Will to Power

No thinker labored more passionately to cast aside Christian wisdom and to promote an alternative atheist narrative than the German philosopher Friedrich Nietzsche (1844–1900). Nietzsche possessed the gift of a powerful critical sense and had much of worth to say about the feebleness of nineteenth-century European morality, which was a shadow of its once robustly Christian self. Nietzsche detested Christianity, whether weakened or robust. Why? Because he saw it essentially as the product of resentment, resentment by the weak of the strong. As strange as it may sound, Nietzsche viewed a Christian virtue such as humility as the attempt by the weak of this world to keep the strong from exercising their strength—not just their physical strength, but all of their creative powers. And because he saw Christianity as the mere projection of this psychological weakness, Nietzsche notoriously declared that "God is dead." By this he meant not so much that God's existence has been disproved (though Nietzsche did believe that). He was principally making a declaration of independence. "Now," he wrote, "it is our preference that decides against Christianity—not arguments."

For Nietzsche, it was the human will that rose up and "murdered" God. Consider the following characteristic passage from his works:

> Whatever has value in our world now does not have value in itself, according to its nature—nature is always value-less—but has been given value at some time, as a present—and it was we who gave and bestowed it. Only we have created the world that concerns man!

This is a stunning proclamation, and in it we can hear Nietzsche giving voice to the atheist claims we considered at the outset. What Nietzsche is saying is that "value," the goodness or badness that we think we find embedded in things, is really something that we put into things by our choices. The value of an education, for example, is therefore not something inherent in the course of instruction or in the person who has been intellectually formed by it. The value of an education, rather, is a decision by someone or by a group of people to prefer and promote that education. We human beings are the creators, not the discoverers, of value. So when it comes to the question of how we ought to live, the Nietzschean answer is that we ought to live as creators of the very meaning of good and bad.

Nietzsche liked to capture this thought with the phrase "will to power." Because he thought European culture no longer needed to take Christian theology as its moral foundation, Nietzsche called for new values, a new way of living, based upon the will to power. "What is happiness?" Nietzsche asked in one of his works, ominously entitled *The Antichrist*. Happiness is "the feeling that power is growing, that resistance is overcome." However sinister such a statement may seem, we should not neglect a clear truth contained in it. We *are* in fact happiest as human beings when we experience progress in the exercise of our powers. No one likes being frustrated in his pursuits; we all want constantly to achieve more in, and to be getting better at, whatever we do. But Nietzsche's conception of the will to power reaches beyond this plain truth. His ideal human being, a character he called the *Übermensch* (the "overman," the "man who transcends") embodies the will to power by putting aside the morality of the slavish "herd," principally Christianity, and masters himself in order to create new values, values that are entirely of this world, not of some transcendent world.

Nietzsche never provided a definitive characterization or list of historical examples of his *Übermensch*. His statements regarding this strange figure are ambiguous. At one point he even speaks of his ideal as "the Roman Caesar with Christ's soul"—whatever that may mean. It is sometimes thought that Nietzsche's *Übermensch* was an inspiration

But he said to me, "My grace is sufficient for you, for power is made perfect in weakness." I will all the more gladly boast of my weaknesses, that the power of Christ may rest upon me. For the sake of Christ, then, I am content with weaknesses, insults, hardships, persecutions, and calamities; for when I am weak, then I am strong.

2 Corinthians 12:9–10

behind Nazism. Although Nietzsche's sister later became an avowed Nazi who appropriated her brother's writings for her cause, there is no clear evidence in Nietzsche's writings themselves that his overman was somehow a prescription for Nazi atrocities. What Nietzsche seemed to have in mind with the *Übermensch* was a man of great spiritedness willing to throw off the yoke of Christian wisdom and to create a new foundation for culture out of his own self-affirmation.

But what guidelines or restrictions are to be placed upon this creative self-affirmation? If Nietzsche himself would have been horrified to learn that his writings had been used as a basis for Nazi propaganda, then what in those writings restricts the *Übermensch's* power?

Because Nietzsche does not provide a clear answer to this question, his thought raises the awful specter of a person with unlimited power dominating others. The image of such a tyrant has no doubt haunted the consciousness of man since the exile of our first parents from the Garden of Eden. It is reflected in popular myths throughout history, down to the myths of our own day. How interesting it is that we never tire of rehearsing the combat between the ultimate force for good and the ultimate force for evil: Frodo versus Sauron; Luke Skywalker versus Darth Vader; Harry Potter versus Voldemort; the host of Marvel superheroes versus their monstrous adversaries and especially Thanos. Such tyrants are, of course, not only the subject of myth. Just staying within the twentieth century, we can name Stalin, Hitler, and Mao Zedong as tyrants exercising a brutal will to power. Indeed, Stalin once declared: "I believe in one thing only, the power of the human will," and from this terrible pronouncement came the deaths of tens of millions of people.

What is also interesting, in the myths as well as in history, is the familiar pattern in which such tyrants rise and fall. Stalin's Communist Russia is no more. And Sauron and all the other mythical nemeses typically get their comeuppance in the final act climax. But perhaps the most moving and most instructive example of the tyrant's rise and fall is in Shakespeare's story of the Scottish warrior Macbeth.

Wisdom or the Will to Power?

Macbeth and his comrade Banquo encounter three witches, who hail Macbeth as the future king of Scotland, but they also predict that Banquo, though he himself will never reign, will give birth to a line of Scottish kings.

A Tale Told by an Idiot

After a great military victory, Macbeth and his comrade Banquo encounter three witches, who utter a two-edged prophecy. The witches hail Macbeth as the future king of Scotland, but they also predict that Banquo, though he himself will never reign, will give birth to a line of Scottish kings. Macbeth does not quite know what to make of the prophecy concerning himself, though he is certainly attracted by its message. When he shares it with his ambitious wife, she goads him on to the assassination—a word invented by Shakespeare for this play—of the reigning king, Duncan, who comes to Macbeth's castle on a state visit. On the night Macbeth is to execute the plan, he hesitates, but Lady Macbeth shames him into following through. Left alone in the castle to prepare himself for the deed, Macbeth then thinks he sees a dagger in the air before him. He convinces himself that it is not real, that "the bloody business" is causing him to see things, and resolves to kill the king. He does so, and though he is haunted by his crime, he brazenly assumes the throne of Scotland.

Once seated, however, Macbeth finds that he cannot rest. His fears concerning Banquo "stick deep." Did not the witches also prophesy that Banquo's line would reign as kings of Scotland? Unable to abide this outcome, Macbeth conspires to do away with his friend. One murder thus breeds a second, yet even after Banquo is dispatched Macbeth's

118   CHAPTER 7

problems are not over. Duncan's son Malcolm, who fled Scotland under suspicion of being his father's murderer, has raised an army in England with which he plans to march on Scotland and reclaim his birthright from Macbeth. The climactic battle takes place in the country near Dunsinane Castle, where Macbeth learns that Lady Macbeth, driven mad by her and her husband's killing spree, has thrown herself from a castle tower. Macbeth is struck by the futility of his tyrannical designs yet, consumed with rage, fights on until he is slain, leaving the way free for Malcolm to take the throne and restore justice.

Lady Macbeth, driven mad by her husband's killing spree, throws herself from a castle tower.

This bare summary of *Macbeth* does not begin to do justice to the depth of the play and especially the psychological and spiritual toll their murderous actions take upon both Macbeth and Lady Macbeth. One speech in particular, delivered by Macbeth on the field of Dunsinane immediately after learning of his wife's suicide, reveals much about the costs of expanding power without limit:

> *Tomorrow, and tomorrow, and tomorrow,*
> *Creeps in this petty pace from day to day,*
> *To the last syllable of recorded time;*
> *And all our yesterdays have lighted fools*
> *The way to dusty death. Out, out, brief candle!*
> *Life's but a walking shadow, a poor player,*
> *That struts and frets his hour upon the stage,*
> *And then is heard no more. It is a tale*
> *Told by an idiot, full of sound and fury,*
> *Signifying nothing.*

Macbeth asserts in these lines that not only his life, but all life, is meaningless, "a tale told by an idiot" that, like Macbeth's own, might be full of "sound and fury" but which in the end signifies "nothing." Is this a view he has always held, or has his ultimately self-destructive path led him to this despair? Earlier in the play, when he is pondering the murder of Banquo, Macbeth refers to his "eternal jewel," his soul, which will be put in further jeopardy by this murder. But by the time he mourns his wife's death on the field of Dunsinane, he has lost all sense of the Christian story giving meaning to his life.

In philosophical argumentation there is a strategy known as the *reductio ad absurdum*, the "reduction to the absurd," in which one refutes one's opponent's argument by showing that it leads to an absurd consequence. In concluding that life has no ultimate meaning or purpose, it is as though Macbeth is pointing out the absurd consequence of an argument—except that the "argument" here is his own life, or the villainous tyranny he has made of his life. The pursuit of power for its own sake and without limits, he argues, leads to the grim reality of despair. Shakespeare's portrayal of Macbeth, therefore, serves as a powerful counter-example to the claim that the will to power leads to any kind of fulfillment. Countless tragic villains through the centuries—in literature and in history—offer the same testimony.

Creators or Characters?

Macbeth, Stalin, Hitler, Nietzsche's *Übermensch*: these figures run to extremes. They are on one end of a spectrum. Most atheists do not go to the extreme of advocating the raw expansion of power as the best way of living a human life. Even while rejecting God or any other source of meaning sewn up into the fabric of the universe, they do not give up on the quest for meaning and truth and justice. Far from being a tale told by an idiot, they believe life can be a tale best told by an enlightened, politically progressive citizen of modern democracy.

It would take us too far afield to examine here even one or two of these intermediate positions. But, in fact, we have already examined one in chapter 2: the claim that happiness is found in authenticity, living the life that is "true" to the person you are meant to be. What we discovered about this modern ideal of authenticity, however, is that it does not

provide sufficient guidelines, guidelines backed up by reasons, for one expression of authenticity over another. And if we were to canvass further intermediate positions—that is, positions that more or less agree with the Nietzschean narrative but still try to provide some justification for a way of living compatible with democratic values—we would come to the same conclusion. How could it be otherwise? Once one accepts that human beings create the stories of their lives through self-affirmation, there is no rational justification for one form of self-affirmation over another. One can only depend upon the (fragile) consensus of like-minded citizens to keep the community from tearing itself apart.

The challenge of the atheist narrative is aimed at the very heart of reality. For if reality has no narrative built into it, if, as the meme says, "the universe doesn't care about you," then we are left to choose a life like Nietzsche's *Übermensch* or some softer version of self-affirmation more suited to the democratic existence we are used to. But what if reality actually takes the form of the narrative discussed in chapter 2 and elaborated in the chapters since then? What if God is the author of the story of creation and we are all characters in his story? As Christian believers, we know this to be true. But how do we convince the atheist, who does not acknowledge God's existence? How do we convince him that we are not creators but characters?

Truth Partial and Obscure

Nietzsche famously said, "There are no facts, only interpretations." Along the same lines he affirmed: "There is only a perspective seeing, only a perspective knowing." What did he mean? He meant that our perception of reality is never unfiltered, that it always involves the point-of-view, the outlook, the perspective of the perceiver. On 9/11, President George W. Bush called the terrorists who attacked the United States cowards. The terrorists who died that day thought of themselves as martyrs, as heroes. Who decides which side is right? Nietzsche would say that we cannot answer this question by appealing to some brute fact "underneath" the conflicting perspectives of President Bush and the terrorists. The facts of nearly 3,000 people killed and 6,000 injured do not alone, Nietzsche would argue, decide the issue: for President Bush saw these dead and injured people as innocent, but the terrorists did not.

It might seem strange to say, but the counter-argument to Nietzsche's view begins by acknowledging a partial truth in what he is saying. Human beings do approach reality from different, often conflicting, perspectives. Sometimes these conflicts occur even at the level of basic sense perception. So how do we break out of the contending perspectives? If Nietzsche is right that there are no facts, only interpretations, then how is truth, the mind's grasp of an objective reality, possible?

Return to the arguments in chapter 2 about happiness. When we consider whether happiness is found in a life of pleasure or in the ideal of authenticity, or even in this chapter as we consider whether happiness consists in the will to power, we are not simply playing with ideas inside our minds that may or may not have something to do with the reality outside our minds. The situation is altogether different. What is really happening as we examine the various candidates for happiness is that we are trying to articulate the reality of happiness completely and clearly, a reality we are already grasping partially and obscurely. Let us put the thought another way. In thinking and speaking, we are already out in the world. The mind is not a piece of software enclosed in the box of one's cranium. Our minds naturally wander, as it were, out in the open field, in public space—though, being a touch near-sighted, they are not always clear on what they see. In a sense, then, we can speak of grasping the truth partially and obscurely. We recognize this all the time when we say things like, "That's true to some extent," or "You're partly right." Accordingly, when someone says that "Happiness consists in pleasure," he or she is saying something partially true-for pleasure is certainly a component, though not the essence, of a happy life.

But hold on. A Nietzschean will complain that in talking about partial and obscure truth we have smuggled into the argument a standard of absolutely clear and complete truth that exists "underneath" or "beyond" conflicting perspectives. After all, it makes no sense to speak of something as partial and obscure without assuming a sense of something complete and clear. No doubt the Nietzschean will accuse us of exercising our own will to power in smuggling into the argument such a standard.

This Nietzschean objection is correct—partially. In speaking of partial and obscure truth we are of course assuming a standard that measures statements as either partially or completely true. But we have not smuggled this standard into the argument without a reason. In point of fact, as we shall now turn to see, it is a reason that the Nietzschean must accept as well.

A Truth That Cannot Be Denied

Everything we do, we do in order to achieve some good, something we believe will perfect or complete us in some way. Whether it is flossing our teeth or studying French irregular verbs, we are always in pursuit of some good. The good, therefore, is that toward which all our actions tend.

This argument shows that, when it comes to our actions, the good is inescapable. We cannot not pursue it. We are, in a sense, bound by it.

So it is not merely a matter of perspective whether a person is bound to pursue the good. On 9/11, both President Bush and the terrorists were attempting to pursue something that at least seemed to them to be good. All their actions were governed by the principle, "Do good and avoid evil." Not that any of them on that terrible day had explicitly formulated this principle. It was so habitual to them, as it is to us, that explicit formulation was unnecessary.

St. Thomas Aquinas (1224–1274) speaks of this principle, "Do good and avoid evil," as the first precept of the natural law. From a theological point of view, the natural law is God's providential law governing the universe as it pertains to human beings. What this means is that God in creating us did not simply give us our human nature; he also directed our nature toward himself by binding it to the good. The word "law" in Latin, *lex*, stems from the verb *ligare*, which means "to bind." That is what good law does, from simple traffic laws to complex federal laws to God's eternal law: it holds us fast, binds us, so that we act in ways that are really conducive to our happiness.

Wisdom or the Will to Power?

From a philosophical point of view, what is apparent is not God as providential lawgiver, but our unavoidable desire for goodness. Anyone, religious believer or not, can recognize the self-evident truth that all his or her actions are governed by the law, "Do good and avoid evil." This precept may also be cast in terms of an affirmative proposition: "Good is to be done, and evil is to be avoided." This principle is so fundamental that its truth cannot be denied. It is so fundamental that the attempt to deny it itself presupposes it. If an objector sets out to defend the thesis, "Not every human being is bound by the law, 'Do good and avoid evil,'" he or she would unwittingly be pursuing the good of a successful objection.

Does this mean that the Nietzschean also is forced to accept the truth of the law, "Do good and avoid evil"? It does. Imagine the Nietzschean trying to convince us that the Christian faith is only a mask for the will to power, the product of resentment. What is the Nietzschean doing? He or she is trying to achieve the good of influencing our way of thinking. There is no action that does not aim at some good. We have, therefore, established at least one truth that cannot be denied by any human agent: the law that says "Do good and avoid evil." By a parallel inquiry, we could also come to recognize the first principle of our very thinking, the well-known and justly-celebrated law of non-contradiction: "A thing cannot be and not be at the same time and in the same respect." As with the first precept of the natural law, those who attempt to deny the law of non-contradiction inevitably assume the principle they are attempting to deny.

See, I have set before you this day life and good, death and evil. If you obey the commandments of the Lord your God which I command you this day, by loving the Lord your God, by walking in his ways, and by keeping his commandments and his statutes and his ordinances, then you shall live and multiply, and the Lord your God will bless you in the land which you are entering to take possession of.... I have set before you life and death, blessing and curse; therefore choose life, that you and your descendants may live, loving the Lord your God.

Deuteronomy 30:15–16, 19–20

124   CHAPTER 7

Consider as well certain fundamental moral norms which are shared by all. These are among the indications that, beyond different schools of thought, there exists a body of knowledge which may be judged a kind of spiritual heritage of humanity.

St. John Paul II, *Fides et Ratio*, 4

Yet it may well be asked, how can this first precept of the natural law help arbitrate between conflicting conceptions of what is good for human beings? For if everyone in the world is bound by it, then this law fails to distinguish anything. Indeed, we seem forced to conclude that everything even a terrorist does is good.

Bound for Heaven

Think back to Aristotle's contention that if there were not some overarching good to our lives, some Best or Highest or Ultimate Good, then we would have no reason to pursue any good whatsoever. If there were not an Ultimate Good that served as the final term or resting place of our desire, then our desire would not be motivated to search for any good, because desire for goodness, by definition, is a quest for total and complete satisfaction. If we are choosing and acting at all, we are necessarily choosing and acting in view of some conception of our Ultimate Good.

So the pursuit of any good and the pursuit of Ultimate Goodness are necessarily linked. Any action, any pursuit of a good, whether well-flossed teeth or mastery of French irregular verbs, is a means to happiness, a step on the quest for Ultimate Goodness. The result is that the natural law binds us not just to "good" in general, but to the hierarchy of goodness that leads to happiness, a happiness that consists in living the virtues. Thus we can conclude that all human beings are necessarily bound to the Christian story, to the life of virtuous activity both as it can be lived in this life and as it is experienced in its ultimate fulfillment in Heaven. The atheist story promoted by Nietzsche is defeated.

The first precept of the natural law alone tells enough of the story of the Christian quest for happiness to rule out certain misguided conceptions of the Ultimate Good. We know from the command to "Do good and avoid evil" that wealth, for example, cannot be the essence of happiness, because wealth is only a means to other goods, not an Ultimate Good in itself. And as soon as we recall the other requirements necessary for a good to be the Ultimate Good of human beings, the narrative arc of human beings comes even more clearly into focus. What are those requirements? The Ultimate Good is:

- specific to our rational nature,
- achievable by our own efforts (not absolutely in isolation from others, however, given that by nature we are social animals), and
- so perfect it can never disappoint us.

Aside from the command to do good and avoid evil, there are other self-evident precepts of the natural law, laws that cannot be denied without rendering the denier incoherent. These precepts are self-evident because they attach to goods that comprise the very essence of happiness. The preservation of life is absolutely fundamental for happiness, and so the natural law commands us to do what is necessary to preserve our existence. The life of moral virtue is essential to happiness, but the seeds of moral virtue are sown in childhood, and so the family's role as the promoter of happiness is assured. Higher still in the hierarchy of goods essential to happiness are the goods of social and political life, and to these goods attach commands of justice that

The life of moral virtue is essential to happiness, but the seeds of moral virtue are sown in childhood, and so the family's role as the promoter of happiness is assured.

The 9/11 memorial pool in New York City, NY.

direct us to care for the common goods of these communities. Lastly there is the natural law commanding us to pursue the highest good we human beings are made for, truth, the pursuit of which frames our pursuit of the virtues in this life and serves as our eternal delight in the next: for God himself *is* Truth.

So what about the terrorists who attacked the United States on 9/11? Does the Christian story that has begun to emerge provide enough of a standard to condemn their actions? It does, and without making any appeal to Christianity in itself. By nature we human beings are made to live in community with others; we cannot be happy in isolation. The natural laws that govern our life in community with others command that we promote and protect, as far as we are able, the good of those with whom we live in community. This, of course, implies that we must work to protect their lives. Wars, when they are just, are undertaken in order to preserve the life of the community and even to do what is best for enemy combatants, which is to deliver them justice. More would have to be said about what constitutes a just war, but it would not take much to argue that in a just war innocent non-combatants can never be targets of military action. This is because the community we share with all human beings is not dissolved when nations go to war with one another; on the contrary, the ultimate aim of war is to preserve the human community. So even before getting into the justice of the terrorists' claims against the United States, we can argue that the killing of innocent non-combatants on 9/11 was unjust and that, as President Bush said, the terrorists' deed was cowardly.

Becoming a Character

This defense of the Christian story shows the weaknesses in the atheist narrative defended by Friedrich Nietzsche, but it is also, in just this sketchy form, somewhat misleading. For what has been left out of the narrative so far is the moral formation required, not only to recognize the natural law, but also to act upon it. The natural law precepts cannot be denied coherently, it is true, but that does not mean they cannot be denied incoherently by poor souls in the grip of twisted ideologies or hobbled by poor moral formation of a more ordinary sort. This is not even to mention the mistakes we human beings make in matters not governed directly by self-evident precepts of the natural law. The best choice of a college, of a career, or of a spouse: there is no self-evident command concerning these things. To make decisions about them we need a virtue that enables us to make good decisions in the midst of complex and shifting circumstances. This virtue is known as prudence, a virtue that only is obtained after long practice. The point is that knowing what our good is, whether at the level of natural law or at the level of prudence, is no mere intellectual exercise like the reading of an instruction manual. To know the good, we have to become a certain sort of person. The first step toward becoming that sort of person is to see ourselves clearly as characters in the Christian story. And so it is to a deeper understanding of what the Christian story is all about that we now turn.

Review Questions

1. Why does Nietzsche think that Christianity is the product of resentment by the weak of the strong? How is this resentment a masked form of the will to power?

2. How does Shakespeare's *Macbeth* argue for the destructiveness in the Nietzschean understanding of the will to power?

3. What is the distinction between the partial and obscure grasp of truth and the complete and clear grasp of truth? Can you think of examples of this distinction other than those having to do with the discussion of happiness (for example, in the realm of science)?

4. In what sense are human beings bound to the Ultimate Good? Is it possible for someone to not want to pursue the Ultimate Good?

5. Why is a denial of the first precept of the natural law, "Do good and avoid evil," necessarily incoherent?

6. Can you list what you think are some natural laws governing family life? Political life? Our love for truth?

7. What are some further examples of situations in which prudence is called for, situations that natural law precepts do not explicitly cover and so demand careful deliberation of circumstances?

Put Out Into the Deep

A forceful defense of the natural law is another feature of a book we have recommended before, C.S. Lewis's *The Abolition of Man*. In the section of the book entitled "Men Without Chests," Lewis contends that without observance of the natural law, a society is vulnerable to being ruled by what Lewis calls "Controllers," a group with strong affinities with Nietzsche's *Übermensch*.

Wisdom or the Will to Power? 129

CHAPTER 8

Creation

In the Beginning

The pronouncements of modern atheists would not have shocked the sages of ancient Israel. There were scoffers aplenty in the ancient world. The Book of Psalms makes that clear, calling "fools" those who told themselves that there is no God (Ps 14:1; 53:1). And in the Book of Wisdom, we find a striking formulation of the secular cast of mind: "They reasoned unsoundly, saying to themselves, 'Short and sorrowful is our life, and there is no remedy when a man comes to his end, and no one has been known to return from Hades. Because we were born by mere chance, and hereafter we shall be as though we had never been; because the breath in our nostrils is smoke, and reason is a spark kindled by the beating of our hearts. When it is extinguished, the body will turn to ashes, and the spirit will dissolve like empty air'" (Wis 2:1–3). The new atheists of our time are not perhaps so new after all. Whatever else an atheistic position may be understood to include or imply, it is plainly opposed to the Jewish and Christian conception of creation, and so our apology or defense of the faith must treat that essential truth.

Our discussion of creation has three parts. First, we will look at the doctrine itself, both as a theoretical position—at once philosophical and theological—and as it relates to various texts in the Bible, including the first chapters of the Book of Genesis. Second, we will examine Darwin's theory of evolution by natural selection, which is often, but erroneously, set in opposition to belief in God. Third, we will consider the Scriptural account of the Fall, which is an essential part of the Church's theology of creation.

The Psalmist's observation that "the heavens are telling the glory of God" (Ps 19:1) was not alien to the first philosophers of ancient Greece. Thales (died ca. 546 B.C.), who thought that all things were made of water, is reported to have said that "the world is beautiful" because "it is of God's making." Anaxagoras (died ca. 428 B.C.), taking the thought of his predecessors one step further, had the beautiful intuition that the myriads of tiny parts of which the world is made—specks of matter of one kind or another—had been put into harmonious order by "mind"

or "thought." Building on these affirmations, Aristotle worked out the arguments that prove that everything we see proceeds from a singular, ultimate cause, the one God, an immaterial mind—in Aristotle's words, "thought thinking itself."

The Catholic understanding of creation has much in common with this philosophical perspective. Consider St. John's formulation of the doctrine in the prologue to his Gospel: "In the beginning was the Word, and the Word was with God, and the Word was God. He was in the beginning with God; all things were made through him, and without him was not anything made that was made" (Jn 1:1–3). From the treasures of revelation contained here, what we should ponder at this juncture is St. John's stirring claim that the Word—in Greek, the *Logos*—was the author of the universe in its entirety, indeed of "everything that was made." Here is an echo of the philosophical doctrine of the uniqueness and the simplicity of God that we have already encountered.

The natural light of reason allows us to arrive at a limited understanding of God by tracing effects back to a first cause. From that reasoning, we learn that the first cause must be uncaused, unique, and immaterial. With confidence, then, we can affirm that God brought the material universe into being from himself, by the entirely unconstrained choice of his will. For if God had been constrained in some way, then that cause outside of God and acting upon God would itself be greater than or prior to God the first cause—a notion which is absurd. Creation from nothing (*ex nihilo*) is, accordingly, what is called a preamble of the faith: it can be known by the natural light of reason, and it has also been revealed to us by God—in Genesis 1, John 1, and by the mother of the seven martyrs of the Book of Maccabees: "I beg you, my child, to look at the heaven and the earth and see everything that is in them, and recognize that God did not make them out of things that existed" (2 Mac 7:28).

The philosophical and theological doctrine of creation *ex nihilo* illuminates the relation in which the world stands to God: as an effect to its cause. The doctrine does not, however, specify how the world

132   CHAPTER 8

proceeded from God as its cause or even when it did so. On this point we encounter a rather startling teaching from St. Thomas Aquinas, who argued that we know by Divine Revelation alone, and not from reasoning, that the world had a beginning in time.

Aquinas treated the question at different times during his life and brought a number of arguments to bear upon it. We will note two of them. The first argument turns upon the fact that while a cause always precedes its effect in being, it does not typically precede its effect in time. In fact, our everyday experiences of causation involve the simultaneity of cause and effect, as when Sally kicks the soccer ball into the net. Her kicking and the ball's being kicked are separate in being—Sally is cause and the ball being kicked is an effect that depends upon that cause—but together in time. On the strength of this observation, Aquinas concluded that it is not self-contradictory to say both that God created the world and that the world has existed forever. (That these two propositions can be held together does not, for that, make them true; it merely makes it possible to hold them both at once.) Thus, if our inquiries are limited to reason alone, we might come to the conclusion that the world always was.

God loves nothing so much as the man who lives with wisdom. For she is more beautiful than the sun, and excels every constellation of the stars. Compared with the light she is found to be superior, for it is succeeded by the night, but against wisdom evil does not prevail. She reaches mightily from one end of the earth to the other, and she orders all things well.

Wisdom 7:28–8:1

The second argument is more difficult: that the world does not declare its newness or beginning in time. Informed by the work of astronomers, we might be inclined to disagree with Aquinas. Surely the world declares its age, we might say, and also its progression from simple to complex, from the "primeval atom" that exploded in the Big Bang to the profusion of galaxies that our telescopes reveal today. Aquinas, however, could note in reply that cosmologists admit that our instruments can only take us back to the first several seconds after the Big Bang, and that the conditions of the universe prior to that moment are only the object of our theories, and not of our empirical investigations. Moreover, it remains at least logically possible to ask what preceded the Big Bang and to theorize about multiverses or an oscillating universe. However much those theories may seem unsubstantiated, the most that can be said against them is that they are fanciful and that they do not repose upon evidence, not that they are self-contradictory. The fact of the matter is simple: we cannot get back behind the beginning to watch it unfold. So, although it is entirely fitting that our cosmological theories should point to a first moment in the history of the universe, such theories neither prove the existence of God themselves, nor are they necessarily going to convince every astronomer and physicist. If we are to have certainty about the temporal origin of the universe, we are going to get that certainty only by believing what God has revealed to us. And so, the twofold "in the beginning" of Genesis 1 and John 1 is not and can never be in conflict with either science or philosophy. It is a revelation that takes us entirely beyond the scope of our scientific investigations and philosophical arguments.

The force of that "in the beginning," as the *Catechism of the Catholic Church* points out with luminous clarity, is as "the first and universal witness to God's all-powerful love" (CCC 288). It constitutes the explicit response of the Christian faith to "the basic question that men of all times have asked themselves: 'Where do we come from?' 'Where are we going?'" This twofold question, as the *Catechism* then notes, is "decisive for the meaning and orientation of our life and actions" (CCC 282). The point, then, of God's having revealed that he created the world from nothing and "in the beginning" was to confirm and to elevate the philosophical truth that he is the world's unique first cause, so that this truth would be accessible not only to the learned, but indeed to all men and women of whatever age or condition (see CCC 286). The truth of creation is what supports and makes intelligible our recourse to prayer, our confidence in Divine Providence, our decisive rejection of false gods, and our equanimity in the face of powers of every kind—whether hurricanes, evil people, or demons—that threaten to harm us. It is because the God who walked among us, suffered and died for us, and rose from the dead is also the God who created the universe that St. Paul was able to profess that "neither death, nor life, nor angels, nor principalities, nor things present, nor things to come, nor powers, nor height, nor depth, nor anything else in all creation, will be able to separate us from the love of God in Christ Jesus our Lord" (Rom 8:38-9).

Aftermath from Hurricane Katrina which devastated New Orleans in 2005. The truth of creation is what supports and makes intelligible our recourse to prayer and our equanimity in the face of powers of every kind.

The Catholic view of this text is and has long been simple: this account is meant to teach us about the dignity of humankind and about the orderliness and goodness of the creation, but not about the details of natural history that are the proper object of scientific inquiry.

In light of the Church's doctrine of creation, we are now able to approach the interpretation of the first three chapters of the Book of Genesis. The Catholic view of this text is and has long been straightforward: this account is meant to teach us about the dignity of humankind and about the orderliness and goodness of the creation, but not about the details of natural history that are the proper object of scientific inquiry (see CCC 283–84).

St. Augustine of Hippo (354–430) was one of the earliest theologians to take up the task of interpreting Genesis 1. In his *Literal Meaning of Genesis*, he spoke with great energy about the danger of Christians "spouting what they claim our Christian literature has to say on these topics," that is, "about the earth and the sky, about the other elements of the world." Those who make such claims risk bringing not only the doctrine of creation into contempt, but the authority of Bible and thus the faith as a whole. St. Augustine's judgment was that this subject requires great caution:

> *Above all we have to remember a point we have already made several times, that God does not work by time-measured movements, so to say, of soul or body, as do human beings and angels, but by the eternal and unchanging, stable formulae of his Word, co-eternal with himself.... In discussing obscure matters that are far removed from our eyes and our experience, which admit of various explanations that do not contradict the faith we are imbued with, let us never, if we read anything on them in the divine scriptures, throw ourselves head over heels into headstrong assertion.*

It should be clear that St. Augustine would not look favorably at attempts to find a "creation science" in the pages of the Bible. Writing fifteen centuries later, the authors of the *Catechism of the Catholic Church* followed his interpretation. The inspired author of the Book of Genesis gave to Israel the account of the six days of creation and of the sabbath rest not to offer a lesson in natural history, but instead to "express in their solemn language the truths of creation—its origin and its end in God, its order and goodness, the vocation of man, and finally the drama of sin and the hope of salvation" (CCC 289).

Theories of cosmic and biological evolution do not come into conflict with the Christian and Jewish belief in God as Creator. By coming to recognize the existence of God, we discover that God causes every other cause and maintains the universe's existence by an act of creation that is entirely outside the realm of matter, motion, and time. Our empirical and theoretical investigations of the natural world can in no way overturn the truth that we are created by God, nor should they prompt us to doubt it.

The pillars of creation in the Eagle Nebula, so named because the gas and dust that they are made up of are in the process of creating new stars.

As to biological evolution, St. John Paul II memorably declared that the idea is "more than a hypothesis." The statement was made in a context in which he could speak only briefly, but it may be taken to have been a gesture to the generally accepted age of the universe (approximately 13.8 billion years) and of the earth (4.5 billion), as well as to the progressive manifestation of the different kinds of living things on the earth that the fossil record reveals. Were he to have elaborated his statement, perhaps he would have said that it seems plain that once there was in the universe nothing but hydrogen and a bit of helium and that from that simple beginning there has unfolded a magnificent tapestry of being, as stars coalesced and gave birth to humble lithium, and eventually to carbon, and then, slowly, as the eons passed, to still heavier elements, and then planets, and at last, on this earth, to life. This story may certainly be called evolutionary, as too the story of the forms of life on earth, for in these stories the simple comes first and the complex afterwards. That the story of the universe has such a shape seems clear; just how we are to go about telling it, however, is not. For his part, St. John Paul II was emphatic: there are "theories" of evolution, in the plural, and the task of adjudicating them requires not only the best possible scientific reflection, but also the illumination offered by philosophy and theology.

Darwinism: Pro and Con

Darwin's theory of evolution by natural selection remains the most celebrated form of evolutionary theory, so we will limit our examination of evolution to it. There is much to be learned from Darwin, but there are also cogent reasons for thinking that his theory is only a partial one, which, like most scientific theories, will profit from further inquiry, reflection, and revision for decades to come.

If an evolutionary account is to be in any way illuminating, it must help us to understand the causes of what we already know to be the case from our common experience. In other words, an evolutionary theory must not only account for the existence of different kinds of living things but also preserve the confidence we gain from our everyday experience that nature does indeed present us with recognizable kinds of living things, such as oak, and robin, and squirrel.

Some of you are perhaps not much in the habit of noticing the kinds of trees, birds, and other living things that surround us. It could be that you are more aware of the differences you see among the people you meet or the automobiles that pass by than of the differences among the various kinds of plants or animals. Many of you, however, may be either avid gardeners and bird watchers yourselves or related to those who are, that is, to people who have learned to scorn such upstarts as the Norway maple and the starling and to prize the rare and beautiful orchid or warbler. It is with just that sort of confidence in knowing the kinds of things and loving them according to what they are that biological inquiry begins.

We take an interest in birds, for instance, precisely because we see in them intelligible patterns that suggest the presence of hidden causes that we can come to understand. For it is not a random set of sounds that we hear every spring in our backyards and neighborhoods, but rather a familiar mixture of the *dee-dees* and *fee-bees* of the chickadees, the sharp cries of the jays, the lilting if monotonous chanting of the robins, and, if we are lucky, the sweet affectionate songs of the bluebirds. If we

Creation 137

are able to distinguish among these various sounds and refer them to their proper performers, then we have begun to attain some knowledge of what the birds in question are, and we have started to learn about their natures, that is, about what kind of bird each of them is.

Darwin's own life as a biologist began with just that sort of experience. He was an accomplished field naturalist whose knowledge of the flora and fauna of Great Britain was already impressive prior to the voyage on the H.M.S. Beagle that took him around the world and showed him so many marvels. After his return to London in 1836, he was plunged into a maelstrom of controversy over the biological and geological history of the world, amidst a climate of opinion that can only be called over-heated. This was the era of Romanticism and Revolution. The Old Regime had been overturned in the French Revolution of 1789, and a new world of gas lights and railroads, utilitarianism and democracy had been born. In this context, it was impossible to theorize about the origins of the different kinds of living things without religious and political questions immediately arising. In England, the most popular form of biological thinking adopted a highly-conservative stance to the changes of the day and asserted the absolute fixity of the natural order: revolutions of all kinds, on this perspective, were unnatural and bad. This was the position contained in William Paley's *Natural Theology* (1802), a book whose arguments were not very astute. The elbow and eye, among other parts and organs, he took to be so many "contrivances" showing the immediate intervention of God in the natural order of things. The idea that an organism bears within itself the cause of its own life, growth, and development—an idea common to Aristotle and St. Thomas Aquinas—was one that Paley did not hold.

We take an interest in birds, precisely because we see in them intelligible patterns that suggest the presence of hidden causes that we can come to understand.

Given that he wrote in the context of Paley's conception of living things as so many machines contrived by God's immediate handiwork, it is understandable that Darwin should have rejected what then passed for creationism. What he chiefly sought to do, it may be argued, was to restore a truly biological view of animals and plants, which, after

138   CHAPTER 8

What Darwin chiefly sought to do, it may be argued, was to restore a truly biological view of animals and plants.

all, we see to be born one from another, with generation following generation reliably and without any evident intervention by the miraculous. Consider this formulation of his conviction: "all the chief laws of paleontology plainly proclaim, as it seems to me, that species have been produced by ordinary generation: old forms having been supplanted by new and improved forms of life, produced by the laws of variation still acting around us, and preserved by Natural Selection." Or, again: "it is far more satisfactory to look at such instincts...as small consequences of one general law, leading to the advancement of all organic beings, namely, multiply, vary, let the strongest live and the weakest die." If Darwinism were nothing more than a persistent seeking for a biological explanation of the emergence of new natural kinds together with an intuition about how the exigencies of life tend to preserve those animals and plants capable of thriving in their ecological settings, it could be accepted by believing monotheists without much need for qualification.

Unfortunately, Darwin's theory, whether in his own formulation or that of other interpreters, has always included much more. Or, perhaps it would be better to say, much less. There was a defect in Darwin's thinking that has shaped most of those who have followed him: he did not sufficiently attend to the reality of natural kinds—that nature does not present us with a bewildering array of unique individuals. Rather, living things fall into more-or-less recognizable families, in the fully-reproductive sense of that word. Although Darwin was constrained to note the tendency of the offspring of an organism to resemble its parents, he never sufficiently reflected upon that great and central truth about living things. He was so troubled by the tendency of his contemporaries to insist upon the absolute fixity of species and the independent creation of them by so many miraculous divine interventions that he effectively set aside the reality of natural kinds, as, for instance here: "I look at the term species as one arbitrarily given for the sake of convenience to a set of individuals closely resembling one another." As Darwin backed away from the intelligibility of natural kinds, he combined and confused

Creation   **139**

varieties, sub-species, and species until the designations became unreliable. Flux and the interrelatedness of living beings preoccupied him, to the point that when he declared "the origin of species" to be the "mystery of mysteries," his accent was on the word origin rather than on the word species. Instead of explaining the different kinds of animals and plants, he had explained them away.

We are even willing to bet our lives on our knowledge of these differences, as when a fisherman in Alaska will brave the presence of a black bear, but flee from a Kodiak.

In the century and half since Darwin wrote *The Origin of Species* (1859), the proponents of Darwinism have gone further in the same line, and their perspective has hardened. Yet however difficult it may be to distinguish one kind of sparrow from another, or however reluctant we may be to declare whether we think the red and the black oak are best thought of as varieties of a single species or as distinct species, we are nevertheless fully confident that animals and plants differ from one another not merely as individuals, but also as groups or kinds. We are even willing to bet our lives on our knowledge of these differences, as when a fisherman in Alaska will brave the presence of a black bear, but flee from a Kodiak, or when the mushroom enthusiast will harvest the morel (*Morchella* sp.) and leave behind the destroying angel (*Amanita bisporigera*).

Professional biologists can help us to wonder even more deeply about the persistent intelligibility of natural kinds. In this vein, biochemist Franklin Harold has called attention to the gut bacterium, *E. coli*. This one-celled creature reproduces itself in generations only minutes long and has DNA that is "notoriously mutable," yet the fossil record offers us the remains of *E. coli* that are dated 100 million years in age but are recognizably the same as today's, even at the level of their DNA. Indeed, a recent scientific article recounting a long-term study of *E. coli* spoke with great confidence about the high rate of evolutionary change that the investigators had been able to witness through careful analysis of the bacteria's DNA, but failed to state the obvious point that, even after an experiment lasting 60,000 generations, the bugs were recognizably what they were before, that is, *E. coli*. Considering this amazing stability of *E. coli* as a natural kind or species, Harold concluded that "biological patterns do change over time" but "not quickly," and so was prompted to bring to his own evolutionary theorizing a question that is remarkably un-Darwinian: "Why, indeed, are there so many *kinds* of organisms large and small, and why do they cluster into discrete species?" If there is a mystery of mysteries in biology, this is it.

The reason for our dwelling on this point is worth reiterating as we bring this section to a close: Darwin's theory of the emergence of new kinds of living things over time by the predominant action of what he called natural selection has unquestionable merit, but it does not tell us everything that we want to know about living things. The Christian response towards Darwinism, therefore, and towards evolutionary theories generally, should be one of lively interest tempered with caution.

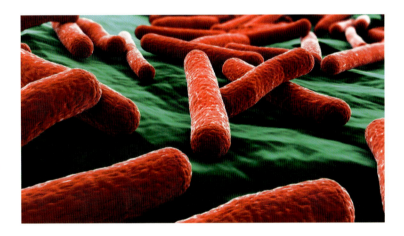

E. coli reproduces itself in generations only minutes long and has DNA that is "notoriously mutable," yet the fossil record offers us the remains of E. coli *that are dated 100 million years in age but are recognizably the same as today's, even at the level of their DNA.*

An example of this kind of response comes from one of America's greatest early scientists, the Harvard botanist Asa Gray (1810–1888), a devout Christian. Gray calmly responded to the claim made by a prominent Protestant minister that Darwin's theory was necessarily atheistic.

> *It is not for the theologian to object that the power which made individual men and other animals, and all the differences which the races of mankind exhibit, through secondary causes, could not have originated multitudes of more or less greatly differing individuals through the same causes. Clearly, then, the difference between the theologian and the naturalist is not fundamental, and evolution may be as profoundly and as particularly theistic as it is increasingly probable. The taint of atheism which, in Dr. Hodge's view, leavens the whole lump, is not inherent in the original grain of Darwinism—in the principles posited—but has somehow been introduced in the subsequent treatment. Possibly, when found, it may be eliminated.*

God is the sovereign master of his plan. But to carry it out he also makes use of his creatures' co-operation. This use is not a sign of weakness, but rather a token of almighty God's greatness and goodness. For God grants his creatures not only their existence, but also the dignity of acting on their own, of being causes and principles for each other, and thus of co-operating in the accomplishment of his plan.

Catechism of the Catholic Church, 306

Here Gray rightly insisted that God's work in creation extends to creating things that are themselves the causes of other things, as whenever we make something, assist someone with a task, or teach. As he pointed out, these secondary causes—the links in the chain we discussed in chapter 6—are themselves causes because of the prior causality of the first cause, which is God. Most effectively, then, did Gray labor to disassociate the speculations of evolutionary biologists from, on the one hand, the irresponsible and unnecessary claims of atheists, and on the other, the intemperate bluster of some of the atheists' opponents. This work of clarifying what science can say and what it cannot will doubtless be an arduous one, but Catholics should be certain that it can be successful. While we are about that work, we should imitate the serenity of Asa Gray, knowing that the doctrine of creation is unassailable and capable of being received on its own merits, that is, both by the natural light of reason and by the truthfulness of the God who has revealed it.

Original Sin: Truth of Reason or of Faith?

If one of the most important lessons of the Book of Genesis is that the creation is good and the result of God's free choice to bring the universe into being, we may naturally wonder why we encounter pain, suffering, death, and evil. For an answer, we turn to the second chapter of Genesis, in which we find God's revelation of another crucial beginning: the origins of the human race and its fall into sinfulness. The findings of archeologists and anthropologists may eventually be able to reconstruct a plausible story of the early history of humankind, and perhaps even say something about the hominid forms that seem to have been our biological precursors. Certainly, the remains of early humans show signs of violent death and at times even ritual sacrifice: we have no archaeological evidence of a lost paradise. What these sciences cannot give us, however, is empirical evidence of the Divine creation of the immaterial intellect of the first man and the first woman or of their equally-invisible descent into sin. Just as is the case with the origins of the universe, to learn about our species's origins, we must listen to God's Word.

The story of the creation and fall of humankind is disarming in its simplicity. Adam was created by God and placed in the garden of Eden with work to do, "to till it and keep it," and a single prohibition: "of the tree of knowledge of good and evil you shall not eat" (Gen 2:15–17). So that Adam would not be alone, God created his spouse, later named Eve. Then disaster struck. The serpent asked a question of Eve that incited her suspicion of God: "Did God say, 'You shall not eat of any tree of the garden?'" (Gen 3:1) And the arrow went home. As the *Catechism* says, with admirable directness, "Man, tempted by the devil, let his trust in his Creator die in his heart and, abusing his freedom, disobeyed God's command. This is what man's first sin consisted of" (CCC 397). Instead of trusting their Creator, Adam and Eve trusted the devil. They had every reason to believe that the God who had created them freely

Creation **143**

out of love would provide for their future needs. But instead, they freely chose to believe Satan, who accused God of duplicity and jealousy (Gen 3:4–5), and intimated that Adam and Eve would be better off if they were the master and mistress of their own fate. The results were soon to make themselves apparent: alienation from God, from one another, and from nature, with continued alienation, sin, pain, and suffering for the generations that followed.

Benjamin West, The expulsion of Adam and Eve from paradise, *1791, Oil on canvas.*

Let us pause to consider what this story purports to explain: the propensity of men and women to choose selfishly and irrationally, to the great harm of themselves and their fellow human beings. G. K. Chesterton (1874–1936) famously quipped that the doctrine of original sin is "the only part of Christian theology which can really be proved." Armed with a necessary distinction, we can surely agree with him. The distinction, however, is essential. What can be proved from experience—both personal and historical—is that there is something wrong with us humans that manifests itself in a tendency toward selfishness and irrationality. What cannot be proved, but can only be learned from Divine Revelation, is the origin and deeper significance of that tendency.

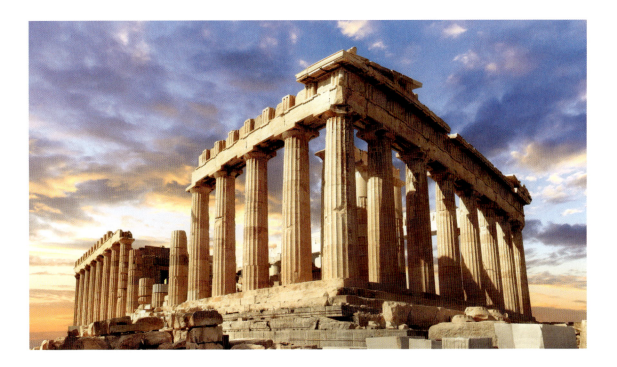

The human race is implicated in some terrible aboriginal calamity.

As to the proof or argument, no one has provided a more eloquent one than Blessed John Henry Newman:

> *To consider the world in its length and breadth, its various history, the many races of man, their starts, their fortunes, their mutual alienation, their conflicts; and then their ways, habits, governments, forms of worship; their enterprises, their aimless courses, their random achievements and acquirements, the impotent conclusion of long-standing facts, the tokens so faint and broken of a superintending design, the blind evolution of what turn out to be great powers or truths, the progress of things, as if from unreasoning elements, not towards final causes, the greatness and littleness of man, his far-reaching aims, his short duration, the curtain hung over his futurity, the disappointments of life, the defeat of good, the success of evil, physical pain, mental anguish, the prevalence and intensity of sin, the pervading idolatries, the corruptions, the dreary hopeless irreligion, that condition of the whole race, so fearfully yet exactly described in the Apostle's words, "having no hope and without God in the world" (Eph 2:12)—all this is a vision to dizzy and appall; and inflicts upon the mind the sense of a profound mystery, which is absolutely beyond human solution. What shall be said to this heart-piercing, reason-bewildering fact? I can only answer, that either there is no Creator, or this living society of men is in a true sense discarded from His presence...[and] since there is a God, the human race is implicated in some terrible aboriginal calamity. It is out of*

Creation   145

joint with the purposes of its Creator. This is a fact, a fact as true as the fact of its existence; and thus the doctrine of what is theologically called original sin becomes to me almost as certain as that the world exists, and as the existence of God.

This haunting passage from Newman's autobiography, *Apologia Pro Vita Sua* (1864), takes the matter of proof as far as it can go. The great tapestry of human affairs depicts a tragedy. Without Christ to save us from ourselves, our lives would be bleak indeed. It is astonishing that Newman should have written in this vein before the horrors of the holocausts of the twentieth century—Hitler's satanic slaughter of the Jews, Stalin's cruel massacre of millions, and the worldwide genocide of abortion over the past half-century.

Sir Anthony Van Dyck, Christ Crucified with St. John and Our Lady, *1619, Oil on canvas, Louvre, Paris, France.*

To conclude that the human race is fatally flawed and to hold the Catholic doctrine of original sin are two different mental acts. Fully to understand the doctrine of original sin is only possible in light of the truth of Jesus Christ (see CCC 388). For in the last analysis, the doctrine of original sin and the Genesis account of the Fall of Man are revealed to us as the key to human affairs that they are only by and in Christ—the Word made flesh—who time and again forgave sins and healed, called for repentance and preached the path of holiness, offered himself as a sacrifice, and, the sacrifice accomplished, returned to the right hand of the Father. To the direct examination of these mysteries, then, we must now turn.

Review Questions

1. How is the doctrine of creation *ex nihilo* (from nothing) a preamble of the faith, that is, at once philosophical and theological?

2. St. Thomas Aquinas argued that we cannot know the newness of the universe—that the world had a beginning in time—from the light of natural reason alone. What do you think he would say about the Big Bang theory?

3. What is the Catholic interpretation of Genesis 1–2, as exemplified by St. Augustine and the *Catechism of the Catholic Church*? How is Catholic "creationism" thus different from other varieties of creationism?

4. How did Charles Darwin's theory of the origin of species by the action of natural selection constitute a more properly biological way of thinking than the belief in the fixity of species that was popular at the time?

5. The Book of Genesis teaches us that humankind's primordial sin was one of disobedience and involved a choice of autonomy or self-rule. What insight does this doctrine offer into the human psychological condition?

6. How does the Catholic doctrine of original sin help to explain the social and political condition of the world today?

Put Out Into the Deep

For an introduction to the theology of creation that briefly treats the interpretation of the first three chapters of Genesis, one can do no better than Joseph Ratzinger's *'In the Beginning…' A Catholic Understanding of the Story of Creation and the Fall*, translated by Boniface Ramsey, O.P. (Eerdmans, 1995). A book that pursues the investigation at greater length and makes a wise foray into the interpretation of evolutionary theories is Christoph Cardinal Schönborn's *Chance or Purpose?: Creation, Evolution, and a Rational Faith*, translated by Henry Taylor (Ignatius, 2007).

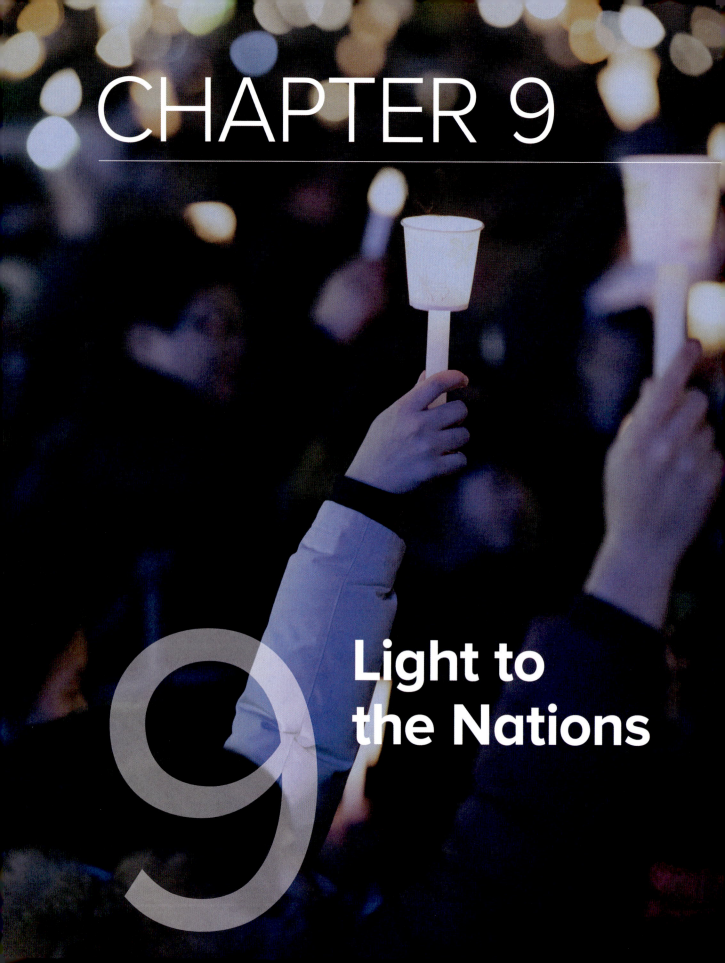

CHAPTER 9

Light to the Nations

One of the most profound autobiographical works ever written is the *Confessions* of St. Augustine, the remarkable story of how finding Christ delivered a young African man from a dead-end life of sin. It was not an easy journey for Augustine, whose disbelief had many facets. One of them was a deep prejudice against the Bible, a book his mother revered as divinely-inspired, but he found to be a bore and a jumble of contradictions. The author he loved to read was Cicero, whose use of the Latin tongue was resonant and stirring. The Bible's "humble style," by contrast, Augustine thought "unworthy of comparison with the nobility of Cicero's writings." It was only when confronted with the learned and eloquent Ambrose of Milan, the Christian bishop, that Augustine realized that the Bible contained more than he had thought. Yet even when he had been convinced that a well-educated person could take the Bible seriously, Augustine still had to face the issue at its heart: the Bible's claim to be the revealed Word of God.

The turning point came when he finally realized that it was reasonable for him to trust the testimony of the Bible's human writers:

> I considered how countless were the things that I believed, although I had not seen them nor was I present when they took place. Such were so many events in human history, so many things about places and cities that I had not seen, so many things about my friends, and so many things about physicians, so many things about countless other men. Unless we believed these things, nothing at all could be done in this life. Lastly, I thought of how I held with fixed and unassailable faith that I was born of certain parents, and this I could never know unless I believed it by hearing about them. By all this you [God] persuaded me that not those who believe your books, which you have established with such mighty authority among all nations, but those who do not believe in them are the ones to be blamed, and not to be given a hearing.

Augustine had no problem believing in God. But to believe God had intervened in history in the way the Bible describes was a much tougher proposition for him to accept.

Light to the Nations   149

The God of Abraham, Isaac, and Jacob

By the natural light of reason, men and women can discover the truth Moses learned at the burning bush, that God is the great "I AM," the source of all things. Thus, without ever reading a page of the Bible, the pagan thinker Aristotle was able to conclude that God must exist. This is why atheism was never an option for Augustine, the one-time hedonist who became one of the most famous theologians of the early Church. Speaking to God, he wrote, "I always believed both that you are and that you have care for us." What Augustine did wrestle with was the claim that the Bible gives us reliable information about God. Scripture insists that the Creator has made himself known by acting in history. Not only does the voice from the bush reveal God as the "I AM," the same voice tells Moses, "I am the God of your father, the God of Abraham, the God of Isaac, and the God of Jacob" (Ex 3:6).

As Augustine knew, this historical dimension of biblical faith requires one to go beyond what reason can demonstrate. The Bible asks us to accept that God has chosen to intervene in specific events in history and in the lives of particular people. Such a claim goes beyond what philosophers can discover. Unlike God's existence or goodness, no process of natural reasoning can prove that God had to intervene at certain points in the course of human events. It was not necessary that God should have spoken to Abraham in the ancient land of Babylon around 2000 B.C., as the Book of Genesis reports. Why not choose to speak to someone else? Why not enter the story at a different point in the timeline? Human reason cannot give us a conclusive answer to these questions.

Moreover, reason tells us that God transcends the limitations of time and space. Why should the God of the cosmos involve himself in petty human affairs at all? Should God act in such ways? And why speak in the plain language of the Israelites? Augustine himself once thought that it seemed beneath God to do such things. Yet these things, which he once called absurd and scoffed at, eventually became compelling to him. Why did Augustine come to believe that the Bible's claims are true? In this chapter, we will make his questions our own.

Not only does the voice from the bush reveal God as the "I AM," the same voice tells Moses, "I am the God of your father, the God of Abraham, the God of Isaac, and the God of Jacob" (Ex 3:6).

The God of Mysteries

The Book of Daniel uses an important word to describe God's revelatory acts in history: "mystery" (Dan 2:18–19). Mystery, in fact, is crucial to Christian faith. Fundamentally, it refers to realities that are either unknown to the human mind or to truths that the human intellect cannot fully comprehend. Some mysteries get solved because they become known to us. Others exceed our capacity to understand. The Bible actually recognizes two kinds of mysteries, natural and supernatural.

The existence of natural mysteries is well known. As any candid scientist will tell you, despite all of the advances made in the physical sciences, mysteries of nature remain. Even a common, everyday reality such as light is puzzling. Indeed, scientists have long been perplexed by the dynamics of this basic ingredient of the cosmos. Is it a wave or a particle? Somehow, defying our expectations, light acts as if it were both. Today, scientists simply accept this as a given even though they cannot fully comprehend why it is so.

Light to the Nations   **151**

We are even often at a loss to explain what is going on in our own hearts, let alone the hearts of others.

One does not have to be a scientist to find natural mysteries. In the Book of Jeremiah, we read: "The heart is deceitful above all things, and desperately corrupt; who can understand it?" (Jer 17:9). Whether or not one believes the Bible contains the word of God, the sentiment expressed here is hardly disputed. The human heart simply defies comprehension. We are often at a loss to explain what is going on in our own hearts, let alone the hearts of others. In the *Confessions*, St. Augustine himself wondered aloud about such mysteries within his own heart, reflecting on various decisions he had made throughout his life and saying more than once that he had become a problem or puzzle to himself.

The Book of Daniel speaks of supernatural mysteries. If natural realities exceed the bounds of human understanding, how much more should we find it difficult to wrap our minds around the things of God. According to the narrative, God intervenes in history to make such mysteries known. As a result, even pagans come to believe in the God of Israel. For instance, the King of Babylon declared to the prophet Daniel, "Truly, your God is God of gods and Lord of kings, and a revealer of mysteries, for you have been able to reveal this mystery" (Dan 2:47). In other words, the Bible makes clear that there are some truths that can only be known because God himself discloses them through special acts of divine revelation. The New Testament explains that God has definitively revealed himself in the person of Jesus Christ: "In many and various ways God spoke of old to our fathers by the prophets; but in these last days he has spoken to us by a Son" (Heb 1:1–2).

Superstition or Revelation?

For many modern thinkers, however, the notion of mystery is nonsense. Rationalists, who insist that reason alone can explain all of reality, recoil at the suggestion that there are truths about God that take us beyond the horizon of our intellects. The philosopher Baruch Spinoza (1632–1677) had another word for belief in mysteries: superstition. According to him, the Bible's accounts of God's miraculous deeds in history are no different than the fantastic stories contained in the mythologies of ancient pagan religions. In Spinoza's view, the biblical narratives have no greater historical value than the spectacular tales of Zeus, Poseidon, or other pagan deities. For such skeptics, the biblical accounts are fairy tales, invented by elites who sought to manipulate the masses through religion.

Augustine lived long before modern thinkers like Spinoza, but he would not have been surprised by their line of thinking. Skeptics in his day raised similar charges. In fact, for a while he too thought scripture's mysteries were absurdities. So, we might ask, what changed his mind?

The Question of Reliable Testimony

Among other things, Augustine eventually recognized that much of what we know to be true comes through the testimony of others. This pertains especially to history. For example, without ever having seen Alexander the Great, Augustine knew that the man truly existed. It would be unreasonable to think otherwise. Why? Because there is a great deal of evidence attesting to his life and deeds, evidence which comes to us through the witness of numerous credible sources. Indeed, without our ability to rely on the testimony of others, there would simply be no possibility of historical knowledge at all.

Light to the Nations   153

Yet recognizing that we need to rely on the witness of others does not mean we can be naïve. It is foolish to trust unreliable sources. Witnesses must be established as trustworthy. Once they have been, however, it is unreasonable to dismiss their accounts. When it comes to Christian faith, then, it is important to know whether it is reasonable to trust the testimony of the biblical authors. How do we know that the biblical stories were not simply the product of overactive imaginations or political agendas? What reasons are there for trusting the Bible and its human authors?

Here we cannot answer every possible objection. We should recognize that there are various genres represented in the Bible. Not all of its stories are intended to teach us history. Indeed, the question of what constitutes responsible biblical interpretation is complicated and cannot be answered in short compass. What can be said here is that sometimes it is clear how a biblical passage was intended to be read and other times it is a matter of debate. Moreover, when it does come to accounts that are meant to be read as history, it should be observed that the biblical authors wrote according to the methods and conventions of their day. Ancient historians did not write history as today's journalists. Historical accounts could be condensed, and chronological details could even be rearranged. Sometimes providing exact quotations of speeches was not possible. In the ancient world, it was common for historians to paraphrase or summarize the main point made by speakers without necessarily using their precise words.

Ancient historians provide us with reliable information about the past. The biblical authors are no different. For our purposes here, let us simply focus on the heart of the story of salvation in scripture, namely, the story of Jesus preserved in the Gospels.

Are the Gospels Reliable?

No reputable historian disputes that Jesus really existed. In addition to the mountains of textual and archaeological evidence from the first three centuries of Christian history, Jesus and early Christians are mentioned by the Jewish historian Josephus and pagan writers like Tacitus and Pliny. As we might expect, however, the most reliable information about him comes from those who were closest to him.

It is worth remembering that Jesus was a teacher. There were, therefore, witnesses to his life and teaching who were something more to him than passing acquaintances. Like any other ancient teacher, Jesus was surrounded by "disciples," a word that literally means "students."

What did students of ancient teachers do? They committed their master's words to memory.

What did students of ancient teachers do? They committed their master's words to memory. Because Jesus had students it would be unreasonable to think that the substance of his message was quickly lost after his death. He was surrounded by people who devoted themselves to learning from him and remembering his words.

While it is difficult for us today to appreciate this common feature of ancient learning, we must not forget that the disciples of Jesus lived in an oral culture, without access to printing presses and technology. Memorization was stressed in their day in ways we no longer do. Though they could rely on tools such as wax tablets, students were nonetheless expected to commit their teacher's words to memory. For example, when a disciple of the philosopher Antisthenes lost his notes, his teacher chided him: "You should have inscribed them on your mind instead of on paper." It was not uncommon for students of Homer to be able to recite all of his works from memory.

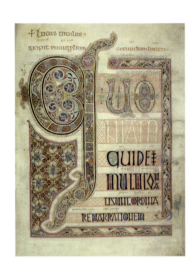

The Lindisfarne Gospel *is an illuminated manuscript produced around 715–720.*

While this seems to set a high bar, we should consider how pervasive skilled memory in the ancient world truly was. Seneca tells us that he could hear a poem and recite it back verbatim. At the end of a long day of auctioneering, Hortensius was known to be able to list every purchaser and their bids. Given such cultural emphasis on the importance of memorization, it is reasonable to conclude that the disciples of Jesus labored to commit to memory what their Master had taught them.

When the authors of the Gospels later sat down to write their accounts of Jesus' life, they did so while the witnesses of Jesus' ministry were still alive. These writers had access to eyewitness accounts of Jesus' ministry from his students. Indeed, Luke's Gospel explicitly refers to such sources:

> *Inasmuch as many have undertaken to compile a narrative of the things which have been accomplished among us, just as they were delivered to us by those who from the beginning were eyewitnesses and ministers of the word, it seemed good to me also, having followed all things closely for some time past, to write an orderly account for you…that you may know the truth concerning the things of which you have been informed (Lk 1:1–4).*

In addition, John's Gospel tells us that it is itself written by an eyewitness of Jesus' ministry (Jn 19:35; 21:24).

Some skeptics might maintain that memories of Jesus were distorted over time. The problem with this claim is that it ignores the fact that Jesus had multiple close disciples—twelve, in fact. To imagine that they all simultaneously suffered a sudden form of amnesia or that they began to mispresent the core of Jesus' message in ways that were unchecked by other eyewitnesses makes little sense. No historian assumes something like that happened with other historical figures, such as Socrates or Cleopatra. There is no reason to suppose that it happened with Jesus.

Others will insist that the Gospels are unreliable because they are written by people who had an agenda. The Gospels were written to help others believe in Jesus (see Jn 20:31). But all ancient historians had agendas. Writers such as Tacitus and Suetonius were funded by the state. Their writings were used as political propaganda. That does not mean, however, that they wrote nothing but fairy tales. Scholars today rely on their accounts because much of what they tell us is credible.

The Gospel writers are credible authors. They give us eyewitness testimony about Jesus' life. These people who testified to Jesus' message knew well that they risked great suffering and even death by identifying themselves as his followers. In fact, the earliest Christians had nothing to gain by testifying to Jesus' life, death, and resurrection and everything to lose—including their lives.

Signs of Credibility

The historical credibility of Jesus' disciples is not the only reason to think the Bible contains divinely revealed truths. In scripture, the testimony of witnesses to divine revelation is accompanied by divine signs of their authenticity. The two most common forms of evidence supporting the reliability of such a messenger's divine commissioning are miracles and prophecies.

Let us return to Daniel. Why does the king of Babylon conclude that the prophet Daniel speaks for the true God? Because Daniel does something that defies explanation. The king had experienced a vivid dream and was perplexed by it. He asked others to interpret its meaning but refused to provide anyone with an account of what it involved. His counselors complained that this was unfair. How could they explain the meaning of the dream if they had no information about it? They complained, "There is not a man on earth who can meet the king's demand" (Dan 2:10). But Daniel came forward and stunned the court, providing the king with an account of his dream right down to its last details. He then went on to tell him what it was about, the future rise and fall of kingdoms. In the face of such a feat, the most reasonable conclusion the king could form was that Daniel was speaking the truth. Moreover, Daniel's truthfulness was confirmed in another way: history played out just as Daniel said it would.

The story of Daniel teaches us why God is willing to stoop down to our level. It is because he cares so much for us. God's omnipotence is not threatened by his decision to act in the particularity of human events.

Light to the Nations   157

Rather, it is further underscored. He need not be concerned that such actions will somehow minimize his glory. This truth is most clearly seen in the event in which the truth of scripture is summed up: the coming of Jesus Christ in the New Testament.

Knowing that those in the Bible who speak for God are able to authenticate their claims with supernatural signs of their divine mandate, the Jewish leaders contested Jesus' authority in the Gospels, asking for a demonstration of his power. Jesus' response to them bears careful examination.

The vessel carrying him was caught in a storm, and he was cast into the sea, where he was swallowed by a large sea creature.

> *Then some of the scribes and Pharisees said to him, "Teacher, we wish to see a sign from you." But he answered them, "An evil and adulterous generation seeks for a sign; but no sign shall be given to it except the sign of the prophet Jonah. For as Jonah was three days and three nights in the belly of the whale, so will the Son of man be three days and three nights in the heart of the earth. The men of Nineveh will arise at the judgment with this generation and condemn it; for they repented at the preaching of Jonah, and behold, something greater than Jonah is here (Mt 12:38–41).*

Jesus promised to demonstrate the truth of his identity by giving the sign of Jonah. What is this mysterious sign? To understand this statement of Jesus, we need to turn back to the story he alluded to, namely, the Book of Jonah. As we shall see, it is easy to miss the full significance of Jesus' use of the story.

Jesus and the Sign of Jonah

The story of Jonah is found in the Old Testament book that bears his name. Jonah received a special mandate to preach a message of repentance to the inhabitants of Nineveh. This task presented Jonah with a conflict of interest. Nineveh was the capital city of the Assyrians, the dreaded enemies of Israel. Jonah was told that if the Ninevites failed to repent, God would destroy their city in forty days. Hoping to rid his people of the Assyrian threat once and for all, the chosen prophet ran away from his calling. Instead of heading east towards Nineveh, he boarded a westbound ship. His plan failed. The vessel carrying him was caught in a storm, and he was cast into the sea, where he was swallowed by a large sea creature.

This is where the story gets especially interesting. Perhaps due to the influence of films like the Walt Disney classic *Pinocchio,* casual readers may assume the story depicts Jonah sitting around in the belly of the whale, awaiting deliverance. This interpretation overlooks key features of the story. The narrative tells us that Jonah cried out to God from "Sheol" (Jon 2:2), the place of the dead. As scholars have observed, this and other indicators suggest that Jonah died when he was swallowed up. Later, the fish coughs him up and the Lord tells him, "Arise, go to Nineveh" (Jon 3:2). The Semitic word translated "arise" is used elsewhere in the Bible to speak of resurrection from the dead, as when Jesus raised Jairus' daughter (see Mk 5:41). Given the context, many interpreters believe the scene involves Jonah being raised from the dead. Although this interpretation has been contested by some, it makes especially good sense of the way Jesus used the story.

Regardless of whether Jonah actually died and was restored to life, one thing is clear: he finally went to Nineveh, proclaiming the message he was originally entrusted with, and his preaching had an astounding result. The Ninevites heeded God's warning, performed public acts of penance, and turned away from their sins. At the conclusion of the story, much to Jonah's chagrin, the city was spared.

The story of Jonah is found in the Old Testament book that bears his name. Jonah received a special mandate to preach a message of repentance to the inhabitants of Nineveh.

Light to the Nations

Now we can better understand why Jesus appealed to this story. The sign of Jonah relates to Jesus' coming death and resurrection. Jesus explained, "For as Jonah was three days and three nights in the belly of the whale, so will the Son of man be three days and three nights in the heart of the earth" (Mt 12:40). With this statement Jesus revealed two ways his message will be authenticated, by prophecy and by miracle. Jesus issued a prophecy whereby he predicted his own death and resurrection. As Jonah went to Sheol and was delivered from Sheol after three days (Jon 2:6), so too Jesus will die and rise again. The reason Jesus said no other sign was needed from him should be evident. If he can deliver on this promise, there should be no further doubt about his identity. Yet the sign of Jonah nevertheless involved something more than a reference to resurrection.

Jesus linked the sign of Jonah to the Ninevites' repentance: "for they repented at the preaching of Jonah" (Mt 12:41). This was no small miracle. The Assyrians were notoriously wicked and corrupt. The idea that Nineveh would repent was unimaginable. Jesus seems to have had a similar outlandish expectation in mind. By linking his resurrection to the sign of Jonah, he indicated that his rising from the dead would lead to the conversion of the Gentiles. Indeed, immediately after he rose from the dead, Jesus sent the disciples out with this commission: "Go therefore and make disciples of all nations" (Mt 28:19).

Both Jesus' resurrection and the conversion of the nations are powerful confirmations of the truth of the Bible's testimony. Indeed, both stand as powerful indicators of the truth of the New Testament's message.

Did Jesus Truly Rise from the Dead?

The biblical story of the resurrection of Jesus cannot be reduced to a spiritual metaphor. The miraculous deliverance of Jesus from death is at the heart of the New Testament's message. St. Paul told the Corinthians, "If Christ has not been raised, then our preaching is in vain and your

After he rises from the dead, Jesus sent the disciples out with this commission: "Go therefore and make disciples of all nations" (Mt 28:19).

160   CHAPTER 9

faith is in vain.... If Christ has not been raised, your faith is futile and you are still in your sins" (1 Cor 15:14, 17).

Skeptics have long attempted to explain away the Easter story. Various theories have been advanced. Some have claimed that Jesus did not really die on the cross and that, after lying unconscious in the tomb for some time, he awoke and returned to his disciples, who misunderstood what had really happened to him. Others claim the resurrection story developed out of a case of mistaken identity. Seeing someone who looked like Jesus, the earliest disciples supposed incorrectly that their Lord had risen from the dead. Others insist the story was an elaborate lie invented by Jesus' followers.

None of these theories holds up under close scrutiny. The suggestion that Jesus survived crucifixion is widely rejected by historians. Prior to being crucified, those sentenced to such a death were first punished by scourging. This was a brutal form of torture. Josephus tells us about an incident in which another man who was similarly flogged had so much flesh torn from his body in the process of scourging that his bones were laid bare. To claim that the Roman soldiers somehow failed to kill Jesus is not credible. They were professional executioners. Moreover, if they had somehow failed to carry out their task and allowed him to escape, they would have been executed (see Acts 16:27).

The contention that the resurrection story was due to a case of mistaken identification is similarly unpersuasive. Jesus' followers lived with him for three years and knew him well. Someone else would not be able to pass as Jesus in their eyes. Indeed, in the accounts of their encounters with the Risen Lord, the disciples are initially skeptical of reports of the resurrection and need some real convincing (see Mt 28:17; Mk 16:14; Lk 24:37–42; Jn 20:25). It is not as if they were quick to accept the idea that he had risen from the dead. They may have wanted to see their Master again, but there is no reason to chalk the resurrection story up to wishful thinking.

To claim that the disciples invented the resurrection as a hoax ignores an obvious problem: they had nothing to gain from such a lie and everything to lose. Faced with horrific torture, not one of them recanted his story. It was not as if people were ready to hear that a man rose from the dead; the claim was obviously a tough sell (Acts 17:32). Why make up such an unbelievable story when it would only lead to certain death?

Prior to being crucified, those sentenced to such a death were first punished by scourging. This was a brutal form of torture.

If the disciples were to invent a story about Jesus' resurrection, it certainly would not look like the ones they told. In the Gospels, the first witnesses to the resurrection are women (Mt 28:1–10; Mk 16:1–8; Lk 24:1–11; Jn 20:1–3). But women were not regarded as reliable witnesses by ancient men. It would have made no sense whatsoever to make up such a detail. St. Paul even said that Jesus later appeared to more than five hundred people (1 Cor 15:6), yet the Gospels never mention this.

Why not? You would expect the Gospel writers to press this point and ignore the women altogether. The best explanation for the account of the women at the tomb is that, as unusual as it was, it represented what actually happened on Easter Sunday.

Moreover, in some of the resurrection appearances the disciples do not recognize Jesus when he first appears to them (Lk 24:13–35; Jn 20:14–16)—another detail that would have never been included if the goal was to make up a convincing story about the resurrection. Why? Because if the first witnesses admitted that they were not initially sure that they had seen Jesus, the obvious objection would be, "Well, maybe you were just confused, and it was not actually him." Again, if the resurrection story was designed to fool people into thinking that Jesus had risen from the dead when he had not, it would not have looked like this.

Actually, not a few writers who have set out to disprove the resurrection have ended up converting to Christianity as a result of their analysis. The more one studies the data, the less it looks like a made-up story. In fact, the best historical explanation for the empty tomb—the one with the fewest problems—is that Jesus actually did rise from the dead just as he said he would. But there is one more aspect to Jesus' prophecy that confirms the truth of his teaching: the utterly astounding fact of the conversion of the nations to Christianity.

Light to the Nations **163**

Light to the Nations

In connecting his resurrection to the conversion of the Gentiles, Jesus signaled the fulfillment of Old Testament prophecy. The Book of Isaiah announces that the day would come when "many peoples shall come, and say: 'Come, let us go up to the mountain of the LORD, to the house of the God of Jacob; that he may teach us his ways and that we may walk in his paths'" (Is 2:3). This was a bold vision, to say the least.

The thought that other nations would worship the God of Israel was nothing less than outrageous. At the time, nations closely identified with their ethnic gods. To worship the deity of another people would be, in effect, to declare that other nation superior to one's own. It is no wonder, for example, that the Greeks insisted that the Jews worship their god, Zeus, when they conquered Jerusalem (2 Mac 6:2). Likewise, the Greek pantheon was quickly re-envisioned after the Romans rose to power. Zeus became Jupiter, Poseidon became Neptune, and so on.

In this context, to imagine all the other nations of the world worshipping the God of Israel seemed extraordinarily unrealistic. After all, Israel was a minor player in the ancient world. The Hittites, Egyptians, Assyrians, Babylonians—even the Philistines—all had much greater civilizations. In many ways, their cultures were far more developed and impressive. Their armies were also far more powerful. In sum, if you were to bet on all the world worshipping the gods of one of these peoples, it certainly would not have been Israel's.

But that is exactly what has happened. Two thousand years after Jesus, you are sitting in a classroom, studying a religion that proclaims that this distant people's God is the one true Creator of the universe. Most of the students in your class—if not all of them—are likely from non-Jewish lineage. Here you are, mostly descendants of Gentiles, living on the other side of the world from where historic Israel existed, studying a religion committed to the God of Israel. This has happened against all odds.

Here you are, mostly descendants of Gentiles, living on the other side of the world from where historic Israel existed, studying a religion committed to the God of Israel.

The sign of Jonah, then, involves something more than the resurrection of Jesus. Although it makes sense to believe that it happened, we were not present to witness that event. We, however, are witnesses to another part of Jesus' prophecy: the conversion of the nations to the God of Israel. For the early Church fathers, this truly miraculous turn of events constituted one of the strongest pieces of evidence supporting the truth of Christianity. St. Ambrose—the bishop whose preaching led to the conversion of St. Augustine—himself declared, "The mystery of the Church is clearly expressed [in Jesus' prophecy of the sign of Jonah]. Her flocks stretch from the boundaries of the whole world. They stretch to Nineveh through penitence....The mystery is now fulfilled in truth."

The spread of the Christian faith cannot be attributed to coercion or force. On the contrary, everyone knows how Christian missionaries sent to pagan lands were typically treated: they were martyred. Nor can it be maintained that this faith remains in various lands because of government mandate. Consider that you are not taking this course at a state-run school. Rather, the only reason you can take this course at all is that people of good will chose to build non-profit alternatives to those places of learning. Indeed, the preaching of the Gospel is not in vain; it is effective and enduring. Empires have risen and fallen but the Church remains. Why is its faith not futile? St. Paul tells us: Christ has been

Fra Angelico, The Conversion of St. Augustine, *c. 1430, Tempera on wood.*

raised from the dead, just as he promised. Because of that we have the greatest evidence of all for the truth of the resurrection—the power it gives by grace to truly be freed from the sins that would otherwise overmaster us. The conversion of the Gentiles is not an abstract concept but one we can experience in our own lives. St. Augustine himself encountered this truth in a personal way when he suddenly found the power to turn away from the sins and the destructive behavior that had long held him in its grip. Encountering the Risen Lord through reading scripture enabled him to escape the unhappy life from which he longed to be free. The truth of scripture thus became undeniable for him, and another Gentile was transformed by the power of the resurrection. In the words of St. Augustine:

> *And lo, I heard from a nearby house, a voice like that of a boy or a girl, I know not which, chanting and repeating over and over, "Take up and read. Take up and read."… I interpreted this solely as a command given to me by God to open the book and read the first chapter I should come upon… I snatched it up, opened it, and read in silence the chapter on which my eyes first fell: "Not in rioting and drunkenness, not in chambering and impurities, not in strife and envying, but put you on the Lord Jesus Christ, and make not provision for the flesh in its concupiscences" (Rom 13:13, 14). No further wished I to read, nor was there need to do so. Instantly, in truth, at the end of this sentence, as if before a peaceful light streaming into my heart, all the dark shadows of doubt fled away.*

Review Questions

1. Why does the notion of God's intervention in history take us beyond reason and into the realm of "mystery"?

2. Why is it plausible to believe the Gospel writers had reliable information about Jesus?

3. What two realities are foretold in Jesus' "Sign of Jonah" prophecy?

4. Why do some people doubt the resurrection? How can those doubts be answered?

5. Jonah did not want to see the Ninevites convert. How might we sometimes have hidden motives for not accepting God's promises of mercy?

6. St. Augustine discovered the power of the Risen Lord in reading the scriptures. How have you experienced God's grace through reading the Bible?

Put Out Into the Deep

If you would like to learn more about the historical reliability of scripture, especially the Gospels, you would enjoy a recent book written by Catholic New Testament scholar Brant Pitre, *The Case for Jesus: The Biblical and Historical Evidence for Christ* (Doubleday, 2016). In the book, Dr. Pitre recounts how he nearly lost his faith as he entered the world of biblical scholarship as a young man. He then details the careful historical research that punctured the skeptics' arguments and led him back to faith in the God of the Bible.

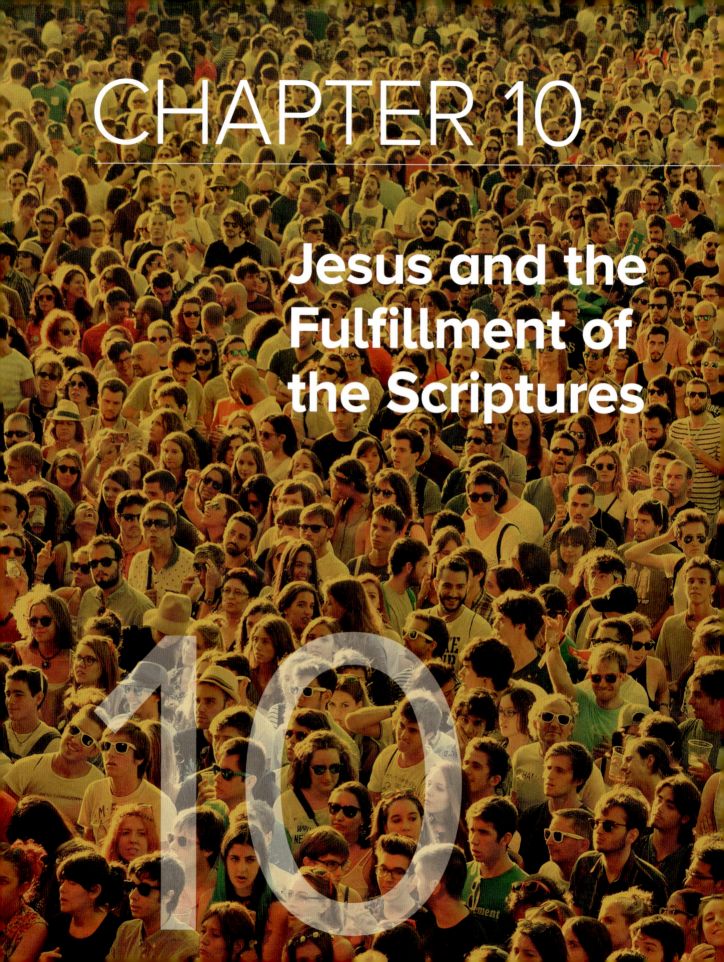

The crowds gathered on a hillside where a teacher from Galilee, the son of a carpenter, delivered his first major discourse. It is remembered today as the Sermon on the Mount and is one of the most famous passages in the New Testament. We can imagine how Jesus' listeners must have hushed one another as he spoke the words that, though familiar to us, were to them astonishing:

Blessed are the poor in spirit, for theirs is the kingdom of heaven.

Blessed are those who mourn, for they shall be comforted.

Blessed are the meek, for they shall inherit the earth.

Blessed are those who hunger and thirst for righteousness, for they shall be satisfied.

Blessed are the merciful, for they shall obtain mercy.

Blessed are the pure in heart, for they shall see God.

Blessed are the peacemakers, for they shall be called sons of God.

Blessed are those who are persecuted for righteousness' sake, for theirs is the kingdom of heaven.

Blessed are you when men revile you and persecute you and utter all kinds of evil against you falsely on my account. Rejoice and be glad, for your reward is great in heaven, for so men persecuted the prophets who were before you (Mt 5:3–12).

Jesus and the Fulfillment of the Scriptures

These sayings, traditionally called the "Beatitudes," have long been recognized as the heart of Jesus' teaching. They have become so well-known to us that we may not stop to consider how truly remarkable they were at the time they were first spoken. In the books known as the "Law of Moses," the first five books of the Bible (Genesis, Exodus, Leviticus, Numbers, and Deuteronomy), Israel had learned that following God's commandments would bring peace and prosperity. Although the Old Testament includes examples of righteous sufferers such as the Patriarch Joseph and Job, it emphasizes the idea that suffering would be the lot of those who were disobedient to God. With the Beatitudes, Jesus flipped the script. He said that the righteous would be sorrowful, persecuted, and reviled. He did not say, "Blessed are the prosperous" or "Blessed are the strong." Why did he speak in such a surprising way?

The more one studies the Beatitudes, the more one discovers their profundity. A careful reading of the Gospels reveals something striking about these sayings: they can all be seen as descriptions of Jesus himself. He insisted that the poor are "blessed" (Mt 5:3) and then lived in poverty; Jesus said that he had no place to "lay his head" (Mt 8:20). Having pronounced a blessing upon the "meek" (Mt 5:5), he spoke of himself as "meek and lowly in heart" (Mt 11:29). He told the crowds, "Blessed are the merciful" (Mt 5:7), and then went on to exemplify this attribute, healing those who called out to him, "Have mercy" (Mt 9:27; 15:22; 17:15; 20:30–31). He promised that the "pure in heart" would "see God" (Mt 5:8) and so, not surprisingly, revealed that he had "seen the Father" (Jn 6:46). Most poignantly, he embodied the final Beatitudes. He declared blessed those who are persecuted, reviled, and falsely accused; in his passion, he was both "reviled" (Mt 27:44) and falsely accused (Mt 26:58–61). Jesus showed us that blessedness is ultimately found in becoming like him.

Nevertheless, Jesus' teaching seems counterintuitive. By and large, the Old Testament promised earthly happiness and security to the righteous. God's people expected triumph and prosperity. St. Paul explained that the notion of a crucified Messiah was a "stumbling block"—literally in Greek, a "scandal"—to Jews (1 Cor 1:22–23). We can understand why Jesus' equation of suffering with blessing would seem puzzling. It would seem that the wicked should suffer, not the righteous. It is no wonder, then, that Jesus followed the Beatitudes with the following statement: "Do not think that I have come to abolish the law and the prophets; I have come not to abolish them but to fulfil them" (Mt 5:17). He clarified this point because his teachings otherwise suggested that he was somehow contradicting Israel's scriptures.

170   CHAPTER 10

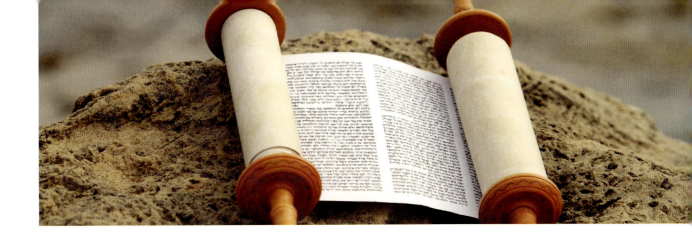

Abolishing the Old Testament?

There are real differences between the Old and New Testaments. For example, immediately after affirming that he did not come to "abolish" the Law, Jesus expressly prohibited practices which the Law had allowed, such as divorce and remarriage (see Mt 5:31–32). In the Gospel according to Mark, we read that Jesus declared all foods "clean" (Mk 7:19), apparently overturning the Old Testament's dietary regulations, which prohibited certain foods, notably pork. Along the same lines, when a woman was caught committing adultery, Jesus did not insist that she be stoned, as the Law required (see Jn 8:3–11). After causing her would-be accusers to walk away, Jesus told her, "Neither do I condemn you" (Jn 8:11).

Moreover, the New Testament shows us that after Jesus' resurrection the apostles taught that certain requirements of the Old Testament—for instance, circumcision, keeping the ritual purity laws, and observing the dietary restrictions of the Torah—were no longer binding in the New Covenant. St. Paul gave the reason: "For in Christ Jesus neither circumcision nor uncircumcision is of any avail, but faith working through love" (Gal 5:6). For this kind of teaching, the early Christians faced persecution from Jewish leaders, who claimed they were rejecting the Law of Moses (see Acts 6:13; 18:13; 21:28).

We may well wonder, therefore, whether the New Testament repudiates the Old. According to many people today, the answer is that it does. Popular opinion holds that the two Testaments present us with two very different portraits of God. The so-called "God of the Old Testament" is said to be characterized by wrath, vengeance, and violence, whereas the "God of the New Testament" is viewed as loving, kind, and merciful. As we shall see, such perceptions are wildly off the mark.

Jesus and the Fulfillment of the Scriptures

For one thing, as in the Old Testament, the New Testament affirms that God's punishment will come upon those who fail to repent. Jesus spoke about Hell just as much as he did about Heaven (see, for example, Mt 7:21–23; 13:40–43; 13:47–50; 18:7–9). Conversely, the portrayal of the God of the Old Testament as impatient and vindictive would have astounded ancient Jews. God had revealed to Moses that he was more than merely the great "I AM," the origin of existence, but that he is "a God merciful and gracious, slow to anger, and abounding in mercy and faithfulness...forgiving iniquity and transgression and sin" (Ex 34:6–7). True, because of his goodness, God explained that he would not "clear the guilty" (Ex 34:7). Yet his defining attributes—even in the Old Testament—are mercy and graciousness. Because the Jews knew their God, they knew how to interpret what he did. Jewish writers never characterized him as primarily impatient and vengeful. They knew that those who sought forgiveness would find it. In short, the comparisons of the supposed different portraits of God in the Old and New Testaments are false.

There is nevertheless something truly new about the covenant established by Jesus. After all, if there were not, there would have been no need for a New Covenant in the first place. What accounts for these differences? There are many ways to answer this question, but Jesus himself provided us with a good place to start.

There is something truly new about the covenant established by Jesus.

For Your Hardness of Heart

In the Gospels, the Jewish leaders recognized that certain aspects of Jesus' teaching were in tension with the Old Testament. Jesus' prohibition of divorce and re-marriage especially rankled. Why? Because in this case Jesus ruled out a practice that was explicitly provided for by the Torah. How could this be? In responding to their challenge, Jesus declared that Moses had permitted divorce with re-marriage for one simple reason: "For your hardness of heart" (Mt 19:8; see Mk 10:5). With this explanation, Jesus shone a spotlight on an important theme in the Old Testament.

In the last chapter, we saw that Jeremiah described the heart as incomprehensible. The prophet complained, "The heart is deceitful above all things, and desperately corrupt" (Jer 17:9). The Book of Deuteronomy makes a similar point. After Moses delivered the Lord's command, "you shall love the Lord your God with all your heart, and with all your soul, and with all your might" (Deut 6:5), he instructed the people to circumcise "your heart, and be no longer stubborn" (Deut 10:16). Israel's disobedience could not be solved apart from a transformation of heart, something that Moses promised in a spectacular prophecy. Anticipating a future day when God would gather his people to himself, Moses proclaimed, "the Lord your God will circumcise your heart and the heart of your offspring, so that you will love the Lord your God with all your heart and with all your soul, that you may live" (Deut 30:6). In other words, Moses promised that God would do what was necessary for his people to be able to love him as they should. He would transform their hearts.

God repeated his promise through the prophets. In the Book of Jeremiah, God announced that he would establish a "New Covenant," adding, "I will put my law within them, and I will write it upon their hearts" (Jer 31:33). Similar assurances are found in the Book of Ezekiel, where such expectations are connected to the idea of the outpouring of the Holy Spirit: "A new heart I will give you, and a new spirit I will put within you; and I will take out of your flesh the heart of stone and give you a heart of flesh. And I will put my spirit within you, and cause you to walk in my statutes" (Ezek 36:26–27).

What these passages underscore is that Israel needed God's help to keep his law. And so they awaited a future day when, as Moses had promised, the Lord himself would transform their hearts. The time would come when God would institute a New Covenant and pour out the Spirit upon them. When this happened, they would finally be empowered to walk in his ways.

God would institute a New Covenant and pour out the Spirit upon them. When this happened, they would finally be empowered to walk in his ways.

Georges de la Tour, Magdalene with the Smoking Flame, *c. 1640, Oil on canvas, Louvre, Paris, France.*

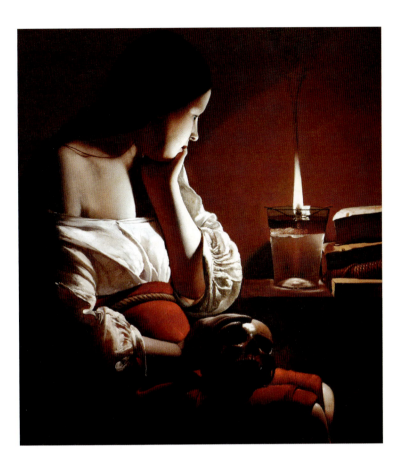

For ancient Jews, these promises were inextricably bound up with the hope for the coming of the Messiah. In the same section of the Book of Jeremiah that contains the New Covenant oracle, the prophet announced that God would "raise up" a new king from the line of David (Jer 30:9). Likewise, both shortly before and after making the promise above, Ezekiel foretold the coming of a future son of David who would "feed" God's people (Ezek 34:23) and usher in an "everlasting covenant" (Ezek 37:25–26). We can understand why the faithful of Israel so desperately longed for the Messiah's arrival: they longed to be free from sin. St. Paul himself wrote poignantly about the interior struggle caused by our tendency to sin, a struggle common to all men and women in every age:

> *I do not understand my own actions. For I do not do what I want, but I do the very thing I hate.... For I know that nothing good dwells within me, that is, in my flesh. I can will what is right, but I cannot do it. For I do not do the good I want, but the evil I do not want is what I do.... Wretched man that I am! Who will deliver me from this body of death? (Rom 7:15, 18–19, 24)*

St. Paul, of course, subsequently identified the solution to this problem, for the promised deliverer had indeed come, Jesus Christ.

Jesus, the "Christ"

It is important to appreciate the significance of Jesus' role as "Christ." The term means "Messiah." In applying it to Jesus, the earliest Christians made two important and interrelated claims. First, by calling him "Christ" the early disciples came to recognize the way Jesus' identity was inextricably wrapped up in the Jewish scriptures, that is, the books we now call the Old Testament. For ancient Jews, the Messiah was the one who would ultimately fulfill the hopes for the future they had derived from their scriptures. Without the Old Testament, we cannot fully grasp who Jesus is, for we cannot understand what it means to say he is the Christ. Why did the Jewish leaders fail to believe in him? Jesus said it was because they did not believe the scriptures. He told them plainly, "If you believed Moses, you would believe me, for he wrote of me. But if you do not believe his writings, how will you believe my words?" (Jn 5:46–47). In sum, if we fail to understand the scriptures of Israel, we cannot truly know the person of Jesus. As the early Church father St. Jerome (347–420) put it, "Ignorance of scripture is ignorance of Christ."

Second, by saying Jesus is the Christ, the disciples testified that Jesus gave the Old Testament its definitive meaning. To say Jesus is the Messiah is to affirm that the Old Testament books are ultimately about him. If Jesus really is the Christ, it means that he is the interpretive key that unlocks the meaning of these ancient books. St. Paul therefore said that those who read the Old Testament without believing in Jesus cannot fully understand it because "a veil lies over their minds" and "only through Christ is it taken away" (2 Cor 3:14–15).

The Law Was Added Because of Sin

As we have seen, Jesus declared that certain laws were given in the Old Testament because of Israel's "hardness of heart," that is, these laws were temporary specifications of how the Ten Commandments were to be applied and interpreted. Jesus also observed that although such provisions were necessary, they were not "from the beginning" (Mt 19:8). In his letter to the Galatians, St. Paul made a similar point. Referring to the Mosaic Law, he wrote, "Why the law? It was added because of transgressions" (Gal 3:19); it was given to teach God's people certain truths they needed to learn prior to the coming of Christ. This idea that the Law was added because of sin has two facets: (1) the Law was added to clarify the unchanging truths that should have already been known by reason, and (2) the Law contained precepts that God added over time that were intended to be temporary remedies for specific sins or concessions to behavioral patterns that were less harmful than their foreseeable alternatives.

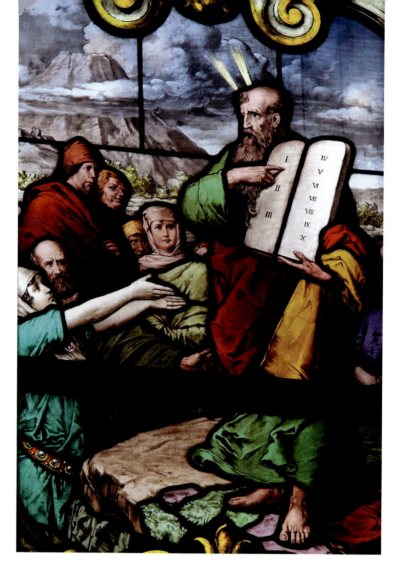

God gave Moses laws that involved truths the Chosen People could have known from reflection upon their experience. The most important of these are the Ten Commandments.

In the first category are the laws given to Moses that involved truths the Chosen People could have known from reflection upon their experience. The most important of these are the Ten Commandments. The human mind should be able to recognize not only that there is one Creator God but that we owe him thanks and praise (the first commandment). Likewise, men and women can understand by the natural light of reason that it is immoral to murder the innocent (the fifth commandment), to commit adultery (the sixth commandment), to bear false witness (the eighth commandment), and so on. Why did God give Moses the Ten Commandments if Israel should have already known their contents? St. Paul explained that sin clouds our intellect and weakens our will. Moral truths that otherwise should be clear to us—what we call Natural Law—are obscured due to sin (Rom 1:21–23). Often, we simply do not want to accept that certain behaviors are bad for us and so we allow ourselves to be confused about morality. God wished the moral law to be known with clarity, and so he appeared to Moses at Mount Sinai to spell it out explicitly.

God also gave precepts to Israel that were temporary in character and were not inherently necessary due to human nature but addressed the particular weaknesses of God's people. For example, when God first brought the Israelites out of Egypt, he did not impose elaborate rules about regular animal sacrifices. Apart from the Passover and the covenant-making ceremony at Mount Sinai, there were no instructions detailing daily offerings. Nor were there rules identifying which foods were to be considered ritually pure and impure. When discussing this episode in sacred history, the Church Fathers pointed to God's words in Jeremiah: "For in the day that I brought them out of the land of Egypt, I did not speak to your fathers or command them concerning burnt offerings and sacrifices" (Jer 7:22). If God did not originally make provisions for ongoing animal sacrifices, why did he do so when he did? It was because Israel had fallen into idolatry by making and worshipping the golden calf (Ex 32).

Why did God make animal sacrifice a staple of Israel's national life after this event? According to the first theologians of the Church, these offerings were intended to teach Israel that the animals worshipped by the Egyptians were not true gods. They had become distractions from the real God of Israel. In his wisdom, God knew how to persuade the people that these animals were not sacred; he had the people kill them—over and over again. For the Egyptians, such sacrifices were abominations (see Ex 8:26). That was indeed the point. Animal sacrifice was meant to wean Israel from its idolatrous ways. Laws such as these were "added because of sin"—they were not from the beginning and, therefore, were not unchangeable. They were intended to be temporary. Unlike the Ten Commandments, these laws were given to address particular struggles against sin in the Old Testament that were tied to Israel's cultural situation.

Why did God make animal sacrifice a staple of Israel's national life? These offerings were intended to teach Israel that the animals worshipped by the Egyptians were not true gods.

Jesus and the Fulfillment of the Scriptures   **179**

The Law as a Tutor

The Law, then, was meant to teach Israel certain truths and to provide a remedy for sin. This is a point St. Paul went on to make in his letter to the Galatians. After explaining that the Law was added due to sin, the Apostle spoke of the Torah as a "custodian" or "tutor":

> The law was our custodian until Christ came....But now that faith has come, we are no longer under a custodian; for in Christ Jesus you are all sons of God, through faith. For as many of you as were baptized into Christ have put on Christ (Gal 3:24–27).

The Apostle's teaching here draws on well-known customs of the Greco-Roman world. In aristocratic households, children were often put under the charge of an educated servant, a "pedagogue" or tutor. Until he or she came of age, the child would be shadowed by this servant, who ensured that the child completed schoolwork, practiced proper etiquette, and, in general, stayed out of trouble. When the child matured, he or she received the full status of a son or daughter and was released from the servant's authority.

We can now better understand some of the differences between the Old and New Testaments. Some of the Old Testament laws were given not because they were good in themselves but because Israel needed to learn certain lessons at particular points in history. In fact, in the Book of Ezekiel, God said that these laws "were not good" (Ezek 20:25), that is, they were precepts that were not intrinsically necessary but were instituted as concessions to Israel's weaknesses. The permission to divorce and remarry under certain circumstances was one such concession. In short, some of the laws changed over time not because God changed but because his people did.

180   CHAPTER 10

God's Fatherly Plan

Let us be clear, however: though the Law changed, it was not because God was caught off guard. In St. Paul's letter to the Ephesians we read, "For [God] has made known to us in all wisdom and insight the mystery of his will, according to his purpose which he set forth in Christ as a plan for the fulness of time" (Eph 1:9–10). This verse makes clear that God was not surprised by the way things turned out; he always had a design for his people. What took place in time was not unforeseen by the Father, including the sending of Jesus Christ. With this in mind we can see how God's plan involved two dimensions. First, it meant dealing with his Chosen People in their specific circumstances, working as a wise father to correct them when they fell away from him. Second, it foreshadowed what would ultimately happen in the New Testament.

God dealt with the Chosen People in their specific circumstances, working as a wise father to correct them when they fell away from him.

God's Education of the Human Race

Following St. Paul, early Christian writers understood God's dealings with the human race according to the analogy of raising children. In the Old Testament, the Chosen People were not asked to understand many complex theological concepts. Instead, God began to reveal himself by speaking to his people in terms they could understand; this is why righteousness was associated with happiness and life, while sin was connected to sadness and death. The early-Christian writer Origen (c. 185–254) wrote that God "condescends and accommodates himself to our weakness, like a schoolmaster talking a 'little language' to his children, like a father caring for his own children and adopting their ways." In other words, God adapts to the needs of his people. In the Old Testament, God stooped down and spoke to his people on their level, so that they might begin to understand him. St. Augustine used a similar image:

> The education of the human race, represented by the people of God, has advanced, like that of an individual, through certain epochs, or, as it were, ages, so that it might gradually rise from earthly to heavenly things, and from the visible to the invisible.

In other words, God's revelation in the Bible was made known to the human race over time. For example, before fully revealing the notion of sin as spiritual death, God punished sinners with physical death to help the people understand the gravity of sin. Over time, God revealed that there is something worse than physical death: spiritual death. As Jesus insisted, "it is better that you lose one of your members than that your whole body go into hell" (Mt 5:30).

Many of the Old Testament strictures which to us sound disproportionate or even savage actually mitigated the barbaric practices specific to the ancient world. Take, for example, the axiomatic principle, "an eye for an eye, a tooth for a tooth" (see Ex 21:24). This precept indicated that the punishment should be proportionate to the crime; if a person gouges out another's eye, his eye shall also be taken from him. This precept was actually meant to restrain retaliation. In most ancient Near Eastern societies, offenses against others—especially the wealthy and elite—were punished with unmerciful severity. A perceived slight against the rich and powerful could result in mutilation and even death. By contrast, the Law of Moses taught the equal dignity of all people. It therefore imposed limits on punishments.

God desires that all people turn to him and repent, but there are always those who will repent only if faced with dire consequences. This reality is portrayed in Psalm 78, which recounts God's dealings with rebellious Israel in the desert: "When he slew them, they sought for him; they repented and sought God earnestly" (Ps 78:34). In other words, staring death in the face caused some Israelites to turn and genuinely repent of their sin. Indeed, sometimes sinners will only gain clarity regarding their state before God once they are facing the inevitability of death. This is why, even today, death-bed conversions are not unusual. For those who view physical death as the end of existence, Psalm 78

God desires that all people turn to him and repent, but there are always those who will repent only if faced with dire consequences.

Jesus and the Fulfillment of the Scriptures

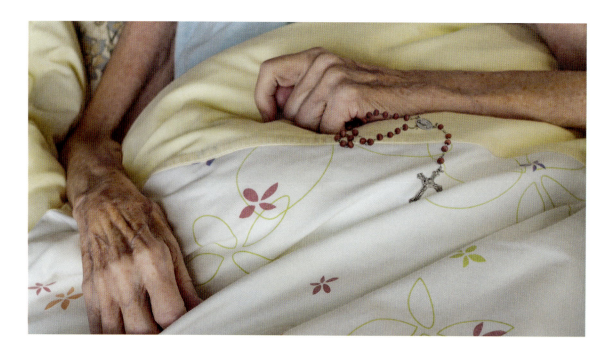

Sometimes sinners will only gain clarity regarding their state before God once they are facing the inevitability of death.

makes no sense. With the eyes of faith, however, we can see how God's punishment is actually a sign of his mercy: it is better to lose one's physical life than to face eternal death in hell. God, in his infinite wisdom, applies this principle wisely. In all that he does, God always acts as a merciful father, one who is "slow to anger" and "abounding in mercy and faithfulness" (Ex 34:6). St. Augustine further described how God carefully brought his people along in other ways as well:

> *It was best, therefore, that the soul of man, which was still weakly desiring earthly things, should be accustomed to seek from God alone even these petty temporal benefits, and the earthly necessities of this transitory life, which are contemptible in comparison with eternal blessings, in order that the desire even of these things might not draw it aside from the worship of him, to whom we come by despising and forsaking such things.*

In other words, in the Old Testament God taught very directly. In effect, he declared to his people, "Be obedient, and you will be blessed—your crops will grow, you will live in good health, and have peace from your enemies. If you are disobedient, you will experience suffering—famine, plagues, and defeat." By teaching in this way, God gave his people the earthly things that they desired so that they would trust him to give them the good things they ultimately needed. This means of teaching ensured that his people—or at least the pious among them—would recognize him as the source of all good things and not prefer temporal goods to him. Ultimately, God wanted to give them something more: supernatural goods.

184   CHAPTER 10

The Law Written on the Heart

According to St. Paul, Israel's heart was finally transformed by Christ, who inaugurated what Jeremiah had foretold, namely, the New Covenant. In his second letter to the Corinthians, St. Paul explained that believers are like "a letter from Christ…written not with ink but with the Spirit of the living God, not on tablets of stone but on tablets of human hearts" (2 Cor 3:3). With these words, he signified that Christ had come to bring what the prophets had announced: God's solution to the problem of the human heart. The Apostle went on to contrast the Old Covenant, which he identified as "the dispensation of death," with the New Covenant, which he called, "the dispensation of the Spirit" (2 Cor 3:7–8). The Old Law had explained what Israel was required to do, but had not conferred the necessary ability. This gift of grace was made available in the sacraments of the New Covenant. Through the Spirit, conferred at baptism, Christ now dwells in believers, enabling them to live a life of faithfulness. As St. Paul wrote in another letter, "it is no longer I who live, but Christ who lives in me; and the life I now live in the flesh I live by faith in the Son of God" (Gal 2:20). Because of this, the custodian or tutor—that is, the provisions of the Mosaic Law beyond the Ten Commandments—is no longer needed. The true Teacher has come, and he abides in our hearts in order to heal them.

The Gospel of Mark, then, tells us that Jesus "declared all foods clean" (Mk 7:19). Likewise, the author of the epistle to the Hebrews explained how, now that Christ has offered himself as the true sacrifice for sins, animal sacrifices are no longer necessary (see Heb 10:13). Christ indeed came to fulfill the Law. Does this mean that the Law is abolished? While certain elements are no longer in force (Eph 2:15), regulations such as

God acts as a wise and merciful father by giving his people remedies for the sins that ail them.

the dietary laws are not to be edited out of scripture. Jesus insisted that nothing would pass from the Law (Mt 5:18). This declaration did not mean that every law is still binding, but it did and does mean that all aspects of the Torah served a particular purpose according to God's wise plan. Among other things, knowing that certain laws were added because of sin helps us to recognize how badly grace was needed. Reading the Old Testament with this in mind, we can begin to see how God acts as a wise and merciful father by giving his people remedies for the sins that ail them.

From Shadows to Reality

The Old Testament's temporary laws "added because of sin" were not only given as a remedy for sin. They often point beyond themselves to Christ. They have a prophetic value, as the epistle to the Hebrews explains: the sacrificial laws of the Old Testament foreshadowed the perfect sacrifice of Christ. The Law thus represented a "shadow of the good things to come" (Heb 10:1). God knew what would transpire in salvation history, and so he placed in the Old Testament realities that foreshadow what would come in the New. We will talk more about this point in the next chapter. For now, it is simply worth noting that the New Testament frequently highlights the way God's actions in the Old Testament anticipate what he would do in Christ. St. Paul, for instance, saw the parting of the Red Sea in the Exodus as a foreshadowing of baptism (see 1 Cor 10:1–6). There is a great lesson here for Christians. Those who are saved through the waters of baptism ought to recall that the Israelites who were saved through the waters of the sea eventually turned away from God and fell into idolatry. Their gratitude to God for so great a deliverance faded. The Apostle was warning the Corinthians not to make a similar mistake; having been delivered through the waters of salvation, Christians must not forget God's marvelous mercy and forsake him.

Becoming Like Christ

Jesus gave the Old Testament its definitive meaning. He is the Christ, the Messiah, the one who fulfills all that was prefigured in the scriptures of Israel. With this truth in mind, we can return to the Sermon on the Mount. There we read that Jesus "went up on the mountain" (Mt 5:1). The language evokes the figure of Moses who also "went up the mountain," that is, Mount Sinai. There Moses received the tablets of the Old Law (see Deut 9:9). As many have recognized, Jesus is presented in Matthew's Gospel as the New Moses, the one who delivered the Law of the New Covenant. What is the purpose of this New Law? It is nothing less than to bring completion to God's design for the human race.

Happiness and fulfillment are found in becoming like Christ. We are called to become perfect as he is. We are called to be true children of God (see 1 Jn 3:1).

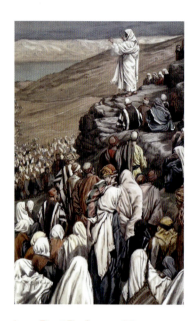

James Tissot, The Sermon of the Beatitudes, *1886–1896, Watercolor over granite on paper, Brooklyn Museum, New York, New York, USA.*

Jesus began his famous discourse with the Beatitudes. Significantly, each Beatitude begins, "Blessed are." In the original Greek, the word translated "blessed" can also mean "happy." In this word, Jesus shows us how the New Covenant brings fulfilment to Israel's longing. Happiness is finally found in living out the Messiah's teachings (see CCC 1718). Moreover, as we have seen, the Beatitudes are first and foremost descriptions of Jesus. Their core teaching tells us how to become like the Son of God. In fact, Matthew 5 ends with Jesus' exhortation, "You, therefore, must be perfect, as your heavenly Father is perfect" (Mt 5:48). Happiness and fulfillment are found in becoming like Christ. We are called to become perfect as he is. We are called to be true children of God (see 1 Jn 3:1).

With the sacraments of the New Covenant and the grace they confer, it is possible to be united to Christ and to receive God's saving power. As the Gospel of John explains, "For the law was given through Moses; grace and truth came through Jesus Christ" (Jn 1:17). St. Paul therefore said that Christians are no longer "under the law" (Gal 3:23) but "under grace" (Rom 6:14), explaining, "For sin will have no dominion over you" (Rom 6:14). With the New Covenant, God's love, identified with the Holy Spirit (Rom 5:5), is poured into our hearts, making it possible for us to fulfill all that the Law intended. St. Augustine's summary of salvation history confirms the teaching: "The Law was given so grace we would seek, grace was given so the Law we would keep."

Jesus calls us to become like him. It is no longer sufficient to follow the mere letter of the law. Jesus insisted that unless the righteousness of Christians "exceeds that of the scribes and Pharisees," we will "never enter the kingdom of heaven" (Mt 5:20). In the New Covenant, our hearts can be changed so that we can actually become holy. Christians are not only called to imitate Jesus but even to participate in his life—to be united to him and live a new life in him. This is what St. Paul meant when he wrote, "I have been crucified with Christ; it is no longer I who live, but Christ who lives in me; and the life I now live in the flesh I live by faith in the Son of God, who loved me and gave himself for me" (Gal 2:20). Believers do not become like sons and daughters of God; we become actual sons and daughters of God by adoption (Rom 8:14–17). In this way, we truly can be the salt of the earth and the light of the world.

Review Questions

1. In what way do the Beatitudes appear paradoxical? How can they be linked to Christ?

2. Why does scripture teach that the Law was added because of sin? Why were some laws changeable and others permanent?

3. How does understanding God as Father help us understand what he is doing in salvation history?

4. Think about some of the distinctive laws given in the Old Testament that are no longer binding in the New Covenant. Why might these have been given?

5. What is the relationship between loving God with all one's heart and serving him with all one's mind?

6. How does the Good News about the happiness Christ announces in the Sermon on the Mount compare with the philosophical understanding of happiness we discussed in Chapter 2? Does the philosophical understanding prepare the way for the happiness expressed in the Beatitudes? In what ways? How do the Beatitudes go beyond the philosophical understanding of happiness?

Put Out Into the Deep

For a clear-eyed overview of God's work in salvation history, see John Bergsma, *Bible Basics for Catholics* (Ave Maria, 2012). In this work, Dr. Bergsma lays out the basic outline of salvation history, offering helpful explanations of the differences between the various covenants God establishes with his people and how they all point to Christ.

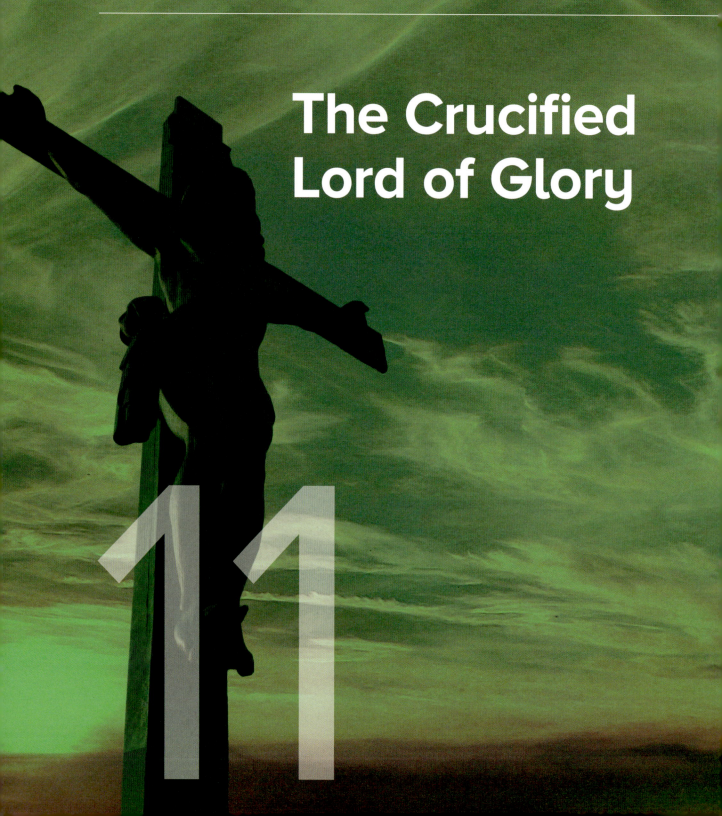

CHAPTER 11

The Crucified Lord of Glory

When I survey the wondrous cross
On which the Prince of glory died,
My richest gain I count but loss,
And pour contempt on all my pride.

Forbid it, Lord, that I should boast,
Save in the death of Christ my God!
All the vain things that charm me most,
I sacrifice them to His blood.

See from His head, His hands, His feet,
Sorrow and love flow mingled down!
Did e'er such love and sorrow meet,
Or thorns compose so rich a crown?

Were the whole realm of nature mine,
That were a present far too small;
Love so amazing, so divine,
Demands my soul, my life, my all.

Isaac Watts (1674–1748)

Israel's One God

In 1857, archaeologists made a discovery on the Palatine Hill in Rome. As they examined the wall of a room once used by the Roman military, the scholars found ancient graffiti. It was apparently anti-Christian propaganda. Though faded, the image's essential elements remain visible today. The image depicts a man worshipping a crucified figure with the head of a donkey. An inscription reads: "Alexamenos worships his god." The message is clear: to worship a crucified man as God is absurd. One might as well worship a donkey. The discovery of the Palatine graffiti is a powerful reminder of how shocking the central claim of Christianity was to ancient Romans. How could Christians worship a crucified Lord?

As off-putting as the notion of worshipping a crucified man was to Romans, it was especially offensive to Jews, to whom it seemed to contradict the commandment to worship one God. This principle is most clearly emphasized in the *Shema,* the famous prayer that stood

The Crucified Lord of Glory   191

Image and rubbing of the Alexamenos graffiti dating back to c. 200.

at the heart of the daily worship of ancient (and modern) Jews. The *Shema* (Hebrew for "Hear") was derived from a passage in the Book of Deuteronomy: "Hear [*Shema*], O Israel: The Lord our God is one Lord" (Deut 6:4). For ancient Jews, there is only one Lord God. English translations of the Bible are always careful to capitalize the word Lord in this verse. In the original Hebrew, the term it translates is the sacred name of God, which is spelled with the consonants YHWH. Instead of spelling out the name of God, our Bibles render the original Hebrew with the term, "Lord." This practice follows Jewish tradition. Ancient Jews refrained from pronouncing the holy name of God. When they saw YHWH, Jewish readers would instead substitute the word, "Adonai," the Hebrew word for "Lord." In keeping this custom, they underscored the uniqueness of God's name. YHWH is God like no other.

The Ten Commandments emphasize this essential belief. They begin, "I am the Lord (=YHWH) your God, who brought you out of the land of Egypt....You shall have no other gods before me" (Ex 20:2–3). The Old Testament regularly speaks of the gods of other nations. Nevertheless, the scriptures emphasize that there is only one true God, and this is the one Lord—YHWH. Moses taught the Israelites that the gods of the nations were not simply false gods, they were demons (see Deut 32:17).

The uniqueness of Israel's God is further underscored in the Book of Isaiah. Speaking through Isaiah, YHWH explains that he is the sole Creator: "I am the LORD (=YHWH), who made all things, who stretched out the heavens alone, who spread out the earth—Who was with me?" (Is 44:24). The question posed at the end of that last verse is plainly rhetorical and makes the point that Israel's God alone created all things. Furthermore, as we discussed in chapter 9, Isaiah insisted that all nations would one day worship YHWH.

> Turn to me and be saved,
>   all the ends of the earth!
>   For I am God, and there is no other.
> By myself I have sworn,
>   from my mouth has gone forth in righteousness
>   a word that shall not return:
> 'To me every knee shall bow,
>   every tongue shall swear.'
> Only in the LORD, it shall be said of me,
>   are righteousness and strength
> (Is 45:22–24).

Israel's One God

St. Paul often applied Old Testament passages that speak of "the Lord" to Jesus. For example, in his first letter to the Corinthians, he quoted one such passage in Isaiah, using it in reference to Christ: "'For who has known the mind of the Lord so as to instruct him?' But we have the mind of Christ" (1 Cor 2:16; quoting Is 40:13, and see also Rom 10:13). Likewise, in his epistle to the Philippians, St. Paul applied the future prophecy of Isaiah to the worship of Jesus. Note the parallel language:

Isaiah 45:23–24	Philippians 2:10
"To me every knee shall bow, every tongue shall swear. Only in the LORD, it shall be said of me, one righteousness and strength."	"at the name of Jesus every knee should bow…and every tongue confess that Jesus Christ is Lord…"

In calling Jesus "Lord" and alluding to Isaiah's famous prophecy, St. Paul made an astounding claim: Jesus is the one God of the *Shema*.

The Crucified Lord of Glory   **193**

St. Paul further emphasized Jesus' divinity in the first letter to the Corinthians. As we have mentioned, ancient Jews understood that there is only one Creator. According to the Old Testament, all things existed through YHWH. St. Paul drew on this tradition when he spoke of God as the source of all things, saying, "from him and through him and to him are all things" (Rom 11:36). In his first letter to the Corinthians, St. Paul used this formula in reference to Jesus.

> *For although there may be so-called gods in heaven or on earth—as indeed there are many "gods" and many "lords"—yet for us there is one God, the Father, from whom are all things and for whom we exist, and one Lord, Jesus Christ, through whom are all things and through whom we exist (1 Cor 8:5–6).*

St. Paul thus re-worked the *Shema* and specifically identified Jesus as the "one Lord" it proclaims. By speaking of Jesus as the one "through whom are all things," he placed Jesus squarely on the divine side of the Creator-creature divide. God is Father, but Jesus Christ is also identified as the God of the *Shema*.

How could someone like St. Paul, raised in the strictest form of Judaism, come to the unlikely conclusion that a carpenter from Nazareth was actually "YHWH"? The Gospels provide the answer.

Pier Francesco Sacchi, St. Paul Writing, *c. 1520, Oil on poplar wood, National Gallery, London, England.*

194   CHAPTER 11

Jesus' Subtle Revelation of His Divinity

In the Gospel accounts, we learn how Jesus of Nazareth revealed that he was more than a mere man. He did not usually do this by making direct claims. Rather, for the most part, Jesus revealed his identity by teaching in a very Jewish way, through scriptural allusions that he could expect his audience to catch. For those who knew the Law and the Prophets, his teaching about his identity was clear.

For example, Mark's Gospel reports that Jesus, caught in a storm with his disciples, caused the wind to cease and calmed the sea. Stunned by what they have witnessed, the disciples asked themselves, "Who then is this, that even wind and sea obey him?" (Mk 4:35). The reader is expected to know that, according to Israel's scriptures, such prerogatives belonged to God alone (see Ps 104:5–7; Ps 107:23–30). In quieting the storm, Jesus performed an action that signaled he is something more than an ordinary human. Through such actions, he slowly prepared the disciples to recognize the astonishing truth of his divine identity.

Another example can be found earlier in the same Gospel, when Jesus told a paralyzed man, "Child, your sins are forgiven" (Mk 2:5). The bystanders were astounded. "Now some of the scribes were sitting there, questioning in their hearts, 'Why does this man speak thus? It is blasphemy! Who can forgive sins but God alone?'" (Mk 2:6–7). The skeptics' response evoked the wording of the *Shema*. In the original Greek used by Mark, their question reads "Who can forgive sins but the one God?" Jesus, however, had the unique ability to read their hearts: "And immediately Jesus, perceiving in his spirit that they questioned like this within themselves, said to them, 'Why do you question like this in your hearts?'" (Mk 2:8). He then proved that he had the divine authority he claimed by healing the paralyzed man (Mk 2:9–11). The response of the crowd was one of sheer astonishment: "We never saw anything like this!" (Mk 2:12). The people were amazed not merely because of the miraculous healing, but also because of Jesus' claim to have forgiven the man's sins. Jesus' audience understood the implications of his actions. To calm the sea and to forgive sins were deeds that God alone could do.

The Crucified Lord of Glory   195

Raphael, The Transfiguration, 1516–20, Tempera on wood, Pinacoteca Vaticana, Vatican City.

The Transfiguration

Jesus normally kept the glory of his divinity hidden, such that it was possible to say of him, without any irony or bitterness, "Is not this the carpenter, the son of Mary?" (Mk 6:3). Yet he once gave Peter, James, and John a glimpse of his true splendor. These three ascended a high mountain with Jesus, where they became witnesses to one of the most spectacular scenes narrated in the Gospels. The apostles watched as Jesus' appearance was suddenly changed. Matthew put it this way: "his face shone like the sun, and his garments became white as light" (Mt 17:2). Those who know the Old Testament well hear an echo of the story of Moses in the Transfiguration. Moses also climbed a mountain, Mount Sinai, where he had an encounter with the Lord. The Book of Exodus tells us that after this divine encounter, the skin of Moses' face was radiant (Ex 34:29–35). There is, however, a major difference between Moses and Jesus: while Moses' face reflected God's glory, Jesus' face is the source of radiance. A careful comparison of the two stories reveals that Jesus is more like God than he is like Moses. Jesus' divine identity is also reinforced in other ways. For example, Matthew tells us that Jesus' garments became "white as light" (Mt 17:2). These words ascribed to Jesus the appearance of God, as told by the Book of Daniel, in which the Lord's clothing was declared to be "white as snow" (Dan 7:9).

The account of the Transfiguration continues with the appearance of Moses and Elijah: "And behold, there appeared to them Moses and Elijah, talking with him" (Mt 17:3). The presence of these two Old Testament saints was no accident. These are the two men in the Old Testament who had ascended mountains to seek the Lord (see Ex 33:18–23; 1 Kings 19:9). While God appeared to both of them, neither were permitted to see his face. Instead, God "passed by" them both. Moses was allowed a look at his back (Ex 33:23), and Elijah experienced his presence in a small voice (1 Kings 19:12). In the Transfiguration, however, both now see the face of God, because in Jesus God has a human face.

Jesus's Divinity in the Gospel according to John

The Gospel of John makes explicit what is implicit in Matthew, Mark, and Luke. The Gospel begins by speaking of Jesus as the "Word of God," telling us directly of his divinity: "the Word was God" (Jn 1:1). It then testifies to the Incarnation: "And the Word became flesh and dwelt among us" (Jn 1:14). As the narrative of John's Gospel unfolds, Jesus referred to his pre-existence by appealing to biblical traditions: "Truly, truly, I say to you, before Abraham was, I am" (Jn 8:58). In speaking of himself as "I am," Jesus applied the divine name to himself. His Jewish audience understood what he was claiming and attempted to stone him to death for blasphemy (Jn 8:59). Later, Jesus reinforced this teaching: "I and the Father are one" (Jn 10:30).

When Jesus performed miracles intended as signs of his divinity, the Jewish leaders picked up on their significance. John tells us, "This was why the Jews sought all the more to kill him, because he…called God his Father, making himself equal with God" (Jn 5:18). The apostle Thomas's words to the Risen Lord at the end of the same Gospel thus make the statement of faith to which the entire narrative has been building: "My Lord

The Gospel of John begins by speaking of Jesus as the "Word of God," telling us directly of his divinity.

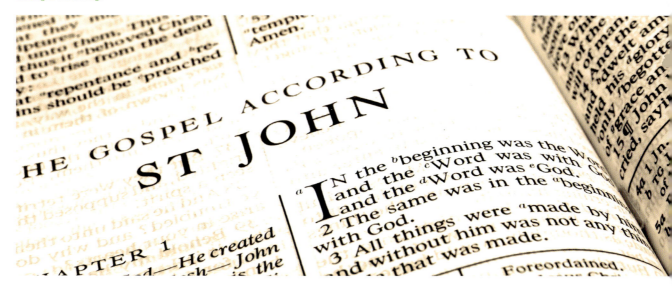

and my God!" (Jn 20:28). Remember, this is an astonishing statement for an ancient Jew like Thomas who daily prayed the *Shema*—his declaration meant nothing less than "You are the one Lord and the one God."

Three Persons, One God

Not only does the New Testament reveal that Jesus is equal to God; it also affirms that the Holy Spirit is a divine person. This truth can be detected in various ways in the New Testament, but it is once again the Gospel according to John that presents this truth most explicitly. In the Last Supper discourse recorded in John's account, Jesus promised that the Father would send the Spirit as "another Counselor" (Jn 14:16). By speaking of "another" such figure, Jesus suggested that he himself is also a Counselor sent by the Father. In fact, the same Greek word, translated "Counselor" in John 14:16 (*paraklētos,* "Paraclete"), is later specifically applied to Christ in 1 John 2:1. By applying the word Counselor to the Holy Spirit, Jesus indicated that the Spirit is like himself—a divine person.

Jesus' teaching, contrary to those who would claim that the Spirit is merely an impersonal force, underscored the Holy Spirit's personhood. He told us that the Spirit "teaches" (Jn 14:26), "testifies" (Jn 15:26), "reproves" (Jn 16:8–11), and "guides" (Jn 16:12). St. Paul and St. Luke also testified to the personhood of the Spirit by speaking of how he "wills" (1 Cor 12:11), "desires" (Gal 5:17), "loves" (Rom 15:30), and "calls" (Acts 13:2). If the Spirit were merely an impersonal power—something like gravity—such language would make no sense. Moreover, the divinity of the Spirit is underscored in the Book of Acts when St. Peter equated lying to the Holy Spirit with lying to God. Rebuking Ananias for withholding the truth from the apostles, the fisherman asked, "Why has Satan filled your heart to lie to the Holy Spirit? . . . You have not lied to men but to God" (Acts 5:3-4).

It is also important to note that when Jesus sent out the apostles to preach the Gospel to the peoples of the world, he commanded them to "baptize them in the name of the Father, and of the Son, and of the Holy Spirit" (Mt 28:19). The fact that Jesus did not speak of the "names" (plural) but used the singular "name" has long been recognized as significant. There are three persons who each have the one name because there are three persons who are one God.

The triquetra, or trinity knot, has been used in Christian tradition since the Celtic revival of the 19th century. The three interconnected loops represent the relationship of the Father, Son, and Holy Spirit while the circle emphasizes the unity of the whole.

The Scandal of a Crucified Lord

We now come to the most difficult question: if Jesus is the Creator God, why did he die on the cross? Those who have taken catechism classes may be able to respond that Jesus' death represents the solution to the problem of sin. This is certainly the teaching of the apostles. Yet the necessity of the cross is not immediately evident. If we are called to forgive one another without counting the cost (see Mt 18:21–22), why is the cross part of God's plan to reconcile the world to himself? Why did God choose such a brutal means of salvation?

After nearly 2,000 years of successful missionary work by Christians, the cross has become the most well-known sign of Christian faith throughout the world. It represents salvation, new life, and the hope of glory. Before Christ's death, however, crucifixion meant none of these things. We would do well to note that for the original readers of the New Testament books, the cross was the ultimate symbol of death, humiliation, and subjugation. Referring to the barbaric scourging that preceded crucifixion and the long, drawn-out suffering it entailed, the Roman statesman Seneca (4 B.C.–A.D. 65) wrote that those sentenced to be executed on a cross would be more likely to commit suicide if given the choice. With good reason the historian Josephus (A.D. 37–100) spoke of crucifixion as the "most wretched of deaths." Its tortures were so ghastly that Cicero (106–43 B.C.) considered it inappropriate even to mention crucifixion in polite society.

Why did the Romans seek to perfect the cruelty of crucifixion with such careful calibration? It was not chiefly because they were sadistic. Although the Romans were known for their savagery, their choice of crucifixion served a purpose beyond satisfying their blood-lust. The cross was a political tool because it was a weapon of terror. "Whenever we crucify the guilty," Quintilian (A.D. 35–100) wrote, "the most crowded roads are chosen, where most people can see and be moved by this fear." The threat of crucifixion helped to keep the world under the Empire's iron rule. Few were willing to think about rebellion when the consequences of failure were so utterly horrific.

The Scandal of a Crucified Christ

We can now better appreciate the challenge the apostles faced. Proclaiming a crucified Lord hardly seemed like "Gospel," that is, good news. St. Paul wrote, "Jews demand signs and Greeks seek wisdom, but we preach Christ crucified, a stumbling block to Jews and folly to Gentiles" (1 Cor 1:22). How could the Messiah—the promised deliverer—be defeated on a cross? The idea was absurd.

We know that the disciples themselves struggled to accept this idea even when they heard it from the mouth of their master himself. According to Mark's Gospel, Jesus only revealed this aspect of his mission to the apostles after Peter had confessed his belief in Jesus' messianic identity (see Mk 8:27–30). Following Peter's profession, we read: "And

How could the Messiah—the promised deliverer—be defeated on a cross? The idea was absurd.

he began to teach them that the Son of man must suffer many things, and be rejected by the elders and the chief priests and the scribes, and be killed, and after three days rise again" (Mk 8:31). To this shocking revelation, Peter responded by attempting to correct Jesus: "And Peter took him, and began to rebuke him" (Mk 8:32). Jesus answered with one of the most stinging corrections ever uttered: "Get behind me, Satan! For you are not on the side of God, but of men" (Mk 8:33).

One wonders if Peter would have been able to recognize Jesus as the Christ had he known in advance what would happen at that last fateful Passover in Jerusalem. It seems that Jesus purposefully waited to reveal the suffering that awaited him until after the apostles had recognized his messianic role. Peter thought he knew what the Messiah would do. But Jesus had to wait until the fisherman became convinced that his teacher truly was the long-awaited King before realigning those expectations.

The story of Peter's misconception about Jesus's messianic role is anticipated in Mark's narrative. Immediately prior to narrating Peter's confession and subsequent rebuke of Jesus, Mark recounts a healing story that, at first glance, transpires in a rather curious way. Jesus spat on a blind man's eyes and laid his hands on him, which caused the man to regain his sight, but imperfectly. He explained to Jesus, "I see men; but they look like trees, walking" (Mk 8:24). Jesus laid his hands upon the man a second time; only then was the man clear-sighted. Why this two-step healing process? Was Jesus' first attempt in some sense a failure? Not at all. The miracle anticipates the account of Peter and the apostles developing a spiritual vision of faith. Peter was able to see that Jesus was the Messiah, but not with clarity. A further healing of spiritual sight would be required. Only later would he understand why his master had to suffer.

The Love of the Crucified Lord

When St. Paul spoke of the scandal of the cross to the Corinthians, he asserted that the rulers of the world were ignorant. They could not fathom how Jesus' death disclosed God's wisdom: "None of the rulers of this age understood this; for if they had, they would not have crucified the Lord of glory. But, as it is written, 'What no eye has seen, nor ear heard, nor the heart of man conceived, what God has prepared for those who love him'" (1 Cor 2:8–9). By referring to Jesus as the "Lord of glory," the Apostle used a title other ancient Jewish works applied to God himself. The truth that God himself would become human and lay down his life was hidden and could not have been anticipated. As the graffiti discovered on the Palatine Hill indicates, the notion of a crucified God was preposterous to pagans.

What the cross ultimately reveals is the deepest truth about God: he is, in his innermost life, love. A crucified God seemed absurd to pagans not because the divine plan was foolish; the real problem was that they had not fully understood who God is. The cross would clarify the meaning of divinity once and for all.

The Crucified Lord

"He who does not love does not know God; for God is love" (1 Jn 4:8). The New Testament discloses that God is love because he is, in himself, a communion of persons. The essence of the divine life itself is love; the three divine persons share their very essence with one another. The Father loves the Son, holding nothing back from him. As Jesus explained, "All that the Father has is mine" (Jn 16:15; see Jn 3:35). The Son reciprocates this love, pouring himself out in love (Jn 10:17). The Holy Spirit is identified as the very gift of love that they share (see

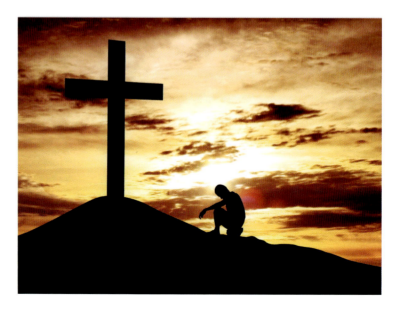

"Therefore God has highly exalted him and bestowed on him the name which is above every name, that at the name of Jesus every knee should bow, in heaven and on earth and under the earth, and every tongue confess that Jesus Christ is Lord, to the glory of God the Father" (Phil 2:9–11).

Rom 5:5). When Jesus offered himself in love for our redemption, he opened a window onto the infinite depth of this Trinitarian love, as St. Paul explained in one of the Bible's most eloquent passages:

> *Christ Jesus, who, though he was in the form of God, did not count equality with God a thing to be grasped, but emptied himself, taking the form of a servant, being born in the likeness of men. And being found in human form he humbled himself and became obedient unto death, even death on a cross. "Therefore God has highly exalted him and bestowed on him the name which is above every name, that at the name of Jesus every knee should bow, in heaven and on earth and under the earth, and every tongue confess that Jesus Christ is Lord, to the glory of God the Father" (Phil 2:6–11).*

Much could be said about this teaching. We will highlight four points of special importance.

First, in these verses St. Paul used language that Christian tradition has long understood as describing the two natures of Christ: he who was in the "form of God" went on to take the "form of a servant" and was "born in the likeness of men." The words declare the essence of the Christian faith: God became man. To be in the "form of a servant" means to become human. When St. Paul spoke of Jesus as being in the "form of God," he affirmed that Jesus is God.

The Crucified Lord of Glory   203

Second, Jesus voluntarily humbled himself not only in becoming human but also in being crucified. St. Paul explained that Christ did not consider "equality with God" a thing to be "grasped." The Greek word for grasped means something like, "a thing to be exploited." So, St. Paul's lesson is that Jesus did not cling to his divinity for his own advantage; he consented to become fully human, to share our nature and the frailties to which it is subject. Yet, at no point did St. Paul suggest that Jesus ceased to be God. What he affirmed is that Jesus was truly God and man. In becoming a man, Jesus aligned his human will with the divine will—he was "obedient." The ultimate expression of this obedience was his death on the cross.

Third, in speaking of how Christ took the "form of a servant" and suffered, St. Paul echoed a famous passage in Isaiah which describes a Suffering Servant who offers his life as a sacrifice that atones for sin:

> *He was despised and rejected by men;*
> *a man of sorrows, and acquainted with grief;*
> *and as one from whom men hide their faces*
> *he was despised, and we esteemed him not.*
>
> *Surely he has borne our griefs*
> *and carried our sorrows;*
> *yet we esteemed him stricken,*
> *struck down by God, and afflicted.*
> *But he was wounded for our transgressions,*
> *he was bruised for our iniquities;*
> *upon him was the chastisement that made us whole,*
> *and with his stripes we are healed...*
>
> *Yet it was the will of the LORD to bruise him;*
> *he has put him to grief;*
> *when he makes himself an offering for sin,*
> *he shall see his offspring, he shall prolong his days*
> *(Is 53:3–5, 10).*

Other New Testament writers also applied this passage to Jesus (see, for example, Mt 8:14–17; Acts 8:26–35; 1 Pet 2:19–25).

Fourth, this passage describes a two-fold movement: (a) as God, Jesus emptied himself in taking the nature of a servant—that is, in becoming human (without ceasing to be God); (b) as man, Jesus emptied himself by dying the humiliating death of crucifixion. What Jesus accomplished

St. John taught that we must respond to God's love, revealed in Christ, by loving one another.

on the cross, then, is an expression of what he always does as God: he pours himself out in love. For St. Paul, this last reason represented the most important truth about the cross, that it reveals God's love for us:

> *While we were yet helpless, at the right time Christ died for the ungodly. Why, one will hardly die for a righteous man—though perhaps for a good man one will dare even to die. But God shows his love for us in that while we were yet sinners Christ died for us (Rom 5:6–8).*

Similarly, St. Paul explained to the Galatians that Jesus' crucifixion proved that Christ "loved me and gave himself for me" (Gal 2:20). God is love, and it is the cross that reveals the immeasurable depth of this love. Jesus himself had prepared his followers to understand the cross, by giving them the instruction he called "my commandment": "that you love one another as I have loved you. Greater love has no man than this, that a man lay down his life for his friends" (Jn 15:12–13). What does it mean to love as Christ loves? It means to lay down one's life for another.

This is precisely St. Paul's point in the passage from Philippians cited above. The account of Christ's sacrificial love is offered to reinforce the exhortation that opens the chapter: "Do nothing from selfishness or conceit, but in humility count others better than yourselves. Let each of you look not only to his own interests, but also to the interests of others. Have this mind among yourselves, which was in Christ Jesus" (Phil 2:3–5). Similarly, St. John taught that we must respond to God's love, revealed in Christ, by loving one another:

> *He who does not love does not know God; for God is love. In this the love of God was made manifest among us, that God sent his only-begotten Son into the world, so that we might live through him. In this is love, not that we loved God but that he loved us and sent his Son to be the expiation for our sins. Beloved, if God so loved us, we also ought to love one another (1 Jn 4:8–11).*

The Crucified Lord of Glory

The Cross and Salvation from Sin

God created us in his "image and likeness" (Gen 1:26). The purpose of life is clear: we were made to share in the divine life, which is characterized by love. St. Paul explains that Adam failed through disobedience, but Jesus is the "New Adam" who conquers through obedience (see Rom 5:14; 1 Cor 15:45). The Second Vatican Council put it this way: Jesus "reveals man to man" (*Gaudium et Spes,* 22). In other words, Jesus shows us what it means to be "fully human"—to be the image of God by pouring out one's life in love. Self-giving is the road to the happiness that we all seek: "For whoever would save his life will lose it, and whoever loses his life for my sake will find it" (Mt 16:25).

At its root, sin is the decision to rebel against this design of love. It is to choose a disordered form of self-love instead of the love of God and neighbor. Sin disrupts God's design for the world and our lives. When God created the world and saw that it was good, death had not yet entered into it. Suffering and death entered the world because of Adam's sin. As St. Paul explained, "The wages of sin is death" (Rom 6:23). Sin rebels against God's will and tries to undermine that plan. It was sin that ushered suffering and death into the world (see Gen 3:14–19; Rom 5:15–21).

Yet the cross reveals to us something else about suffering: God can redeem it. The greatest tragedy can be transformed into a means of salvation. Death can become a gift of love. By embracing the cross willingly, suffering death, and rising on the third day, Jesus defeated death once and for all.

Whatever distress, sadness, and suffering we experience, we know that God is not indifferent to our pain. He understands betrayal, rejection, torture, and even death. Christ took the form of a servant—the Suffering Servant—and truly is the "Man of Sorrows" (Is 53:3). Suffering is not an indicator that God has somehow lost control of the world or that he has ceased to care for our plight. The Father has a plan. Although we cannot always understand how, suffering serves his greater plan. It may not have looked like it on Good Friday, but what appeared to be a brutal execution was actually the means by which God would save the world. He permitted his Son to give himself up for us in order to reveal his love for us: "For God so loved the world that he gave his only-begotten Son, that whoever believes in him should not perish but have eternal life" (Jn 3:16).

The cross is now the ultimate sign of love.

The cross is now the ultimate sign of love. And, by the grace of God, we too can suffer obediently. In Christ, we too can learn to renounce selfishness—the root of sin—and to love like God, giving ourselves away: "Therefore be imitators of God, as beloved children. And walk in love, as Christ loved us and gave himself up for us" (Eph 5:1–2). In accepting the suffering of his Passion, Jesus defeated sin with divine love. God does not delight in seeing us suffer, but permits it because it provides the opportunity to overcome sin and become like Christ. If we only love when it is easy to do so, we ultimately only love ourselves. Love without suffering is empty; and suffering without love is unendurable. Suffering perfects love. By means of the Spirit who unites us to Christ, we are conformed to his image (Rom 8:29) and enabled to love like him: "For all who are led by the Spirit of God are sons of God. For you did not receive the spirit of slavery to fall back into fear, but you have received the spirit of sonship." (Rom 8:14–15).

In a pagan world, this perspective was absurd. To Rome the highest good was conquering and ruling over others. The imperial forces sought not life-giving love, but domination. The ultimate sign of that goal was, arguably, the Roman cross. Because of it, all would bow to Caesar. To worship a man who hung upon it was, therefore, the height of foolishness and absurdity. But, as St. Paul explained, "the foolishness of God is wiser than men, and the weakness of God is stronger than men" (1 Cor 1:25). By accepting crucifixion, Jesus overturned Rome's supposed power and revealed the way to true victory. The love that Christ is, the love revealed in his cross, is more powerful than earthly empires, our suffering, and our sin. It is even more powerful than death itself. Christ opens the door to our participation in eternal life, a sharing in the life of the Triune God.

Review Questions

1. What was the *Shema,* what does it teach us about Israel's God, and how does the prophet Isaiah reinforce the beliefs it emphasizes?

2. What evidence is there in St. Paul's writing and in the New Testament for belief in the divinity of Christ and the Holy Spirit?

3. Why was the notion of a crucified Lord so preposterous? Explain the two-fold movement of Philippians 2:6–8 and how its message relates to the truth about God articulated in 1 John 4:8–11.

4. What does the cross teach us about suffering?

5. What suffering have you experienced in your life and how does meditating on the cross shed light on that experience?

6. If death is due to sin, but sin has been forgiven in Christ, why do you think God still permits death?

Put Out Into the Deep

To learn more about the theology of the Trinity and Redemption, see Frank Sheed, *Theology for Beginners* (1957; reprinted Ignatius, 2017). Sheed (1897–1981) for many years preached the faith on a soapbox in London's Hyde Park, developing the clear and forcible style that he deployed in this classic work.

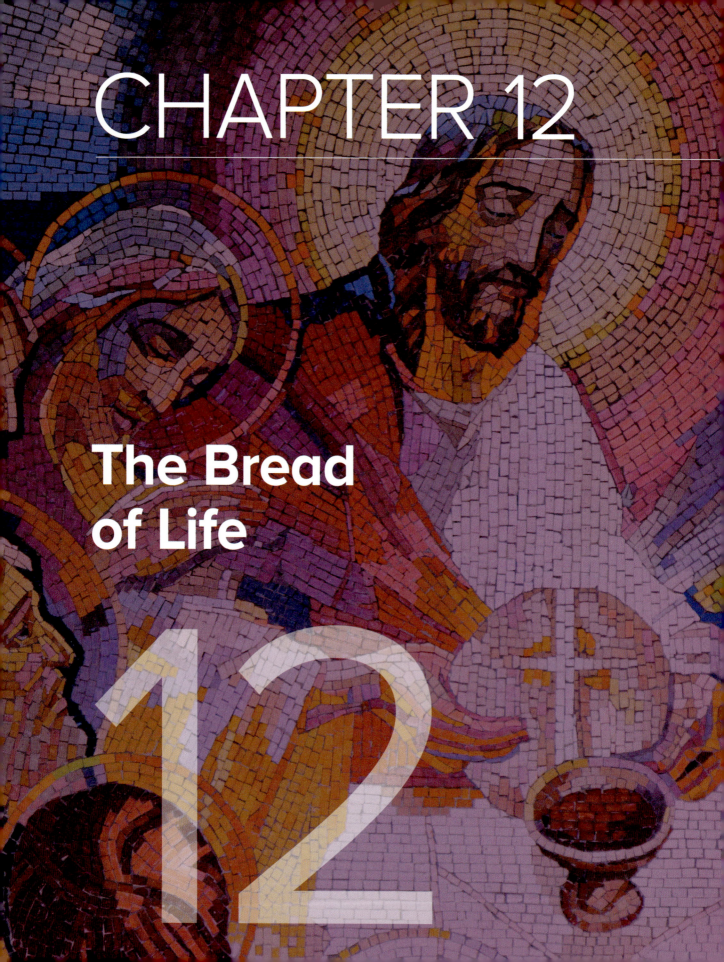

CHAPTER 12

The Bread of Life

*And the whole congregation of the sons of Israel murmured against Moses and Aaron in the wilderness, and said to them, "Would that we had died by the hand of the L*ORD* in the land of Egypt, when we sat by the fleshpots and ate bread to the full; for you have brought us out into this wilderness to kill this whole assembly with hunger."*

*Then the L*ORD* said to Moses, "Behold, I will rain bread from heaven for you; and the people shall go out and gather a day's portion every day, that I may test them, whether they will walk in my law or not. On the sixth day, when they prepare what they bring in, it will be twice as much as they gather daily." So Moses and Aaron said to all the sons of Israel, "At evening you shall know that it was the L*ORD* who brought you out of the land of Egypt, and in the morning you shall see the glory of the L*ORD*, because he has heard your murmurings against the L*ORD*. For what are we, that you murmur against us?" And Moses said, "When the L*ORD* gives you in the evening flesh to eat and in the morning bread to the full, because the L*ORD* has heard your murmurings which you murmur against him—what are we? Your murmurings are not against us but against the L*ORD*."*

*And Moses said to Aaron, "Say to the whole congregation of the sons of Israel, 'Come near before the L*ORD*, for he has heard your murmurings.'" And as Aaron spoke to the whole congregation of the sons of Israel, they looked toward the wilderness, and behold, the glory of the L*ORD* appeared in the cloud. And the L*ORD* said to Moses, "I have heard the murmurings of the sons of Israel; say to them, 'At twilight you shall eat flesh, and in the morning you shall be filled with bread; then you shall know that I am the L*ORD* your God.'"*

*In the evening quails came up and covered the camp; and in the morning dew lay round about the camp. And when the dew had gone up, there was on the face of the wilderness a fine, flake-like thing, fine as hoarfrost on the ground. When the sons of Israel saw it, they said to one another, "What is it?" For they did not know what it was. And Moses said to them, "It is the bread which the L*ORD* has given you to eat. This is what the L*ORD* has commanded: 'Gather of it, every man of you, as much as he can eat; you shall take an omer apiece, according to the number of the persons whom each of you has in his tent.'" And the sons of Israel did so; they gathered, some more, some less. But when they measured it with an omer, he that gathered much had nothing over, and he that gathered little had no lack; each gathered according to what he could eat.*
(Ex 16:1–18)

The Bread of Life   **211**

Jesus incorporates us into his work of redemption, especially through his presence and work in the sacraments.

Jesus' Miraculous Sign

We have already considered the unity of God's plan of salvation in the Old and New Testaments. It is important also to understand that we ourselves belong to the same story. Although it is true that all of salvation history finds its fulfillment in Christ, his ministry did not bring about the end of salvation history. Alive and active still today, Jesus incorporates us into his work of redemption, especially through his presence and work in the sacraments. We will ponder this mystery by looking at one of the most important and controversial chapters in the New Testament, the sixth chapter of St. John's Gospel.

The chapter begins with an account of Jesus performing "signs" the word John used for Jesus' miracles (see Jn 2:11)—in this case, healing the sick (Jn 6:2). As we have seen, Jesus' healings were an important means by which he revealed his identity. The Jews had learned from their prophets that the Messiah would demonstrate his identity by performing miraculous works such as curing the blind and lame (see Mt 11:5, citing Is 35:5–6 and Is 61:1). This is one reason John called Jesus' miracles signs: they point beyond themselves to deeper truths about Jesus and his mission. As John continued his narrative, he recounted one of the most famous miracles of Jesus: the feeding of the five thousand, the only miracle recounted in all four Gospels. This miracle was a sign that pointed in two directions: backward in one respect and forward in another. On the one hand, the miracle reminded those present (as it reminds us who read it today) of God's providential care for the Israelites in the wilderness. On the other hand, the feeding of the five thousand points forward to what would later transpire at the Last Supper.

Jesus and Israel in the Wilderness

To help the hearer or reader of the Gospel understand the miraculous feeding with reference to the story of the Exodus, John began by situating the event in time: "Now the Passover, the feast of the Jews, was at hand" (Jn 6:4). He thus linked the miracle to a festival in which the events of the Exodus were commemorated. As we shall see, there are many connections between the story of the manna that God gave to the people of Israel during their long march through the desert and the account of Jesus' feeding of the multitudes. John then reinforced his allusions to the manna by mentioning certain details in the lead-up to the miracle itself. First, both stories take place in the wilderness. John reported that Jesus was on the far side of the Sea of Galilee, which was known as a deserted place (Mt 14:13; Mk 6:32, 35; Lk 9:12). Second, in both episodes there was a problem of too many people and not enough food. John recorded the following exchange between Jesus and his disciples:

> Lifting up his eyes, then, and seeing that a multitude was coming to him, Jesus said to Philip, "How are we to buy bread, so that these people may eat?" This he said to test him, for he himself knew what he would do. Philip answered him, "Two hundred denarii would not buy enough bread for each of them to get a little. One of his disciples, Andrew, Simon Peter's brother, said to him, "There is a lad here who has five barley loaves and two fish; but what are they among so many?" (Jn 6:5–7)

James Tissot, The Miracle of the Loaves and Fishes, 1886-1894, Watercolor on granite on paper, Brooklyn Museum, New York, New York, USA.

Philip's protest bears the mark of desperation. Jesus has given the disciples a task that exceeds their abilities. A denarius was the wage for a day's worth of work. It would simply be cost-prohibitive to feed all the people (Jn 6:10). The few items offered by the boy were woefully insignificant to feed such a vast multitude. Like Moses, Jesus was faced with a group of hungry people in the wilderness. Finally, John explained that the purpose of Jesus' question was to "test" his disciples (Jn 6:6). By choosing this word, John linked the miracle to the Exodus, which was also an instance of divine testing: "[God] fed you in the wilderness with manna which your fathers did not know, that he might humble you and test you" (Deut 8:16).

The Bread of Life

The Manna as Miraculous Food and Foretaste of the Promised Land

What happened next was that Jesus satisfied the people's hunger by performing one of his miraculous signs (Jn 6:14), multiplying the loaves and fish. The evangelist leaves no doubt about the supernatural nature of this action. In the aftermath, we learn that the disciples "filled twelve baskets with fragments from the five barley loaves" (Jn 6:13). In other words, the numerous fragments all came from the original five loaves. Although there are echoes here of a miracle performed by Elisha (2 Kings 4:42–44), the notion of a miraculous feeding involving bread also evokes the gift of the manna. In the Book of Exodus, we are told that each Israelite collected the bread from heaven in an omer—that is, a jar. Yet "he that gathered little had no lack" (Ex 16:18); that is, no matter how little was gathered, no one's jar ever ran out. There was a sort of multiplication of the manna. The manna was truly miraculous.

Ancient Israel considered the manna to have been heavenly bread. The Psalmist reminisces about how God gave his people "bread from heaven in abundance" (Ps 105:40). In Psalm 78, the manna is even called the "bread of angels" (Ps 78:25). Further special properties of the manna were conveyed by the Book of Wisdom:

> You gave your people food of angels, and without their toil you supplied them from heaven with bread ready to eat, providing every pleasure and suited to every taste. For your sustenance manifested your sweetness toward your children; and the bread, ministering to the desire of the one who took it, was changed to suit every one's liking (Wis 16:20–21).

The Miracle of the Loaves and Fishes performed by Jesus echoes God's gift of manna to Moses and the Israelites in the desert.

View of the Promised Land as seen from Mount Nebo.

Here the manna is said to have had another miraculous feature: the manna was "changed" to satisfy "everyone one's liking." We do not know whether this special occurrence happened the entire time Israel ate the manna or if this quality disappeared over time. What it does emphasize is that the manna was more than mundane bread. It was supernatural food.

It is also worth pointing out that the gift of the manna was accompanied by the additional gift of "flesh" (Ex 16:8). While the manna fell every morning, God also saw to it that the Israelites received quail every evening, which was found laying over all the ground, ready to be cooked. The Book of Numbers tells us more about their mysterious origin. Moses complained to the Lord about the insufficiency of food to feed the people, asking "shall all the fish of the sea be gathered together for them?" (Num 11:22). In response to Moses, God not only sent the manna but the quail as well. In an apparent allusion to Moses' off-hand remark, the Book of Numbers specifies that God brought the quail "up from the sea" (Num 11:31; see also Wis 19:12). Ancient Jewish tradition thought that this suggested that the quail actually arose from the water itself, describing the quail as sea-creatures of a sort. It is no surprise, therefore, that Jesus chose to multiply both bread and fish.

What happened to the manna? It ceased to fall when the Israelites arrived at the border of the Promised Land (Ex 16:35). This was no accident. The Bible repeatedly calls the Promised Land a place "flowing with milk and honey" (Ex 3:8; 13:5; 33:3; Lev 20:24). Significantly, the manna is said to have tasted like "wafers made with honey" (Ex 16:31). The manna was, therefore, a foretaste of the Promised Land and so was no longer given to the people of Israel after their arrival there.

The Bread of Life   215

The Manna and the Messiah

The story of the manna eventually became wrapped up with hopes for God's future deliverance of Israel. God had informed the people that he would one day raise up another prophet like Moses (Deut 18:15–18). Jesus' contemporaries read this announcement as a reference to the coming of the Messiah. If the manna had fallen from heaven under Moses' leadership, it made sense to think that something similar would happen when the Messiah was revealed. This kind of thinking was common in Jesus' day. It is attested to not only in the ancient collection of texts contained in the Dead Sea Scrolls, but also in this passage from a late first century non-biblical book known as *2 Baruch:*

> *And it will happen that when all that which should come to pass in these parts has been accomplished, the Anointed One will begin to be revealed. And Behemoth will reveal itself from its place, and Leviathan will come from the sea, the two great monsters which I created on the fifth day of creation and which I shall have kept until that time. And they will be nourishment for all who are left ... And those who are hungry will enjoy themselves and they will, moreover, see marvels every day ... And it will happen at that time that the treasury of manna will come down again from on high, and they will eat of it in those years because these are they who will have arrived at the consummation of time.*

This text links the coming of the Anointed One (the Messiah) and the gift of the manna to feasting on the sea monster, Leviathan. The imagery here builds on Jewish traditions about the fish-like nature of the quail in the Book of Numbers.

Given these expectations the crowd's response to Jesus' miracle is understandable. We read, "When the people saw the sign which he had performed, they said, 'This is indeed the prophet who is to come into the world!'" (Jn 6:14). The "prophet who is to come into the world" is a reference to the figure mentioned by Moses in Deuteronomy 18, a prophecy ancient Jews understood as describing the Messiah. The Jews who were fed by Jesus in the wilderness remembered the prophecy, which is why "they were about to come and take him by force to make him king" (Jn 6:15). Jesus, however, slipped away. Like Peter, the crowds were expecting the Messiah to be a political and military victor. But Jesus was seeking a heavenly kingdom (see Jn 18:36).

The Bread of Life

The Miracle of the Feeding and the Eucharist

Catholics believe that Jesus' greatest miracle involving bread was the Last Supper. Matthew reveals by his choice of words that it was a reprise of the multiplication of the loaves:

The Feeding of the Five Thousand	The Last Supper
And *when it was evening*… (Mt 14:15)	And *when it was evening*… (Mt 26:20)
"Then he ordered the crowds to *sit* down on the grass…" (Mt 14:19)	"he *sat* at table with the twelve disciples…" (Mt 26:20)
"and *taking the five loaves*…" (Mt 14:19)	"Jesus *took bread*" (Mt 26:26)
"*and blessed, and broke and gave the loaves to the disciples*" (Mt 14:19)	"*and blessed, and broke it, and gave it to the disciples*" (Mt 26:26)

Similarly, John's account of the multiplication of the loaves and fish contained a number of echoes of the accounts of the Last Supper found in the previous Gospels. The chart below highlights the similarities between the Last Supper in Luke's Gospel and John's version of the miracle.

The Last Supper in Luke 22	The Multiplication of the Loaves in John 6
"And when the hour came, he *sat* at table, and the apostles with him" (Lk 22:14)	"Make the people *sit* down" (Jn 6:10)
"I have earnestly desired to eat this *Passover* with you before I suffer" (Lk 22:15)	"Now the *Passover*, the feast of the Jews was at hand" (Jn 6:4)
"And he *took bread*" (Lk 22:19)	"Jesus then *took the loaves* (Jn 6:11)
"and when he had *given thanks* [*eucharisteo*]" (Lk 22:19)	"and when he had *given thanks* [*eucharisteo*]" (Jn 6:11)
he "*gave*" (Lk 22:19)	"he *distributed* them to those who were seated" (Jn 6:11)

Catholics believe that Jesus' greatest miracle involving bread was the Last Supper.

In light of these parallels, we should conclude that John intended his account of the miraculous feeding to be read in the context of existing written accounts of the Last Supper. Two important connections should not be overlooked. First, John sets the Passover festival as the backdrop of the miracle. This is the same feast at which Jesus celebrated his Last Supper. John thus helps us to recognize that Jesus was planning far in advance what he would accomplish in the Upper Room. Second, the Greek word *eucharistēsas*—the origin of the English word "eucharist"—appears in John's account of the miracle.

We learn from the *Catechism of the Catholic Church* that Jesus' miracles "announced and prepared what he was going to give the Church when all was accomplished" (CCC 1115). As we have seen, the visible cures Jesus worked pointed to his power to bring spiritual restoration. A clear instance of this connection occurs in the miracle of the healing of the paralyzed man (see Mk 2:10). By raising the man up, Jesus demonstrated his ability to forgive sins and proved his ability to bring spiritual healing. Now, with the miracle of the multiplication of the loaves and fishes, Jesus has demonstrated his ability to feed his people, to provide us with an everlasting fount of grace—that is, of divine favor, strength, and life—in the eucharist.

The Bread of Life

Jesus proclaims the Bread of Life discourse. In the first part of the speech Jesus invited the crowds to faith. In the second part he pointed to the eucharist that he would fully reveal at the Last Supper.

The Bread of Life Discourse and Faith

After eating their fill of bread and fish, the crowds sought Jesus and found him on the other side of the Sea of Galilee. Yet Jesus knew that their intentions in seeking him were less than pure: "Truly, truly, I say to you, you seek me, not because you saw signs, but because you ate your fill of the loaves" (Jn 6:26). Jesus revealed their carnal motives; the crowds were simply looking for a free lunch. Jesus, therefore, attempted to take their minds off their earthly appetites: "Do not labor for the food which perishes, but for the food which endures to eternal life, which the Son of man will give to you; for on him has God the Father set his seal" (Jn 6:27). What followed is one of the most famous sermons in the Gospels, the Bread of Life discourse. This speech of Jesus has essentially two parts. Both sections begin with the words, "I am the bread of life" (Jn 6:35, 48). In the first part of the speech Jesus invited the crowds to faith. In the second part he pointed to the eucharist that he would fully reveal at the Last Supper.

The crowd's startled response to the first part of the sermon reminds us of the manna story: "The Jews then murmured at him, because he said, 'I am the bread which came down from heaven.' They said, 'Is not this Jesus, the son of Joseph, whose father and mother we know? How does he now say, "I have come down from heaven"?'" (Jn 6:41–42). The language of murmuring is reminiscent of the manna story, which uses the word repeatedly to describe how the Israelites complained about God and Moses (Ex 16:2, 7–8). The people are thus presented as hardhearted like the generation that trekked through the wilderness. Jesus intimated that God would do what the Jews expected: give them bread from heaven. But they did not like his description of how this would take place. How could Jesus be the bread of life that came down from heaven? They protested and began to reject Jesus' new teaching because they did not believe in his divinity.

In response, Jesus emphasized the theme of faith, which he described as a gift from the Father: "Do not murmur among yourselves. No one can come to me unless the Father who sent me draws him; and I will raise him up at the last day.... Truly, truly, I say to you, he who believes has eternal life" (Jn 6:43–47). The first part of the Bread of Life discourse should be understood as extending the Father's invitation to faith. Without faith, the "hard saying" of the second part of the sermon cannot be accepted.

The Bread of Life Discourse and the Eucharist

Jesus then delivered the shocking news that to receive eternal life, we are required to eat his flesh and drink his blood:

> I am the bread of life. Your fathers ate the manna in the wilderness, and they died. This is the bread which comes down from heaven, that a man may eat of it and not die. I am the living bread which came down from heaven; if any one eats of this bread, he will live for ever; and the bread which I shall give for the life of the world is my flesh (Jn 6:48–51).

The Jews had been awaiting the day when the Messiah would bring down the bread from heaven. Their Messiah had come, and now he had told them that the bread to be consumed was his own flesh.

With these words, Jesus went from frustrating his audience to losing them entirely. Consuming human flesh was abhorrent to Jews who obeyed the Torah. The people were mystified, asking: "How can this man give us his flesh to eat?" (Jn 6:52). One might expect at this point a further clarification that would have indicated that the words were merely symbolic or metaphorical. But the crowd received no such comfort. Instead, Jesus deployed even more graphic imagery:

> Truly, truly, I say to you, unless you eat the flesh of the Son of man and drink his blood, you have no life in you; he who eats my flesh and drinks my blood has eternal life, and I will raise him up at the last day. For my flesh is food indeed, and my blood is drink indeed. He who eats my flesh and drinks my blood abides in me, and I in him. As the living Father sent me, and I live because of the Father, so he who eats me will live because of me. (Jn 6:53–57).

This passage is the Scriptural foundation of the Church's theology of the eucharist. There are, however, interpreters who reject the Church's teaching and argue that Jesus was speaking symbolically here. In replying to that argument, we will first take a careful look at the passage itself.

We note that Jesus chose increasingly visceral language to communicate his teaching. In the first few instances of speaking about the need to eat his flesh, he used the Greek term *esthiō* (Jn 6:50–51, 53). This common word describes the consumption of food. In John 6:54, however, he altered his terminology, employing the term *trōgō* ("he who eats [*trōgō*] my flesh"). This verb meant to vigorously gnaw at something, such as gnawing meat off a bone. Moreover, Jesus declared "my flesh is real food, and my blood is real drink" (Jn 6:55). The Greek word translated "real" could also be understood as "true" or "actual." This is the term, for example, that appears in Jesus' declaration earlier in the Gospel that Nathanael is an "Israelite indeed" (Jn 1:47). Nathanael was an actual Israelite, a true descendent of the Patriarch Jacob. Jesus' choice of words makes it very difficult for non-Catholic Christians to maintain that Jesus was speaking only symbolically. He insisted "My flesh is real food." Though some still resist the conclusion, it is hard to see how the literal dimension of his teaching could be any clearer. Imagine for a moment that Jesus actually meant believers would need to consume his flesh. What more would he have had to say than "My flesh is real food"?

John 6:53–57 is the scriptural foundation of the Church's theology of the eucharist.

The Words of Spirit and Life

Utterly perplexed and offended by this teaching, a number of Jesus' followers cried out upon hearing this teaching, "This is a hard saying; who can listen to it?" (Jn 6:60). Some have interpreted Jesus' response as signaling that his teaching was intended only symbolically: "Do you take offense at this? Then what if you were to see the Son of man ascending where he was before? It is the Spirit that gives life, the flesh is of no avail; the words that I have spoken to you are Spirit and life. But there are some of you that do not believe" (Jn 6:61–64). To interpret this verse as indicating that his sermon was only meant metaphorically, however, is unconvincing. "Spirit and life," here, resonate with the earlier verses in the same discourse: they are terms that signal the divine presence, eternal life, and grace. The key to the interpretation of the passage is that this "Spirit and life" are equated with "the words I have spoken to you," that is, with the command to eat the flesh and drink the blood of Jesus. The statement that "the flesh is of no avail," then, is not at all a reference to the flesh of Jesus—he did not say "my flesh is of no avail"—it is a reference to the fleshly mind of the man or woman who lacks faith. It is divine faith or "the Spirit" that gives "life," that is, the utterly unprecedented life-giving truth that the Incarnate Son of God will feed his people by the miraculous multiplication of his flesh and blood, down through the centuries, in Holy Communion.

Jesus knew that the disciples were leaving him because of what he had said about eating his flesh and drinking his blood.

At the end of all of this we read that many disciples "drew back" from Jesus (Jn 6:66). He did not stop them. He knew that they were leaving him because of what he had said about eating his flesh and drinking his blood. Jesus did not stop them by back-tracking or offering explanations that would render his teaching merely symbolic and thereby much easier to accept. He did not stop them because he meant exactly what he had said.

The Bread of Life

The Supper of the Lamb

In addition to these considerations, another feature of John's Gospel also reinforces the eucharistic meaning of Jesus' teaching in the Bread of Life discourse: John's identification of Jesus as the Lamb of God. At the very beginning of the narrative, St. John the Baptist sees Jesus coming towards him and says, "Behold, the Lamb of God" (Jn 1:29). He reiterates this identification a second time only a few verses later (see Jn 1:36). Why identify a man as a lamb? Throughout John's Gospel, the point is made that Jesus is the new Passover sacrifice.

It is helpful to recall that it was the blood of an unblemished lamb sprinkled on the doorframe which saved Israel's firstborn sons from the last and most terrible plague that God sent upon the Egyptians. The angel of death passed over the houses marked by the blood of the lamb. The directions for the Passover ritual can be found in Exodus 12. There the Israelites are essentially directed to do three things: (1) to sacrifice an unblemished lamb, that is, one with no broken bones (Ex 12:5, 46); (2) to sprinkle its blood on the family's doorposts using a hyssop branch (Ex 12:7, 22); (3) to consume the lamb (Ex 12:8–11).

When the evangelist John describes Jesus' death, he depicts him as the true Passover sacrifice. Not only is the Passover festival the backdrop for Jesus' final meal, arrest, and trial, its imagery is especially pronounced at the crucifixion scene. John tells us that Jesus died before the soldiers could break his legs to hasten his death. This is said to fulfill the scriptures, namely, the regulations regarding the paschal lamb in Exodus 12: "Not a bone of his shall be broken" (Jn 19:36; see Ex 12:46). In addition, John points out that when Jesus is offered a drink on the cross it is raised up to him on sponge attached to a hyssop branch—the same kind of branch that was to be used to sprinkle the blood of the Passover lamb on the doorposts in Exodus 12.

Jesus' Bread of Life discourse was delivered in the time of Passover. Much later in the same Gospel, Jesus is established as the Passover lamb. But remember that the Passover ritual required that the lamb be consumed. If Jesus is the Passover lamb sacrificed on the cross, then, following the ritual, the completion of the saving sacrifice is the consumption of the lamb. But how are we to eat the lamb? John answers that question: in the eucharist. St. Paul himself made a similar point in his first letter to the Corinthians. He began by declaring that "Christ, our Paschal Lamb, has been sacrificed." He thus underscored the sacrificial character of Jesus' death. He then added in the very next line: "Let us, therefore, celebrate the festival" (1 Cor 5:7–8). If Christ is the Passover sacrifice, there must be a meal at which we consume the lamb, and indeed there is: the Holy Sacrifice of the Mass.

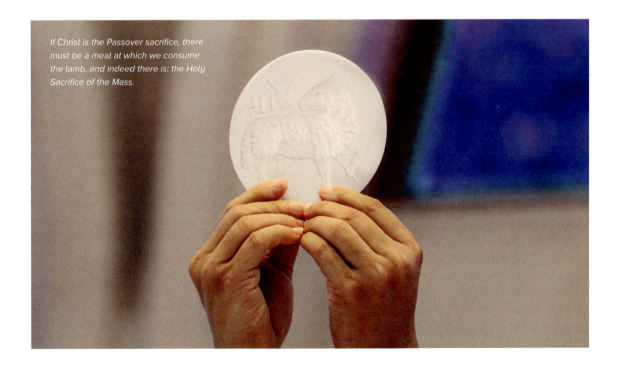

If Christ is the Passover sacrifice, there must be a meal at which we consume the lamb, and indeed there is: the Holy Sacrifice of the Mass.

The Bread of Life   225

Becoming Part of the Story

The divine plan to save humanity from sin is fulfilled in Christ, but that does not mean that the story is now over. Through the sacraments we are taken up into that same story. The deliverance of Israel from Egypt that occurred in the Passover, their passing through the Red Sea, their reception of the manna: all of these realities pointed forward not only to Christ's earthly ministry but also to the sacraments (see 1 Cor 10:1–5). In the Our Father, Jesus taught us to pray for our "daily bread." The language evokes the imagery of the manna, which fell every morning except for the Sabbath. A closer look at the Greek text of the Lord's Prayer, however, reveals an even more profound dimension. As St. Jerome noted, the term Jesus uses, *epiousios*, can mean a number of things. It can refer to the food God gives us each day—God provides for our daily spiritual and material sustenance. It can have another meaning: "super-substantial". In this word, accordingly, the Church finds a reference to the eucharist, our supernatural food and drink (see CCC 2837).

God gave Israel the manna as a foretaste of the Promised Land, the land flowing with milk and honey. In the eucharist—which is nothing other than communion with Christ (1 Cor 10:16)—we receive something even greater than a foretaste of earthly delights. Catholic tradition recognizes the eucharist as a foretaste of the kingdom of heaven, where we will forever be in the presence of Christ the Lamb. Moreover, just as the manna satisfied the desires of Israel, so too does Christ in the eucharist satisfy us. All that we have been longing for is found in him. The road home may seem wearying. Yet by his power God can transform our meager resources and multiply them far more abundantly than we could ever ask or imagine (see Eph 3:20). As we make our way as pilgrims through this world, like the Israelites in the desert, we too are given bread from heaven. Only we receive something they never could have imagined: the God-man gives us his very flesh and blood so that we may have eternal life in him through the working of the Spirit.

In the eucharist, we receive something even greater than the foretaste of earthly delights, we receive a foretaste of the kingdom of heaven, where we will forever be in the presence of Christ.

Review Questions

1. What is the relationship between Jesus' miracles and the sacraments?

2. How does the story of the feeding of the five thousand both look backwards to the Old Testament and point forward to the Last Supper?

3. What are the two parts of the Bread of Life discourse? How do the two parts of the discourse work together to communicate the truth of Jesus' real presence in the eucharist?

4. What connection is there between the imagery of Jesus as the Lamb of God in John's Gospel and the Bread of Life discourse?

5. Besides the manna and the Passover, what other Old Testament events foreshadow the institution of the eucharist?

6. What other miracle stories of Jesus can you think of that might have sacramental significance and why?

Put Out Into the Deep

One of the finest and most readable books on the eucharist in scripture is Brant Pitre's *Jesus and the Jewish Roots of the Eucharist: Unlocking the Secrets of the Last Supper* (New York: Doubleday, 2011). This book is a page-turner; with every chapter, the reader learns new things about the Old Testament and Judaism which shed exciting light on eucharistic passages in scripture.

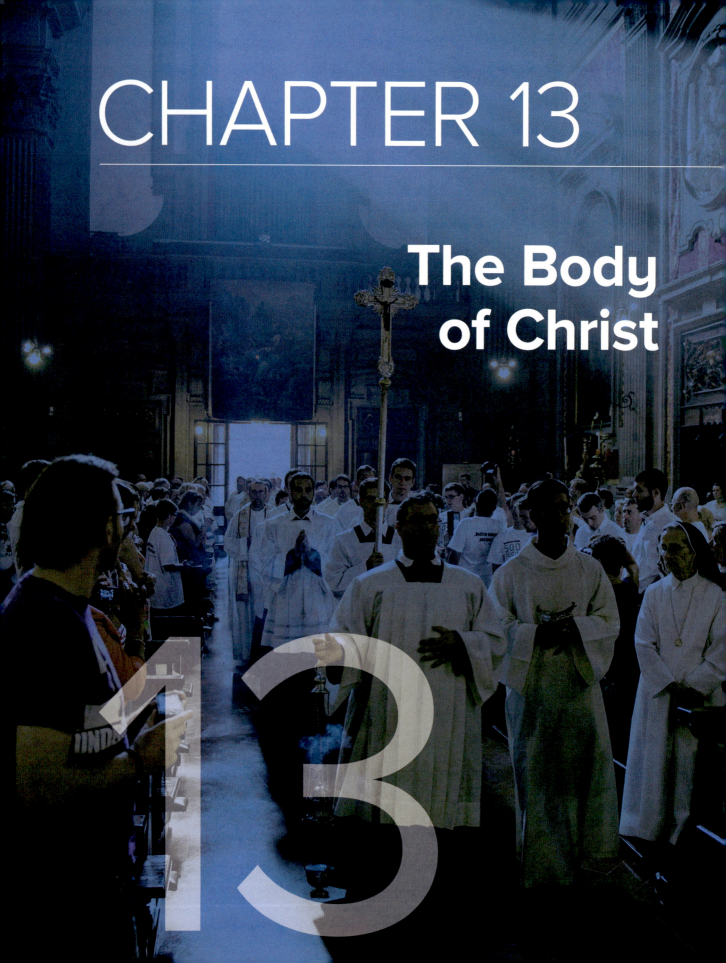

CHAPTER 13

The Body of Christ

On Friday about suppertime the mounted police and horsemen set out, armed with their usual weapons as though chasing after an armed rebel. And closing in on him late in the evening, they found him in bed in an upstairs room in a small cottage; and though he still could have escaped from there to another place, he refused, saying, "May God's will be done." So when he heard that they had arrived, he went and talked with them, while those who were present marveled at his age and his composure, and wondered why there was so much eagerness for the arrest of an old man like him. Then he immediately ordered that a table be set for them to eat and drink as much as they wished at that hour, and he asked them to grant him an hour so that he might pray undisturbed. When they consented, he stood and prayed. Those who heard him were amazed, and many regretted that they had come after such a godly old man.

Now when at last he finished his prayer, it was time to depart, and so they seated him on a donkey and brought him into the city on the day of a great Sabbath. Herod, the police captain, and his father, Nicetes, came out to meet him. They tried to persuade him, saying, "Why, what harm is there in saying, 'Caesar is Lord,' and offering incense" (and other words to this effect) "and thereby saving yourself?" Failing to persuade him, they began to utter threats and made him dismount in such a hurry that he bruised his shin as he got down from the carriage. And without even turning around, he went on his way eagerly and quickly as if nothing had happened to him, and as he was led to the stadium there was such a tumult that no one could even be heard.

The proconsul asked if he were Polycarp. And when he confessed that he was, the proconsul tried to persuade him to recant, saying, "Have respect for your age," and other such things as they are accustomed to say: "Swear by the Genius

The account of the martyrdom of St. Polycarp (69–155) is one of many such narratives that come down to us from the Church's first centuries. It reminds us that fidelity to Christ has always exacted a cost, at times the very highest.

of Caesar; repent; say, 'Away with the atheists!'" So Polycarp solemnly looked at the whole crowd of lawless heathen who were in the stadium, motioned toward them with his hand, and then (groaning as he looked up to heaven) said, "Away with the atheists!" But when the magistrate persisted and said, "Swear the oath, and I will release you; revile Christ," Polycarp replied, "For eighty-six years I have been his servant, and he has done me no wrong. How can I blaspheme my King who saved me?"

So the proconsul said: "I have wild beasts; I will throw you to them, unless you change your mind." But he said: "Call for them! For the repentance from better to worse is a change impossible for us; but it is a noble thing to change from that which is evil to righteousness." Then the proconsul said to him again: "I will have you consumed by fire, since you despise the wild beasts, unless you change your mind." But Polycarp said: "You threaten with a fire that burns only briefly and after just a little while is extinguished, for you are ignorant of the fire of the coming judgment and eternal punishment, which is reserved for the ungodly. But why do you delay? Come, do what you wish."

The proconsul was astonished, and sent his own herald into the midst of the stadium to proclaim three times: "Polycarp has confessed that he is a Christian." When this was proclaimed by the herald, the entire crowd cried out with uncontrollable anger and with a loud shout: "This is the teacher of Asia, the father of the Christians, the destroyer of our gods."

Then the materials prepared for the pyre were placed around him; and as they were also about to nail him, he said: "Leave me as I am; for he who enables me to endure the fire will also enable me to remain on the pyre without moving." So they did not nail him, but tied him instead. Then he looked up to heaven and said: "O Lord God Almighty, Father of your beloved and blessed Son Jesus Christ. I bless you because you have considered me worthy of this day and hour, that I might receive a place among the number of the martyrs in the cup of your Christ, to the resurrection to eternal life, both of soul and of body. May I be received among them in your presence today, as a rich and acceptable sacrifice, you who are the undeceiving and true God. Amen."

When he had offered up the "Amen" and finished his prayer, the men lit the fire. And as a mighty flame blazed up, we saw a miracle. For the fire, taking the shape of an arch, like the sail of a ship filled by the wind, completely surrounded the body of the martyr; and it was there in the middle, not like flesh burning but like bread baking or like gold and silver being refined in a furnace. For we also perceived a very fragrant odor, as if it were the scent of incense or some other precious spice.

When the lawless men eventually realized that his body could not be consumed by the fire, they ordered an executioner to go up to him and stab him with a dagger. And when he did this, there came out a large quantity of blood, so that it extinguished the fire; and the whole crowd was amazed.

This account of the martyrdom of St. Polycarp (69–155) is one of many such narratives that come down to us from the Church's first centuries. It reminds us that fidelity to Christ has always exacted a cost, at times the very highest. Indeed, in the pages of the New Testament, we learn that the Church has suffered persecution from the very beginning.

In the ninth chapter of the Acts of the Apostles, we read how Saul of Tarsus—a zealous persecutor of the Church—set out for Damascus "still breathing threats and murder against the disciples of the Lord" (Acts 9:1). Damascus was the gateway to the eastern part of the Roman empire, and Saul knew that if Jesus' followers were established there, they would be able to spread far to the east and north. And so with authority from the Jewish high priest, he rode off, hoping to stamp out this dangerous sect once and for all (Acts 9:2). Along the way, he had an encounter that forever changed him and the world:

Suddenly a light from heaven flashed about him. And he fell to the ground and heard a voice saying to him, "Saul, Saul, why do you persecute me?" And he said, "Who are you, Lord?" And he said, "I am Jesus, whom you are persecuting; but rise and enter the city, and you will be told what you are to do" (Acts 9:3–6).

Appearing to Saul, Jesus asked, "Why do you persecute me?" Saul might have responded: "But Lord, I am not persecuting you, only these people who believe in you." Yet somehow, he did not dare to say it. He was unable to resist Jesus' claim that he is united to his Church. What Saul had done to the Church, he had done to Christ himself, and now Christ had come to change Saul's heart and thereby put an end to his murderous ways. This experience transformed Saul of Tarsus into St. Paul, the apostle to the Gentiles, and informed one of his central teachings, that the Church is the body of Christ.

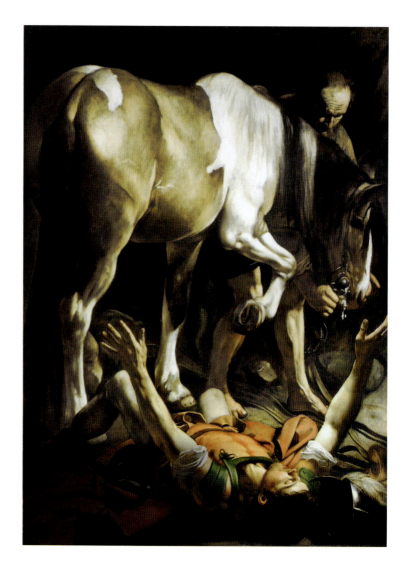

Michelangelo Merisi Da Caravaggio, Conversion on the way to Damascus, 1601, Oil on canvas, Santa Maria del Popolo, Rome, Italy.

232   CHAPTER 13

Jesus and the Church in Acts

The close connection between Jesus and the Church is underscored in various ways in the Book of Acts. At the outset, we are reminded that this book is meant to be read as the second volume in a two-part story. In the book's prologue, its author, St. Luke, linked the Acts of the Apostles to his Gospel: "In the first book, O Theophilus, I have dealt with all that Jesus began to do and teach" (Acts 1:1). But Acts is more than a sequel. We should note Luke's choice of words. By saying that his Gospel reports what Jesus "began" to do, he signaled that in this second book, Jesus would continue to be at work. How? Through the life of the Church. As one reads the Book of Acts, one can see how Luke established this point by highlighting parallels between Jesus' ministry and that of the Church.

For example, in his Gospel, Luke began his narrative of Jesus' public ministry with his baptism. Although the report is brief, the story is full of striking details:

> Now when all the people were baptized, and when Jesus also had been baptized and was praying, the heaven was opened, and the Holy Spirit descended upon him in bodily form, as a dove, and a voice came from heaven, "You are my beloved Son; with you I am well pleased. . . . And Jesus, full of the Holy Spirit, returned from the Jordan (Lk 3:21–22; 4:1).

Luke's account of the Church's first actions is strikingly similar to this narrative. In Acts we read about the coming of the Spirit upon the Apostles at Pentecost, an event St. John the Baptist had foretold when he explained that the Messiah would "baptize you with the Holy Spirit and with fire" (Lk 3:16). Indeed, Jesus explicitly called Pentecost a baptism, saying "before many days you shall be baptized with the Holy Spirit" (Acts 1:5). In addition, as Jesus' baptism is portrayed as an occasion of public prayer, so too is Pentecost. After hearing how the

The Body of Christ   233

Jean II Restout, Pentecost, *1732, Oil on canvas, Louvre, Paris, France.*

first Christians had "devoted themselves to prayer," we then read: "And suddenly a sound came from heaven like the rush of a mighty wind, and it filled all the house where they were sitting. And there appeared to them tongues as of fire, distributed and resting on each one of them. And they were all filled with the Holy Spirit" (Acts 1:12–14; 2:1–4). Both Jesus' baptism and Pentecost included a visible manifestation of the Spirit. And just as Jesus was said to be "full of the Holy Spirit" in the Jordan (Lk 4:1), so now the disciples are declared to be "filled with the Holy Spirit" (Acts 2:4). Finally, the miracle of Pentecost is accomplished with fire, thus fulfilling the prophecy made by St. John the Baptist.

There are many more parallels between Jesus' life in Luke's Gospel and the account of the Church's ministry in the Acts of the Apostles. For instance, Jesus began his public ministry with a sermon, which he delivered in a Jewish place of worship, the synagogue, announcing, "Today this scripture has been fulfilled in your hearing" (Lk 4:21). Although they ultimately turned on him, the people at first responded with amazement and "wondered at the gracious words which proceeded out of his mouth" (Lk 4:22). The beginning of the Church's mission is described in similar terms in the Acts of the Apostles. After the Spirit came down at Pentecost, the ministry of the apostles commenced with a speech delivered by St. Peter at the Temple where, like Jesus' audience in the synagogue, the crowd was stunned by the apostles' miraculous ability to speak in different languages: "And all were amazed and perplexed, saying to one another, 'What does this mean?'" (Acts 2:12). Echoing Christ, St. Peter announced that the scriptures had been fulfilled in Jesus: "but this is what was spoken by the prophet Joel" (Acts 2:16).

Again, after his proclamation in the synagogue, Jesus went out and performed miracles. Among his first in the Gospel was the healing of the paralyzed man.

And behold, men were bringing on a bed a man who was paralyzed, and they sought to bring him in and lay him before Jesus.…[Jesus said:] "that you may know that the Son of man has authority on earth to forgive sins"—he said to the man who was paralyzed—"I say to you, rise, take up your bed and go home." And immediately he rose before them, and took up that on which he lay, and went home, glorifying God. And amazement seized them all, and they glorified God and were filled with awe, saying, "We have seen strange things today" (Lk 5:18–26).

Similarly, the first miracle performed by the apostles after Pentecost occurred when Peter practically replicated Jesus' action.

Laurant De La Hyde, Saint Peter Healing the Sick with His Shadow, 1635, Oil on canvas, Louvre, Paris, France.

And a man lame from birth was being carried, whom they laid daily at that gate of the temple which is called Beautiful to ask alms of those who entered the temple. Seeing Peter and John about to go into the temple, he asked for alms.… But Peter said, "I have no silver and gold, but I give you what I have; in the name of Jesus Christ of Nazareth, rise and walk." And he took him by the right hand and raised him up; and immediately his feet and ankles were made strong.… And all the people saw him walking and praising God…and they were filled with wonder and amazement at what had happened to him (Acts 3:2–10).

The story has numerous parallels with Jesus' healing of the paralyzed man. In both cases, Luke mentioned that the injured man was brought forward by friends, told to rise or walk, and was immediately healed, and that the onlookers were amazed. The Gospels, then, tell us how Jesus began his work, and the Acts of the Apostles teach us that his work continues through St. Peter, the apostles, and indeed the whole Church.

The Body of Christ

Jesus and St. Stephen

It is not only Jesus' miracles that are reproduced in the Church, but also his sacrificial death. This pattern is first seen in the story of the death of the proto-martyr, St. Stephen, in a story that is reminiscent of Luke's account of Jesus' passion. Both Jesus and Stephen were brought before the Jewish council of elders and were accused by false witnesses (Lk 22:66; Mk 14:53; Acts 6:13). Luke tells us they "set up false witnesses who said, 'we have heard [Stephen] say that this Jesus of Nazareth will destroy this place, and will change the customs which Moses delivered to us'" (Acts 6:14). Moreover, just as Jesus told the high priest, "But from now on the Son of man shall be seated at the right hand of the power of God" (Lk 22:69), Stephen told the council: "Behold, I see the heavens opened, and the Son of man standing at the right hand of God." (Acts 7:56). The final scene of Stephen's martyrdom itself also brought him into close conformity to Christ:

> Then they cast [Stephen] out of the city and stoned him; and the witnesses laid down their garments at the feet of a young man named Saul. And as they were stoning Stephen, he prayed, "Lord Jesus, receive my spirit." And he knelt down and cried with a loud voice, "Lord, do not hold this sin against them." And when he had said this, he fell asleep (Acts 7:58–60).

Annibale Carracci, The Stoning of St. Stephen, *1603-1604, Oil on canvas, Louvre, Paris, France.*

The echoes here of Jesus' final moments in the Gospel of Luke are unmistakable. Stephen's act of entrusting his spirit to Jesus was in imitation of the words Jesus had spoken from the cross: "Father, into your hands I commit my spirit!" (Lk 23:46). Even more stirring is Stephen's prayer on behalf of his killers, a petition also made by his crucified Lord: "Father, forgive them; for they know not what they do" (Lk 23:34). Finally, Jesus' death resulted in the change of heart of a Roman centurion, who declared "certainly this man was innocent" (Lk 23:47). Something similar is reported in the Book of Acts. "The witnesses laid down their garments at the feet of a young man named Saul" (Acts 7:58), the same Saul who would soon receive the grace of conversion on the road to Damascus. St. Augustine explained that it was no coincidence Saul makes his first appearance in Acts at this moment, and he attributed Saul's transformation by grace directly to Stephen's prayer: "If Stephen had not prayed thus, the Church would not have had Paul." In short, Stephen participated in Christ's redemptive work.

Christ Working in Believers

Saul's encounter with the Risen Lord on the way to Damascus made a lasting impression on him. In his letters, we see the fruit of his continued reflection upon Jesus' question: "Why do you persecute me?" First and foremost, St. Paul emphasized the notion of "grace," which, in Greek, is synonymous with "gift." As we have seen, for St. Paul, Christ "gave himself" by offering his life as a sacrifice on the cross (Gal 2:20), an act that revealed his divine love. But his gift of self does not end on the cross. Paul also taught that, in the Spirit, the Risen Christ gives himself to believers by living within them: "it is no longer I who live, but Christ who lives in me" (Gal 2:20). This sharing in Christ's life is purely the result of God's graciousness—nothing we do could ever earn it. "For by grace you have been saved through faith; and this is not your own

The Body of Christ

doing, it is the gift of God" (Eph 2:8). Yet once given this gift, believers are empowered by it to cooperate with Christ. Contrary to the claims of some Christians, our good works have true salvific effect because of this union with Christ. Thus St. Paul admonished the Philippians, "work out your own salvation with fear and trembling; for God is at work in you, both to will and to work for his good pleasure" (Phil 2:12–13). Salvation is not merely avoiding Hell; it is becoming a son or daughter of God by being united to the Son of God. In him, we become co-workers with him. Catholic teaching holds that salvation, although initially given to us as a pure gift in grace (CCC 2003), is realized through our participation (see CCC 2010–11). If Christ dwells in us, our works become his works. To say our good works do not truly have salvific value is to say Christ's work does not have salvific effect—and that is impossible.

Grace is what enabled St. Stephen to participate in Christ's redemptive work. His pious death and faithful prayer played a pivotal role in the conversion of Paul. This contribution was not in place of Christ's work, as if that had somehow been incomplete. Rather, it is precisely because of Christ that Stephen's works are capable of having effective results. Because Christ is working with him—he was a man who was "full of grace" (Acts 6:8)—Stephen can be taken up into Christ's own work.

If Christ dwells in us, our works become his works.

The Church as the Body of Christ

But individual believers are not united only to Christ. St. Paul taught that those who are in the Lord are also closely bonded to one another in the body of Christ: "For just as the body is one and has many members, and all the members of the body, though many, are one body, so it is with Christ. For by one Spirit we were all baptized into one body" (1 Cor 12:12–13). Christ not only lives in each believer; he also lives in the corporate body of believers. In other words, what Christ did in his personal body, he now does in his mystical body, the Church. Thus, just as St. Paul described Christ's suffering as having redemptive value (see Rom 6:3–4), he also commanded us that as members of his mystical body, we are to make sacrifices of ourselves: "I appeal to you therefore, brethren, by the mercies of God, to present your bodies as a living sacrifice, holy and acceptable to God, which is your spiritual worship" (Rom 12:1). Notice that in this verse the sacrifices of the many are offered as one. St. Paul did not say "present your bodies as living sacrifices" but, rather, "present your bodies as *a* living sacrifice." All believers offer themselves together as one body in Christ.

Furthermore, because Christ's bodily suffering redounds to the benefit of others, St. Paul also taught that believers share in one another's redemptive works: "If one member suffers, all suffer together; if one member is honored, all rejoice together" (1 Cor 12:26). In his second letter to the Corinthians, he offered a meditation on this point: "If we are afflicted, it is for your comfort and salvation; and if we are comforted, it is for your comfort, which you experience when you patiently endure the same sufferings that we suffer. Our hope for you is unshaken; for we know that as you share in our sufferings, you will also share in our comfort" (2 Cor 1:6–7). The Church suffers together and shares together in the effects of its members' righteous deeds.

St. Paul's teaching explains how St. Stephen's death fits into the larger story of the Book of Acts. Through Stephen, Christ offers himself to the Father as he did on the cross. Christ's passion is reproduced in the first martyr. Because of his participation in Christ, Stephen's death has redemptive effects. He prays for his killers, and God hears that request. Although no one knew it at the time, God would use Stephen's suffering to trigger the grace of conversion for the man who would become St. Paul. The very person who would explain the nature of the Church as the body of Christ in the New Testament was saved through the graces called down by the sanctity of another member.

The Church as the Bride of Christ

To further explicate the meaning of the Church's role as the body of Christ, St. Paul used another image; according to him, the Church is also the Bride of Christ. Of the many passages that contain this image, perhaps none is clearer than the one in his letter to the Ephesians from which we learn that Christian marriage is a sign of the marriage between Christ and the Church:

> "Husbands, love your wives, as Christ loved the Church and gave himself up for her.... Even so husbands should love their wives as their own bodies. He who loves his wife loves himself. For no man ever hates his own flesh, but nourishes and cherishes it, as Christ does the Church, because we are members of his body.... "For this reason a man shall leave his father and mother and be joined to his wife, and the two shall become one flesh." This is a great mystery, and I mean in reference to Christ and the Church" (Eph 5:25).

"Husbands, love your wives, as Christ loved the Church and gave himself up for her." (Eph. 5:25)

240   CHAPTER 13

Here St. Paul indicated that the mystery of marriage is ultimately realized in Christ's relationship with the Church. The union of Christ to believers is so real and intimate it can be described in terms of marital love. In fact, the marriage between Christ and the Church is the true marriage. Human marriages are meant to be signs of the union of Christ to his Church. St. Jerome's famous Latin translation of this passage makes this especially clear. Where the English has St. Paul describing the marital bond of Christ and his Church as "a great mystery," St. Jerome used the phrase *magnum sacramentum*—a "great sacrament." Christ's union to the Church is the great sacrament, the one all sacramental marriages are meant to mirror.

Founding his teaching upon the Book of Genesis, St. Paul indicated that in marriage two become "one flesh." At its most profound level, this is why the Church is Christ's "body." The Church is the body of Christ because she is the bride of Christ. St. Paul's images of the Church are mutually illuminating: the Church's identity as Christ's body is inseparable from her marital union with him. St. Paul also described how Christ "nourishes" his body, that is, how he "feeds" her. How does Christ do this? The answer is clear from his other letters: in the eucharist, Christ feeds the Church with his own body. The Church is the body of Christ because of the eucharist. This is precisely what he taught in his first letter to the Corinthians: "Because there is one bread, we who are many are one body, for we all partake of the one bread" (1 Cor 10:17).

"Because there is one bread, we who are many are one body, for we all partake of the one bread" (1 Cor 10:17).

Mary, Icon of the Church

Although Luke highlighted St. Stephen's role as an *alter Christus* (another Christ), there is another person whose role is even more important in helping us to understand Christ's work in the Church: Mary. Jesus' mother's unique role can be seen in the story of the Annunciation.

In the sixth month the angel Gabriel was sent from God to a city of Galilee named Nazareth, to a virgin betrothed to a man whose name was Joseph, of the house of David; and the virgin's name was Mary. And he came to her and said, "Hail, full of grace, the Lord is with you!" But she was greatly troubled at the saying, and considered in her mind what sort of greeting this might be (Lk 1:26–29).

Mary's unease was due to more than the sudden appearance of a celestial figure; she was troubled at the angel's "saying" and was confused about "what sort of greeting this might be." What was so strange about it?

It is important to observe that the angel Gabriel did not say, "Hail, *Mary*, full of grace," using the words of the famous Marian prayer. Rather, the angel's greeting was simply "Hail, full of grace." The difference is crucial. The term "full of grace" stood in the place of her name, as if it were a title or the name of an office. The Greek expression here is unique. The term used for Mary, *kecharitōmenē,* implied that Mary has always been full of grace; "full of grace" is who she is. No one else in the Bible is said to be "full of grace" in the same way. This point was recognized as early as the third century, when Origen wrote, "the angel greeted Mary with new expressions, which I have never encountered elsewhere in the scriptures." He went on to point out, "Such a special greeting was reserved only for Mary." It is also significant that St. Paul used a form of the term in his letter to the Ephesians:

He destined us in love to be his sons through Jesus Christ… to the praise of his glorious grace which he freely bestowed [echaritōsen] on us in the Beloved. In him we have redemption through his blood, the forgiveness of our trespasses, according to the riches of his grace which he lavished upon us (Eph 1:5–8).

Leonardo Da Vinci, Annunciation, *c. 1472–75, Oil and tempura on panel, Uffizi, Florence, Italy.*

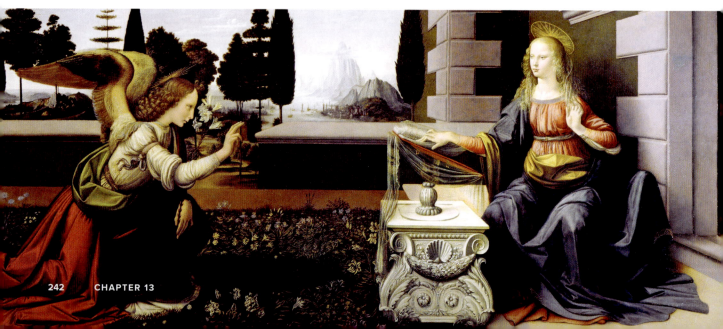

Duccio Di Buoninsegna, Maestá, 1308-11, Tempera and gold on wood, Museo Del 'Opera Metropolitana Siena, Italy.

In St. Paul's vocabulary, to be given God's grace is to be free from sin. We see here the Biblical roots of the Church's doctrine of the Immaculate Conception of the Blessed Virgin Mary, which was definitively promulgated by Bl. Pius IX in 1854 (see CCC 490–93).

All Christians receive grace. Mary is therefore a model for all believers, though she is "full of grace" in a unique way. As such, Mary is an icon of the Church and the first Christian believer. Before the Holy Spirit came upon the Church at Pentecost, he had already "overshadowed" Mary (Lk 1:34). Mary is also the first communicant, the first to receive Christ's body and blood. What the eucharist enables believers to share in, Mary was given at the Annunciation. In fact, scripture tells us that all generations would call her "blessed" (Lk 1:48).

Indeed, throughout the ages myriads of Christians have sung their praises to the Mother of God, for she has a unique relationship to all believers. As he hung from the cross, Jesus looked down at Mary and the "beloved disciple" and spoke to them:

> *When Jesus saw his mother, and the disciple whom he loved standing near, he said to his mother, "Woman, behold, your son!" Then he said to the disciple, "Behold, your mother!" And from that hour the disciple took her to his own home (Jn 19:26–27).*

When Jesus called his disciple Mary's "son," he was speaking spiritually. Mary had no other physical children. Although the Gospels describe some relatives of Jesus as "brothers" (*adelphoi*), in ancient Judaism relatives such as cousins could also be spoken of in this way.

The Body of Christ   243

Significantly, James and Joseph, two men identified as Jesus' "brothers" are later said to be sons of a different Mary (see Mt 13:55; 27:56). The fact that Mary had no other children is also precisely the reason behind Jesus' actions on the cross. Jesus was identifying a guardian for his mother, a person to care for her after he was gone. We also note that Jesus identified the disciple as more than merely Mary's guardian. Jesus could have said, "Take care of my mother." Instead, he told the disciple that Mary is *his* mother. Why? Because he wanted us to know that we are truly made part of his family. His mother is now our mother.

Some non-Catholics complain that Catholics give too much honor to Mary. The charge is often made that Catholics detract from the glory of God and the power of God's grace by viewing Mary as having been given such unique holiness. The truth is, however, that for Catholics Mary is only special because of God's grace. The Church's teaching about Mary is intended to highlight and clarify its faith in Christ and in his work (CCC 487). What Mary teaches us first and foremost is that God's grace can make someone so holy that she can truly be called "Full of Grace." As Mary herself explained, "My soul magnifies the Lord" (Lk 1:46). Following her example, Catholics honor God's work when they honor Mary. To claim that Catholics have elevated Mary too highly is to imply that God's grace is not effective enough to conform a person to Christ in such a close and exemplary way. In Mary, we recognize the true power of what God's grace can accomplish. By asking for her prayers, we acknowledge that we are all one in the Church and that we are empowered by grace to help one another. In her we discover what grace is truly capable of making us to be: witnesses to Christ as steadfast as St. Stephen and St. Polycarp.

Bartolomé Estaban Murillo, The Madonna and Child with the Rosary, *c. 1670–80, Oil on canvas.*

Review Questions

1. How does the story of the martyrdom of St. Polycarp echo the passion and death of Christ?

2. How do Jesus' words to Saul on the road to Damascus indicate his union with the Church and how is this theme developed in Luke's Gospel and the Acts of the Apostles?

3. How does Acts show us how St. Stephen participates in Christ's redemptive work and how does St. Paul's teaching on the Church further explain how Stephen was empowered to do this?

4. How is St. Paul's explanation of the Church as the Bride of Christ related to his teaching that the Church is also the Body of Christ?

5. What problems emerge when one views salvation in individualist terms?

6. How is St. Paul's teaching about the Church as the Bride of Christ important for understanding what marriage should be?

7. In what way is Mary presented as uniquely holy in Luke's narrative? How is she presented as the model disciple of Christ and the mother of all believers?

Put Out Into the Deep

If you would like to learn more about the nature of the Church and its role in salvation, see Christoph Schönborn's *Loving the Church: Spiritual Exercises Preached in the Presence of Pope John Paul II*, trans. John Saward (Ignatius, 1998). This collection of addresses offers an insightful and profound overview of theology, drawing from the teaching of scripture, the documents of the Second Vatican Council, and the *Catechism of the Catholic Church*.

CHAPTER 14

He Who Hears You, Hears Me

14

An angel of the Lord said to Philip, "Rise and go toward the south to the road that goes down from Jerusalem to Gaza." This is a desert road. And he rose and went. And behold, an Ethiopian, a eunuch, a minister of Candace the queen of the Ethiopians, in charge of all her treasure, had come to Jerusalem to worship and was returning; seated in his chariot, he was reading the prophet Isaiah. And the Spirit said to Philip, "Go up and join this chariot." So Philip ran to him, and heard him reading Isaiah the prophet, and asked, "Do you understand what you are reading?" And he said, "How can I, unless some one guides me?" And he invited Philip to come up and sit with him. Now the passage of the scripture which he was reading was this: "As a sheep led to the slaughter or a lamb before its shearer is silent, so he opens not his mouth. In his humiliation justice was denied him. Who can describe his generation? For his life is taken up from the earth." And the eunuch said to Philip, "Please, about whom does the prophet say this, about himself or about some one else?" Then Philip opened his mouth, and beginning with this scripture he told him the good news of Jesus. And as they went along the road they came to some water, and the eunuch said, "See, here is water! What is to prevent my being baptized?" And he commanded the chariot to stop, and they both went down into the water, Philip and the eunuch, and he baptized him. And when they came up out of the water, the Spirit of the Lord caught up Philip; and the eunuch saw him no more, and went on his way rejoicing. But Philip was found at Azotus, and passing on he preached the gospel to all the towns till he came to Caesarea (Acts 8:26–40).

When Philip asked the Ethiopian if he understood the scripture he had been reading, the eunuch responded in humility, "How can I, unless someone guides me?" Indeed, understanding that God has revealed himself in the scriptures is one thing. Understanding what those scriptures mean, however, raises a host of complex questions. How can we be sure that we understand what we read? An even more difficult question is this: how do we even know which books belong in the Bible in the first place? We would do well to remember that the Bible did not fall out of heaven with all of its books intact. The various works that it includes were written over a long period of time by many different people.

Even in Jesus' day there was much debate among Jews about which books should be considered Sacred Scripture. The Sadducees accepted only the five books attributed to Moses (Genesis, Exodus, Leviticus, Numbers, and Deuteronomy). The Pharisees embraced a wider list of books, including most of what are considered the books of the Old Testament today—though not all of them. Other Jews, however, appear to have recognized an even larger set of books. The ancient Jewish work 4 Ezra, which is not found in our Bible, speaks of ninety-four books. And that number did not include the books of the New Testament. So not only must we ask how we interpret the Bible, but also how we know which books belong to it in the first place. More generally, the question we are faced with in this chapter is to know what God has revealed and how we are to understand it. Where we seek the answer is in Christ.

The Word Made Flesh

Before we discuss the biblical books as Sacred Scripture, let us remember what we have already learned: the Gospels give us reliable historical information about Jesus. Our conviction that they are also inspired—that is, works written by human authors who were moved by the Holy Spirit—should not obscure their value as an historical record. Prior to reading these books in the light of faith, we can know that they are important historical witnesses to the life of Jesus.

One of the things that the Gospel record reveals is that Jesus entrusted his teachings to others; there is no report of a book written by him. Jesus taught that the fullness of divine revelation had come in him: "no one knows...who the Father is except the Son and any one to whom the Son chooses to reveal him" (Lk 10:22; see also Mt 11:27). Jesus even insisted that he is the only way by which the Father can be known: "I am the way, and the truth, and the life; no one comes to the Father,

Jean-Baptiste Jouvenet, The Raising of Lazarus, *1706, Oil on canvas, Louvre, Paris, France.*

but by me" (Jn 14:6). John echoed this teaching: "No one has ever seen God; the only-begotten Son, who is in the bosom of the Father, he has made him known" (Jn 1:18). At the end of the day, then, Christianity is first and foremost about Jesus, as the *Catechism of the Catholic Church* explains: "the Christian faith is not a religion of the book. Christianity is the religion of the Word of God, a word which is not a written and mute word, but the Word which is incarnate and living" (CCC 108).

Living Witnesses

Instead of committing his teachings to paper, Jesus recruited disciples and taught them. "And when his disciples asked him what this parable meant, he said, "To you it has been given to know the secrets of the kingdom of God; but for others they are in parables" (Lk 8:9–10; see also Mt 13:10–11). According to the Book of Acts, this private instruction continued even after the Resurrection: "To [the apostles] he presented himself alive after his passion by many proofs, appearing to them during forty days, and speaking of the kingdom of God" (Acts 1:3). The fullness of revelation comes in Christ, and Christ in turn entrusted all of it to his apostles.

At first glance this conclusion may not seem comforting. After all, the disciples repeatedly proved themselves to be deficient students. Although Jesus repeatedly prepared them for his coming passion, the actual event took them by surprise: "While they were all marveling at everything he did, he said to his disciples, 'Let these words sink into your ears; for the Son of man is to be delivered into the hands of men.' But they did not understand this saying" (Lk 9:43–45). The apostles' inability to comprehend Jesus at times even manifested itself as a kind of obtuseness.

Thus he spoke, and then he said to them, "Our friend Lazarus has fallen asleep, but I go to awake him out of sleep." The disciples said to him, "Lord, if he has fallen asleep, he will recover." Now Jesus had spoken of his death, but they thought that he meant taking rest in sleep. Then Jesus told them plainly, "Lazarus is dead" (Jn 11:11–14).

Here Jesus spoke of death, using the common image of sleep. The apostles, however, missing the metaphor, thought he was speaking about actual sleep. What is even more outrageous is that they tried to explain to Jesus the way sleep works: "Lord, if he has fallen asleep, he will recover." Episodes such as these do not inspire great confidence. Jesus may be the fullness of revelation, but, given the apostles' human limitations, how do we know that his teaching has been transmitted to us accurately? Why did not Jesus just write it all down himself? Would that not have been a better strategy for preserving his teachings?

But if Jesus had written a book, what would it communicate? For one thing, it might lead us to think that the fullness of divine revelation could be contained in a book. It cannot. John's Gospel tells us, "there are also many other things which Jesus did; were every one of them to be written, I suppose that the world itself could not contain the books that would be written" (Jn 21:25). Moreover, by not writing a book himself, Jesus showed us how much he truly wants his Church to share in his ministry. As we saw in the last chapter, Christ is still alive and present in the world in his sacraments and thus in his Church. If Jesus had written a book, it would have suggested that the Church is insufficient to the task of proclaiming his message. It is not. It is truly his Mystical Body.

For Jesus was not only the greatest teacher who ever lived, he was the Creator God. Because of that, he could see to it that his disciples' limitations were remedied; he could send the Gospel's most powerful Advocate, by whose grace his teaching would be preserved and his disciples strengthened to become teachers themselves. He promised to send them the Holy Spirit so that they would accurately remember all that he taught.

These things I have spoken to you, while I am still with you. But the Counselor, the Holy Spirit, whom the Father will send in my name, he will teach you all things, and bring to your remembrance all that I have said to you (Jn 14:25–26).

Jesus knew that the apostles would need help not only remembering all that he said but also understanding the meaning of what he had taught them. Because of this he promised that when "the Spirit of truth comes, he will guide you into all the truth (Jn 16:12–13). With these words, we can be fully assured that Jesus arranged for his teachings to be faithfully preserved. Sacred Scripture itself bears witness to the presence of the Spirit in the Church.

He Who Hears You, Hears Me

Jesus called his apostles to the special vocation of representing him to the people and invested them with special authority for this task. "He who hears you hears me, and he who rejects you rejects me, and he who rejects me rejects him who sent me" (Lk 10:16). This kind of authoritative teaching office was already present in Judaism. Though the Jews had scriptural books, they recognized the need for authoritative teachers who could correctly interpret them. Jesus alluded to this Jewish custom when he gave the counsel that "the scribes and the Pharisees sit on Moses' seat; so practice and observe whatever they tell you, but not what they do; for they preach, but do not practice" (Mt 23:2–3). This passage is of great significance. We are so often reminded of Jesus' condemnations of the Pharisees that we forget that he nevertheless recognized their truly divine teaching authority. Even though Jesus condemned the hypocrisy of the Jewish leaders, he did not dispute the authority of their office. The Pharisees' problem was not that they lacked divine authority; it was that they did not measure up to their own teaching.

Jesus invested even greater authority in his apostles. Consider the passage in Matthew's Gospel with which our common study began. Peter had just made his great confession of Christ's divinity, and Jesus responded with a stunning promise:

> I tell you, you are Peter, and on this rock I will build my church, and the gates of Hades shall not prevail against it. I will give you the keys of the kingdom of heaven, and whatever you bind [deö] on earth shall be bound [dedemenon] in heaven, and whatever you loose on earth shall be loosed in heaven" (Mt 16:18–19).

Pietro Perugino, Delivery of the Keys, 1481-1482, Fresco, Sistine Chapel, Vatican City.

Jesus' words mirrored what he would subsequently declare about the teaching authority of the scribes and Pharisees: "They bind [*deö*] heavy burdens, hard to bear, and lay them on men's shoulders; but they themselves will not move them with their finger" (Mt 23:4). In a statement that reflects the authority of the Jewish teachers' to "bind," Jesus promised to give Peter that same authority: "whatever you bind [*deö*] on earth shall be bound [*dedemenon*] in heaven." Likewise, Jesus tells the Jewish teachers, "you shut [literally, 'shut with a key,' *kleiete*] the kingdom of heaven against people" (Mt 23:13). And Jesus transferred that authority too, promising that Peter would be given the "keys" of the "kingdom." Later, the rest of the apostles also were given this authority to "bind" and "loose" (Mt 18:18). The authority that belonged to the Jewish teachers in the Old Covenant was now given to Peter and the apostles in the New.

His Office Let Another Take

That authority did not die out with the apostles. It is clear from scripture that the apostles had successors. After Judas died, Peter stood up and, quoting the scripture, said, "His office let another take" (Acts 1:20). As Judas had a successor, Peter and the other apostles had successors as well. They passed on the authority they had been given by Christ to others by laying their hands on them and thus effecting the outpouring of the same Spirit (see 2 Tim 1:6). They established others with the office of their teaching authority, namely, the offices of bishops (1 Tim 3:1; Phil 1:1) and "elders," in Greek, "presbyters" (Jas 5:14–16), the term from which we get the English word "priests."

Jesus spoke of the authority of the Jewish teachers by referring to the fact that they sat on "Moses' seat" (Mt 23:2). The Greek word used for "seat" in this verse is *kathedra*. If the word looks familiar, it is probably because you know an English term that comes from it: cathedral. A cathedral is a bishop's church. In cathedrals we find the bishop's seat, which is a large ceremonial chair. In the Old Covenant, the Jewish teachers sat on the "seat of Moses." In the New, they can be said figuratively to sit on the chair of Peter and those which belonged to the other apostles.

It does not follow, however, that the divine authority invested in the occupant of the chair renders him sinless. We remember that Jesus instructed the Jews to follow the preaching, but not the practice, of the scribes and Pharisees. By virtue of their office, they were given special authority to teach, despite their sinfulness. John's Gospel tells us that even the wicked high priest who had Jesus executed, Caiaphas, prophesied. This was not due to his personal holiness but to the holiness of his priestly ministry: "being high priest that year he prophesied" (Jn 11:51). The same is true in the New Covenant. Peter professed that Jesus is the Messiah, and then betrayed him in his hour of need. His confession of Jesus' identity was true, even if his later deeds did not always manifest that truth. Later, long after the Resurrection, St. Paul rebuked St. Peter for acting hypocritically at Antioch (see Gal 2:11–14). The first pope, of course, went on to die a martyr's death, fulfilling a prediction of Jesus (Jn 21:18–19), and he truly was a saint. But even St. Peter sinned.

Gian Lorenzo Bernini, Chair of Saint Peter, *1647–53, Gilt Bronze, St. Peter's Basilica, Vatican City.*

This pattern would continue to play out in Church history after the apostolic age. The successors of Peter and the apostles, the pope and the bishops united to him, exercise the teaching authority that Jesus bestowed on their predecessors. Nevertheless, history is full of examples of scandals and hypocrisy among the clergy. Even so, the teaching of Jesus is preserved in the Church through the ministry of the pope and bishops. Jesus himself ensured that his teaching would be correctly preserved. Speaking of the Church to Peter, he guaranteed that "the gates of Hades will not prevail against it" (Mt 16:18). Jesus continues to speak through the successors of the apostles even if they do not always live up to his teachings. And there is another important lesson here: St. Peter himself knew what it meant to need mercy. The Church thus always extends it to us freely. Petrine authority is fundamentally defined by participating in the mercy of God and the forgiveness of sins.

Go Therefore Teaching

Jesus sent out the apostles first and foremost to preach, as we see in the famous "Great Commission": "Go therefore and make disciples of all nations, baptizing them in the name of the Father and of the Son and of the Holy Spirit, teaching them to observe all that I have commanded you; and behold, I am with you always, to the close of the age" (Mt 28:19–20). Here we see that Jesus promised to be with the Church and to make the Church's ministry an extension of his own. It was to be through the travels and labors of the apostles that the nations would be able to hear the Gospel of Christ and receive the sacraments of salvation. Jesus, therefore, had prayed to the Father for their ministry:

> *I have given them your word; and the world has hated them. . . . I do not pray for these only, but also for those who believe in me through their word, that they may all be one; even as thou, Father, are in me, and I in you, that they also may be in us, so that the world may believe that you have sent me (Jn 17:14, 20–21).*

From these two passages, we can learn the essential contours of the apostolic office. Jesus commanded the apostles to preach, to teach, and to baptize, thus setting down the important guideline that Christian teaching is ordered to sacramental communion. When he told the apostles to teach "all that I have commanded you," he did *not* say, "Go therefore and *write* to all nations." As we have earlier noted, John

254   CHAPTER 14

declared that if everything Jesus had said were to be written down, "the world itself could not contain the books that would be written" (see Jn 21:25; 20:30). So, the fullness of divine revelation is meant to be communicated directly by the apostles, not chiefly through books. In his second epistle, John underscored the importance of this point: "Though I have much to write to you, I would rather not use paper and ink, but I hope to come to see you and talk with you face to face, so that our joy may be complete" (2 Jn 12). Not surprisingly, most of the apostles never wrote a book; instead they founded communities of Christians.

Vladimir Borovikovsky, St. John the Evangelist, *1809, Painting, The State Russian Museum, St. Petersburg, Russia.*

Tradition and the Church

So, we begin to understand that the Bible does not contain all the treasures of God's revelation to the human race. Writing to the Thessalonians, St. Paul explained, "So then, brethren, stand firm and hold to the traditions which you were taught by us, either by word of mouth or by letter" (2 Thess 2:15). Notice here that St. Paul indicates that the traditions he passed on to believers were not only conveyed through his letters. They were also conveyed in person, by speech. Catholic teaching has thus always recognized that the fullness of revelation comes to us not only through scripture but also through Sacred Tradition.

The New Testament affirms the importance of tradition. In scripture, the Greek word for tradition, *paradosis*, plays an important role. The verbal form of the term (*paradidōmi*) is also significant. St. Paul used the latter term both to talk about how the Father "gave" (*paradidōmi*) his Son to us (Rom 8:32) and to speak of how Jesus "gave" (*paradidōmi*) himself on the cross (Gal 2:20). Likewise, John employed it to speak of how the Son "gave up" (*paradidōmi*) the Spirit (Jn 19:30). What is "Sacred Tradition"? It is nothing less than God giving himself to us. It is not simply the communication of data or teachings; it is the Word himself who is communicated to us.

"For I received from the Lord what I also delivered [paradidōmi] to you, that the Lord Jesus on the night when he was betrayed took bread, and when he had given thanks, he broke it, and said, 'This is my body which is for you. Do this in remembrance of me'" (1 Cor 11:23–24).

St. Paul also used the terminology of *paradidōmi* and *paradosis* in his first letter to the Corinthians: "I commend you because you remember me in everything and maintain the traditions [*paradosis*] even as I have delivered [*paradidōmi*] them to you" (1 Cor 11:2) Again, he did not reject tradition. He heartily commended the Corinthians for maintaining it. But how is this tradition passed along?

> "For I received from the Lord what I also delivered [paradidōmi] to you, that the Lord Jesus on the night when he was betrayed took bread, and when he had given thanks, he broke it, and said, 'This is my body which is for you. Do this in remembrance of me.' In the same way also the chalice, after supper, saying, This chalice is the new covenant in my blood. Do this, as often as you drink it, in remembrance of me" For as often as you eat this bread and drink the chalice, you proclaim the Lord's death until he comes (1 Cor 11:23–26).

St. Paul thus linked the idea of traditioning (*paradidōmi*) to the eucharist. As we have seen, the teaching of the apostles is ordered to sacramental communion. Sacred Tradition is not simply information about Jesus; it is Jesus himself. Sacred Tradition is inextricably bound up with the eucharistic celebration.

Catholic teaching clearly distinguishes between the notion of Sacred Tradition, that is, the transmission of the Word of God, and various Church traditions that are merely customs or disciplines. The latter change with time and historical circumstances. For example, it was once the practice of all Catholics to refrain from eating meat on Fridays. This was a changeable Church discipline, not an aspect of divine revelation regarding who God is, what he has done for us, and what are universal moral laws. Dogmas such as the Trinity will not change. Various customs, however, can. How do we distinguish between the two? The task of defining what actually belongs to Sacred Tradition belongs to the teaching authority of the Church, called the magisterium (from the Latin word for teacher, *magister*). Specifically, this term refers to the successors of St. Peter and the apostles, namely, the pope and the bishops united to him.

The Bible and the Church

With the authority given to it by Jesus, the Church's magisterium has recognized certain books as belonging to the canon of Sacred Scripture. Collected together, these books are what we now call the Bible (from the Greek term *biblos*, meaning "book"). The Church teaches that all of the books of the Bible are inspired. The terminology comes from St. Paul: "All scripture is inspired by God and profitable for teaching, for reproof, for correction, and for training in righteousness, that the man of God may be complete, equipped for every good work" (2 Tim 3:16–17). The Greek word translated as "inspired" literally means "God-breathed" (*theopneustos*). Some non-Catholic Christians have misinterpreted this passage to mean that the Bible *alone* suffices, yet St. Paul did not teach that. Indeed, neither St. Paul nor any other Biblical author provided us with a list of what the phrase "all scripture" meant. And if such a list were present in one of the books of the New Testament, we would still be faced with another question: how would one know *that* book should be placed in the Bible?

There was much debate in the early Church about which books should be included in scripture. Some included the Book of Revelation, others did not. Some included a book called 1 Enoch, which seems to have been wildly popular among many first-century Jews. It is even alluded to in the New Testament Book of Jude. Of course, 1 Enoch did not make it into the Bible. It took the authority of the Church to settle the question of which books belong in the Bible. Without the Church, we simply would not know which books belong in the canon (that is, the list of biblical books) and should be received as Sacred Scripture, as bearers of God's Truth.

The Gutenberg Bible, the first substantial printed book in this royal-folio two-volume Bible, comprising nearly 1,300 pages, printed in Mainz on the Central Rhine by Johann Gutenberg in the 1450's.

Protestant Bibles today omit certain material (books and parts of books) found in the Catholic Bible. In this, Protestant Bibles mirror the modern Jewish Bible, which leaves aside the same material. Some have explained this by insisting that Catholics have added books to the Old Testament. The historical issues here, however, are far more complex than that claim suggests. First, Jews in Jesus' day did not agree on which books belonged in scripture. The final collection that now represents the modern Hebrew Bible was determined long after the time of Jesus. In fact, in the Talmud, a famous collection of rabbinic teachings whose authority in Judaism is second only to the biblical books, the Book of Sirach is recognized as scripture. This is remarkable since this book was not ultimately included in the Bible of Judaism. It should be noted, however, that Sirach does appear in the Catholic Bible. Second, if one were to look at the first bibles that came off the Gutenberg printing press (1450s)—the famous *Gutenberg Bible*—one would find something remarkable: they include the books no longer found in Protestant Bibles. Why? Because prior to the Protestant Reformation (1517), these books were widely read as Christian scripture. In short, the claim that Catholics simply added these books is entirely misleading.

The Bible and the Church

Church dogmas are consistent with one another and can, therefore, shed light on one another, and the Church teaches that the Incarnation can shed light on biblical inspiration. Just as the Word incarnate—Christ—is both fully God and fully human, the Word of God inspired has both a truly divine and a truly human dimension.

On one hand, scripture is inspired, or "God-breathed." God is the author of the Bible. As explained in the Second Vatican Council's document on Sacred Scripture, the human authors thus wrote down "whatever [God] wanted written, and no more" (*Dei Verbum*, 11). This applies to all the parts of the Bible. The Church teaches that God is the author of all the books of the Old and New Testaments, "whole and entire, with all their parts" (*Dei Verbum*, 11). There are no "un-inspired" parts of the Bible. On the other hand, like the Word Incarnate, Sacred Scripture is "fully human." Thus, to quote in full the passage we have been drawing from, the Church teaches:

> *To compose the sacred books, God chose certain men who, all the while he employed them in this task, made full use of their own faculties and powers so that, though he acted in them and by them, it was as true authors that they consigned to writing whatever he wanted written, and no more (*Dei Verbum*, 11).*

The Lindisfarne Gospel of St. Luke.

The human authors of the biblical books cannot be reduced to stenographers. Their distinctive personalities, genius, and concerns are clearly present in their books. They are true authors.

In Catholic teaching this view of inspiration applies only to the Bible. Although the Church believes various doctors and saints are witnesses to Sacred Tradition, the Church only recognizes scripture as inspired in this way. God is never said to be the author of a Church document. The Holy Spirit preserves the Church from error. When using its full authority to speak in Christ's name, the Church's magisterium exercises a special charism of infallibility. But only scripture contains the Word of God in the very words of God. This is why in the liturgy we read only from scripture. In the Mass, the Church does not substitute the writings of St. Thomas Aquinas, the documents of a Church council, or the writings of a pope for scripture. The goal of the Church's magisterium is to be a servant to the Word of God and to help us understand what God has revealed to us in it. The Church's authority does not replace it.

Furthermore, the Church teaches that the dual dimension of scripture also has important implications for interpretation. Because God speaks to us through the human writers, it is necessary to work hard to understand what they themselves have tried to communicate to us. This means paying close attention to the historical circumstances in which they wrote. The Second Vatican Council taught that interpreters of the Bible must give "due attention...to the customary and characteristic styles of feeling, speaking and narrating which prevailed at the time of the sacred writer, and to the patterns men normally employed at that period in their everyday dealings with one another" (*Dei Verbum*, 12). Indeed, because the biblical books have a truly human dimension we must study them with all the methods typically employed to understand human literature.

At the same time, the divine dimension of the biblical books must also be carefully kept in mind. The Church thus gives us three crucial "criteria" for properly interpreting Sacred Scripture (see CCC 112–114). First, we must pay attention to the "content and unity of the whole of Sacred Scripture." Since all the biblical books were composed under the inspiration of the Holy Spirit, they are mutually illuminating. Second, the biblical books should read in light of "the living Tradition of the whole Church." To read scripture in a way that would ignore the authority of Sacred Tradition is to misunderstand it. Finally, Catholics should be mindful of the "analogy of faith." This refers to the way in which all the truths of divine revelation shed light on one another. Reading scripture in the light of the Spirit thus means reading it in a way consistent with the teaching of the Church's magisterium, which is preserved by the same Spirit who initially inspired the biblical authors.

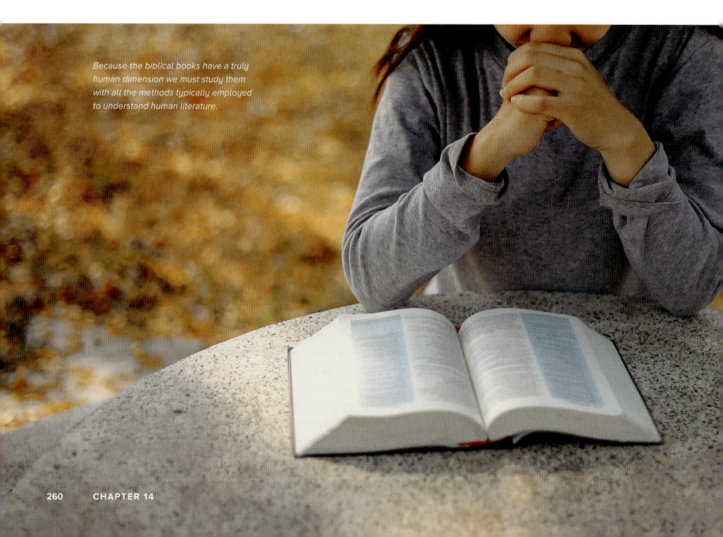

Because the biblical books have a truly human dimension we must study them with all the methods typically employed to understand human literature.

Jesus and Philip

At the end of the Gospel of Luke, the Risen Lord appeared to two disciples who were walking on the road to Emmaus. They failed to recognize him. As he began to walk with them, he inquired into their discussion. They told him of their disappointment over what had happened to Jesus at Jerusalem: "our chief priests and rulers delivered him up to be condemned to death, and crucified him. But we had hoped that he was the one to redeem Israel" (Lk 24:20–21). They mentioned the report that Jesus had risen from the dead, though it does not appear that they then believed it.

Jesus responded, "O foolish men, and slow of heart to believe all that the prophets have spoken! Was it not necessary that the Christ should suffer these things and enter into his glory?" And then, "beginning with Moses and all the prophets, he interpreted to them in all the scriptures the things concerning himself" (Lk 24:25–27). What a truly remarkable journey this must have been. The disciples, though they did not realize it, were given a crash course in interpreting scripture by Jesus. Yet in spite of this unique opportunity to hear the inspired Word explained by the Word himself, they failed to recognize him until they sat down at table. In a scene reminiscent of the institution of the eucharist at the Last Supper, we read: "When he was at table with them, he took the bread and blessed and broke it, and gave it to them. And their eyes were opened and they recognized him; and he vanished out of their sight" (Lk 24:30–31).

The explanation of scripture is meant to lead us to an eucharistic encounter. Indeed, the entire story of Jesus' appearance on the road to Emmaus is repeated for us in a way during every eucharistic liturgy. There we begin by hearing the scriptures (the Liturgy of the Word), which orient us toward receiving him at table (the Liturgy of the eucharist). As the disciples would later explain, Jesus "was known to them in the breaking of the bread" (Lk 24:35). In the eucharist, we too discover the presence of the one we have already encountered in the scriptures.

He Who Hears You, Hears Me **261**

Joseph von Führich, Der Gang Nach Emmaus, *1837, Oil on canvas, Kunsthalle Bremen, Bremen, Germany.*

In the last chapter, we saw the parallels between the account of Jesus' life and ministry in the Gospel of Luke and the story of the Church in the Book of Acts. The account of the story of Jesus' appearance on the road to Emmaus also has a parallel in the Book of Acts: the story of Philip and the eunuch, presented at the beginning of this chapter. The following chart illustrates some of the parallels:

Jesus in Luke 24	Philip in Acts 8
Accompanies the disciples on the road to Emmaus (v. 15)	Accompanies the eunuch on a road (v. 26–30)
Begins the conversation with a question, asking what the disciples have been discussing (v. 17)	Begins the conversation with a question, asking if the eunuch understands what he has been reading in the scriptures (v. 30)
Jesus explains the scriptures "beginning with" Moses and the prophets (v. 27)	Philip explains scripture, "beginning from" a passage in Isaiah (v. 35)
Jesus explains why his passion was necessary (vv. 25–27)	Philip is pressed to discuss why Jesus' passion was necessary (v. 34)
He is invited to stay with the disciples (v. 29)	Philip is invited into the eunuch's chariot (v. 31)
Jesus' blesses and breaks bread (v. 30)	Philip baptizes the eunuch (vv. 36–39)
Jesus disappears from their sight (v. 31)	Philip is miraculously taken up and the eunuch sees him no more (v. 39)

Again, as Luke makes clear, what Jesus did for the disciples at Emmaus is now accomplished through the ministry of the Church: scripture is explained and we are brought into communion with Christ through the sacraments. We too ask how we can understand what we read in scripture. To help us, Jesus gives us the Church to lead us into correct understanding and union with him. With the Church, we are guided into all Truth through the Spirit. Remaining close to the successors of St. Peter and the apostles, we can be confident that the gates of hell will never prevail against the Church. In her, we hear the voice of Christ who comes to be present with us.

Review Questions

1. Why is it significant that Jesus himself never wrote a book? What does this tell us about his plan for the apostles and the Church?

2. What important promises did Jesus make that should give us confidence that the teachings of Jesus were accurately remembered and transmitted by the apostles?

3. Why do Catholics reject the idea that the Bible alone is sufficient to know and understand what has been divinely revealed in Christ?

4. How is the communication of Divine Revelation more than merely the transmission of "data"? What is the connection of Sacred Scripture and Sacred Tradition to the sacraments?

5. How is the Word Inspired analogous to the Word Incarnate? What are the implications for interpreting the Bible correctly? What errors might we fall into if we ignore these lessons?

6. How can reading the Bible apart from the Church lead to problems regarding biblical interpretation?

Put Out Into the Deep

If you would like to learn more about what it means to read the Bible in a way that is faithful to Catholic tradition, see Scott Hahn's *Consuming the Word: The New Testament and the Eucharist in the Early Church* (Doubleday, 2013). In this rich and engaging book, Dr. Hahn introduces some of the important insights the early Church Fathers left us on the close connection between the Bible and the Church.

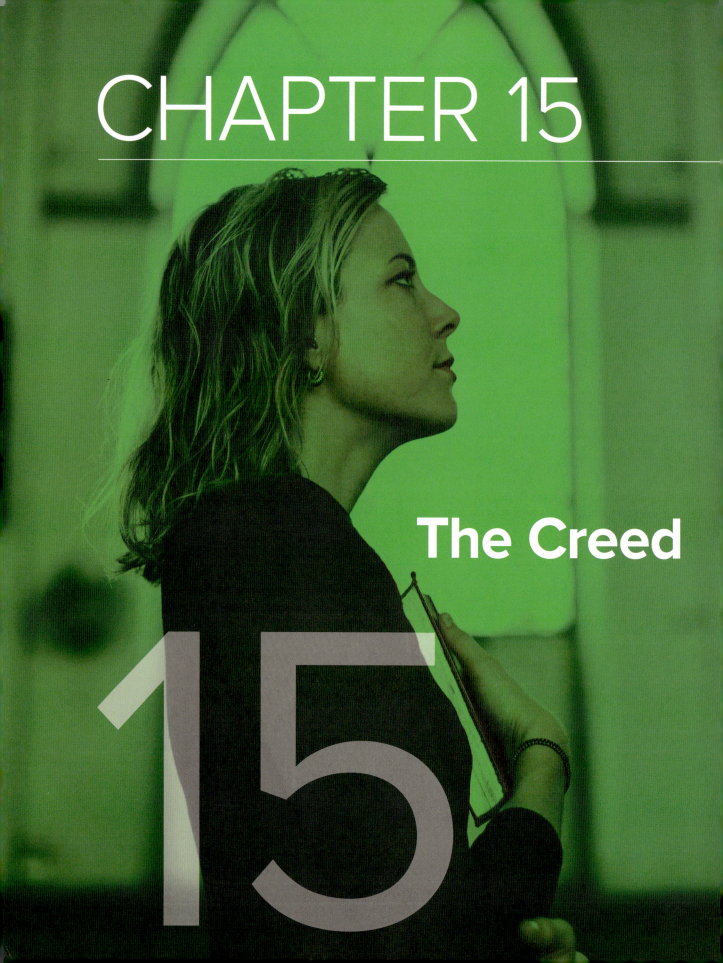

CHAPTER 15

The Creed

The year was 386, and Augustine knew he was on the cusp of something big. For years he had wrestled with questions that go to the heart of human existence. Who am I? Where do I come from? Why do I exist? Who is God, and how can I know Him? After profound and sometimes painful searching, Augustine had acknowledged that the Catholic faith offered answers to his deepest yearnings. But something still held him back from committing himself to Christ.

Augustine decided to ask the advice of a wise old priest named Simplicianus. To nudge Augustine toward conversion, Simplicianus told him a story about Victorinus, a philosopher and orator who was so famous that the Romans placed a statue of him in their Forum. Like Augustine, Victorinus had become convinced that Christianity was true. Yet he did not enter the Church, for he did not think it necessary for him to do so.

> [Victorinus] said to Simplicianus, not openly, but privately and as a friend, "You should know that I am already a Christian." But he answered, "I will not believe it, nor will I reckon you among Christians, unless I see you in the Church of Christ." The other laughed and said, "Is it walls, then, that make men Christians?" He often said that he was already a Christian; Simplicianus just as often made his reply: and just as often he made his joke about the walls.

The Creed   **265**

Constantine's Basilica in Trier, Germany early 4th century.

Eventually Victorinus admitted to himself that he was afraid to be known to be a Christian. What would the crowds think? What would his elite friends think? Would they mock him? Realizing that he needed to make a decision, he returned to Simplicianus and declared, "Let us go to the church. I wish to become a Christian." After Victorinus had been catechized and prepared, the night of his baptism finally arrived. But before he received the sacraments, there was something else to be done.

> *At length the hour came for him to make his profession of faith. At Rome, those who are about to approach [God's] grace usually deliver this profession from an elevated place, in the sight of [God's] faithful people, in set words which they have learned and committed to memory.*

Exceptions were made, however, for those who were too uncomfortable. They could recite the words privately. But Victorinus—now emboldened by his faith—refused to be ashamed. He stood up in front of the gathered Christians of Rome. Everyone recognized him as he professed his faith in Christ. What happened next came as a beautiful surprise: "they all desired to clasp him to their hearts. By their love and joy they clasped him to themselves." For years Victorinus had won acclaim by using words of his own choosing. Now, overcoming his shame and confessing his faith in Jesus, Victorinus recited words that had been given to him by Mother Church and which he had accepted and memorized. And when he professed those words, he found himself welcomed into something stronger, deeper, and richer than his successful career could ever provide.

The Profession of Faith

The profession of faith that Victorinus made that night in Rome is better known as "the Creed." There are several important Catholic creeds, but the most familiar ones are the Nicene Creed, which is usually recited at Mass on Sundays and solemnities, and the Apostles' Creed, which is used in the Rosary. Simply put, a creed summarizes and proclaims what Christians believe. The word "creed" itself comes from the Latin *credo*, meaning "I believe," the word with which many creeds begin.

The roots of Christian creeds can be traced back to the Old Testament. In the Book of Deuteronomy, the Israelites were preparing to cross over into the land promised them by God. Early in the book, Moses gave the people the following commandment: "Hear, O Israel: The Lord our God is one Lord; and you shall love the Lord your God with all your heart, and with all your soul, and with all your might" (Deut 6:4–5). You may recall that, when Jesus was asked what the greatest commandment was, this is the very answer he gave (see Mk 12:29–30). This basic affirmation of the oneness of God and of the obligation to be faithful to him, the *Shema*, serves as a constant reminder of what it means to belong to God's people Israel. It functions not only as a statement of fact or opinion, but as a statement of relationship with God, and therefore as a claim on one's identity.

Hundreds of years later, St. Paul wrote to the Christians of Corinth to address a series of problems that he saw as symptoms of a deeper malady. The Corinthians needed to remember who they were. As part of his reminder of their identity as belonging to God in Christ, Paul adapted the ancient Israelite *Shema*: "for us there is one God, the Father, from whom are all things and for whom we exist, and one Lord, Jesus Christ, through whom are all things and through whom we exist" (1 Cor 8:6). We can recognize here the first building blocks of the creeds we use today. Later in the same letter, he provided another important part of the structure of our creeds: "I delivered to

The Creed

you as of first importance what I also received, that Christ died for our sins in accordance with the scriptures, that he was buried, that he was raised on the third day in accordance with the scriptures" (1 Cor 15:3–4). A couple of things are worth noticing in these verses. First, following the example of the *Shema*, St. Paul presented Christian faith in God as making a claim on the believer: God is the one "for whom we exist" and Jesus the one "through whom we exist." Second, he did not present his teaching as a matter of personal opinion, even personal opinion that has been reached through careful study and thought. Instead, he spoke of what he "received" and had now "delivered" to the Corinthians. As discussed in chapter 14, the word for "delivered" here can also be translated "handed on," and it refers to the reality that we call "tradition" (*traditio* means "handing on" in Latin). In other words, Jewish and Christian faith depend on a community that hands on the truths that God has revealed, and these truths, in turn, make a claim on those who accept them.

Hebrew plaque with the first words of the Shema Prayer.

As the apostles preached, they also ordained trustworthy men to continue to lead the churches.

The Rule of Truth

While we can recognize in his first letter to the Corinthians the beginnings of a Christian profession of faith, it is nonetheless true that St. Paul did not present us with a full-fledged creed. Creeds as we know them emerged gradually as the Gospel spread and the Church grew. It is important to understand how and why this took place. But to do that, we need to take a step back and consider how the Church's beliefs have been handed on over time.

The Catholic Church has always understood itself to have been uniquely entrusted by Christ with the task of faithfully preserving and teaching "the faith which was once for all delivered to the saints" (Jude 3). The origin of this faith is the Father's eternal plan of salvation (see Eph 1:9–10), according to the words of Jesus himself: "My teaching is not mine, but his who sent me" (Jn 7:16; see 14:24). Jesus, in turn, sent his chosen apostles just as the Father had sent him (Jn 20:21), and he gave them his Holy Spirit to empower them to teach the saving Gospel with his own authority (see Mk 3:14–15; Mt 28:19–20; Jn 14:26; 15:26–27; Acts 1:8). Just a few decades after Christ's ascension, one the earliest bishops of Rome, Pope St. Clement I, put these pieces together: "The apostles received the gospel for us from the Lord Jesus Christ; Jesus the Christ was sent forth from God. So then Christ is from God, and the apostles are from Christ." He went on to say that, as the apostles preached, they also ordained trustworthy men to continue to lead the churches. In turn, they provided that, when these men died, "other approved men should succeed to their ministry." The principle laid out here is known as "apostolic succession." Traces of this procedure are visible already in the New Testament (see Acts 1:24–25; Phil 1:1; 1 Tim 3:1–13; 2 Tim 1:6–7, 13–14). Apostolic succession provides a living guarantee of continuity in the Church's teaching across generations and centuries.

The Creed   269

The Lord's provision of this guarantee turned out to be extremely important. You may have noticed how many different groups and individuals offer interpretations of Christianity and of the Bible that sometimes differ wildly from one another and nevertheless all claim to be the truth about Jesus. Sorting out these competing views can be bewildering. This situation is not new. In the first centuries after Christ, the Church faced the challenge of responding to numerous teachers and sects who claimed to teach the true Gospel. One of the greatest figures to rise to this challenge was St. Irenaeus (130–202). Born in modern-day Turkey, St. Irenaeus eventually became bishop of Lyon in what is now France. Around the year 180, he tackled the question of identifying reliable Christian teaching in a work called *Against Heresies*. As most of his opponents read and interpreted the same scriptures he did, he could not simply appeal to the Bible. The question was how the Bible was to be understood. St. Irenaeus proposed a simple criterion, which he referred to as the "rule of truth." This "rule," or "standard," was a summary of the meaning of the Bible as a whole, and so it could be used to measure the validity of claims about the meaning of specific parts of the Bible. St. Irenaeus argued that the rule of truth was itself reliable because it was taught by churches across the known world whose bishops could trace their lineage back to the apostles. In other words, he appealed to apostolic succession as a guarantee of the trustworthiness of the rule of truth.

St. Irenaeus argued that the rule of truth was itself reliable because it was taught by churches across the known world whose bishops could trace their lineage back to the apostles. In other words, he appealed to apostolic succession as a guarantee of the trustworthiness of the rule of truth.

Artist Unknown, Council of Nicaea 325, 1590, Fresco, Capella Sistina, Vatican, Vatican City.

What did this rule of truth say? St. Irenaeus did not always use a single, set formula, but here is one of his clearest expressions of it:

> The Church, though dispersed throughout the world, even to the ends of the earth, has received from the apostles and their disciples this faith: [She believes] in one God, the Father Almighty, Maker of heaven, and earth, and the sea, and all things that are in them; and in one Christ Jesus, the Son of God, who became incarnate for our salvation; and in the Holy Spirit, who proclaimed through the prophets the dispensations of God.

Again, this is not identical to the creeds as we know them now. But it is plain that early Christians were expanding on the building blocks set down in Sacred Scripture—as, for instance, in St. Paul's first letter to the Corinthians—and moving us toward the Apostles' and Nicene Creeds.

The Symbol of Faith

As with the *Shema* in the Old Testament and St Paul's teaching in the New, the teaching of the first creeds is not the handiwork of the authors who appeal to them. They have been "handed on" across the generations, and they are "received" by every new believer. When especially sharp disagreements arose within the Church about the meaning of specific points of Christian teaching, the then-existing creed

The Creed   271

St. Athanasius

was expanded so as to explain its meaning more fully. The most famous instance of this kind of development took place at the Council of Nicaea in 325. In the creed they promulgated, the Nicene Creed, the bishops at the Council used the word "consubstantial" to describe the Son's relationship to the Father. The bishops who defended the use of this word—which is not present in Sacred Scripture—were confident that they had not altered the faith, but only expressed its meaning more clearly. In this case, St. Athanasius (296–373) argued that the word "consubstantial" was necessary to guard against false understandings of the Catholic faith and so to preserve the integrity of the Church's received teaching. Much more recently, the Second Vatican Council taught that such clarifications represent a deepening grasp of the faith, for "there is a growth in the understanding of the realities and the words which have been handed down" (*Dei Verbum*, 8). In this way, the Creed offers us the amazing assurance that the faith we profess today is the same "faith which was once for all delivered to the saints" (Jude 3), the same faith that was "handed on" to St. Paul and that he handed on in turn to the Corinthians, and the same faith that Victorinus stood up and professed in Rome. It is awe-inspiring to call to mind the innumerable and diverse crowd of believers who have professed the same Catholic faith over the last twenty centuries, and to realize that you stand in their company whenever you recite the Creed.

This consideration brings us back to St. Irenaeus, who noted that there is a type of person who is unlikely to be deceived by counterfeit teachings. That person is the one "who retains unchangeable in his heart the rule of the truth which he received by means of baptism." By associating it with the decisive moment of baptism, St. Irenaeus helps us to understand that the Creed represents more than true information. It is the charter of the new identity that is given to us in baptism. When we are baptized, we die and are raised with Christ (Rom 6:3–4). We "put on Christ," so that we are "born anew" to share by the power of the Holy Spirit in Jesus' identity as Son of the Father (see Jn 3:3; Gal 3:27; 4:6; Titus 3:5). To confess faith in the Trinity is therefore to confess the new life you received in baptism. This is why the early Church taught the Creed to those preparing for baptism, and they publicly professed it as their own on the occasion of their baptism.

These considerations might help us understand why, in ancient Christianity, the most common word for "creed" was "symbol" (in Greek, *symbolon*). The Church Fathers delighted in pointing out that this term bore a double meaning. It meant a "collection" because the Creed collects in summary form the principal articles of Christian faith. But it could also refer to a seal, or token of identity. Since being baptized into Christ means being baptized into his one Body (1 Cor 12:13), the Creed is not only the charter of your own personal relationship with Jesus. It is also a "seal," or "token," ("symbol") that identifies you as belonging to Christ's Body, the family of God—the Church.

Like the ashes we recieve on Ash Wednesday, the Creed is not only the charter of your own personal relationship with Jesus, it is also a "seal," that identifies you as belonging to Christ's Body, the family of God—the Church.

The Content of the Creed

What can be said about the contents of this charter of Christian identity? What does the Creed say? This is not the place to discuss each line of the Creed in detail, but it would be worthwhile to consider a few of its key features. These features are shared by both the Apostles' Creed and the Nicene Creed, and we will draw from both.

Throughout this book, we have considered the intricate and interdependent relationship between reason and faith. At its outset, the Creed reflects this relationship. The Letter to the Hebrews says that "whoever would draw near to God must believe that he exists and that he rewards those who seek him" (11:6). In other words, the bare minimum for a relationship with God is belief, first, in his existence, and second, that he acts within his creation according to a plan for our happiness. This is precisely what we express in the first words of the Nicene Creed: "I believe in one God, the Father almighty." God is real, he is one, and he exercises fatherly care for his creatures. Despite many obstacles and opportunities for error, we can know these things through the use of reason. We can know that there is one God. We can know that he created the universe. We can know that he is omnipotent. And we can even recognize him as "father" insofar as we can discern his provident care for us as part of his creation (see Acts 14:16–17; 17:22–28; CCC 238). The rest of the Creed concerns itself with matters that we only know because God has freely revealed them. But it is very important that the Creed begins with things we can know naturally about God, for this bears witness to the unity of faith and reason. Our reason is a good gift from God, a way of bearing the divine image, and God honors our reason. Revelation purifies, stretches, and exceeds our reason, but it does not violate it. This feature of the Creed assures us that the God we can glimpse through sound philosophy, even if only dimly, is not a different God from the One we know by faith, the God of Abraham, Isaac, and Jacob.

Nonetheless, the knowledge of God available to us by faith is far deeper and more intimate than what reason alone can offer. The rest of the articles of the Creed expand and heighten our understanding of the meaning of the two basic points of God's existence and his providence. St. Thomas Aquinas explained it well: "the existence of God includes all that we believe to exist in God eternally, and in these our happiness consists; while belief in His providence includes all those things which God dispenses in time, for man's salvation, and which are the way to that happiness."

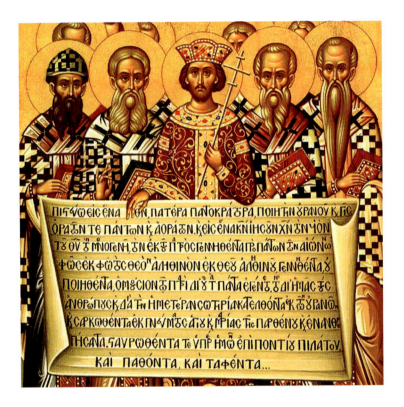

Icon depicting the Emperor Constatine, accompanied by the bishops of the first council of Nicaea (325), holding the Nicene-Constantinopolitan Creed of 381.

The culmination and fulfillment of God's providence, what he "dispenses in time," is Jesus Christ, the eternal Son of God made man. The Letter to the Hebrews begins, "In many and various ways God spoke of old to our fathers by the prophets; but in these last days he has spoken to us by a Son" (Heb 1:1–2). This is why the longest section of the Creed, and the only part of it to include narrative, is the paragraph on Jesus Christ, which summarizes his Incarnation and his Paschal Mystery. Sometimes people wonder, if the Creed is supposed to encapsulate the meaning of the whole Bible, why it excludes such important events as the fall of our first parents, the call of Abraham, the Exodus, and descriptions of Jesus' earthly teaching and ministry. But this is to misunderstand the purpose of the Creed. By zeroing in on the very pinnacle of God's plan—Christ's Incarnation, death, resurrection, and ascension—the Creed provides us with the proper lens through which we can accurately evaluate and appreciate the true meaning of all those other biblical realities.

The Creed 275

Albrecht Dürer, All Saints, 1511, Oil on poplar wood, Kunsthistorisches Museum, Vienna, Austria.

Not only does Christ fulfill God's plan for our salvation; as we saw in chapter 11, he also reveals a startling truth about the one God. Jesus himself is the very same God as the Father who sent him, and the Spirit whom Jesus gave to his Church is also that very same God. The one God in whom we believe is an eternal communion of love among three Divine Persons: the Father, the Son, and the Holy Spirit. According to the *Catechism of the Catholic Church*, this truth is God's "innermost secret" (CCC 221). Since it specifies who the one God is, the doctrine of the Trinity is also "the central mystery of Christian faith and life" (CCC 234). It is the mystery into which we are baptized "in the name of the Father and of the Son and of the Holy Spirit" (Mt 28:19).

This is why the Creed follows a Trinitarian pattern. It is essential to recognize that the three paragraphs of the Creed, devoted to the three Persons of the Trinity, are not independent, for these three Persons are truly one unique God, and the plan of salvation is the work of this one, Triune God. This is another way in which the Creed offers important perspective for reading the Bible. The entire arc of salvation history from creation, through the history of Israel, and to the coming of Christ and the founding of the Church is a single, coherent story crafted by the one God who is three Persons. Accordingly, the three paragraphs interlock intricately and beautifully. We noted above that awareness of God's fatherhood is, in a sense, available to natural reason. But through Christ, we have come to know God as Father in an amazing, new way. He is not only "father" as provident creator of the universe. He is eternally Father of the eternal Son. Even more amazing, he has offered us a share by grace in Christ's Sonship, so that, as his adopted sons and daughters, we can call God Father in the same way that

Jesus calls God his Father. This offer has been made to us through the Incarnation and Paschal Mystery of Jesus Christ, the topic of the second paragraph of the Creed.

In this new relationship with God, we not only know him as creator and all-powerful caretaker of the universe, but we participate in his eternal life, sharing in the communion of the Father and the Son, through the Holy Spirit, sent by the Father and the Son. The articles of faith in the Creed's third paragraph, which are associated with the Holy Spirit, might seem at first glance to be a bit of a hodgepodge. They are not. These realities—the Catholic Church, the communion of saints, baptism, the forgiveness of sins, the resurrection of the dead—describe the work of the Holy Spirit in uniting us to the life of Jesus and thereby making us ever more truly sons and daughters of the Father. The Holy Spirit makes the story of Jesus real in our lives, not as isolated individuals, but as members of the Body of Christ, the Church.

In the Gospel of John, Jesus prays to his Father, "And this is eternal life, that they know you the only true God, and Jesus Christ whom you have sent" (Jn 17:3). Knowledge of God as the eternal communion of love of Father, Son, and Holy Spirit and knowledge of Jesus Christ as the supreme revelation of God's providence is not mere information. It is "eternal life," for we are called not only to know about who God is; we are called, through his plan of salvation, to "become partakers of the divine nature" (2 Pet 1:4), to enter into the joy of his eternal reality. That is the real meaning of the Creed.

To know God is to "become partakers of the divine nature" (2 Pet 1:4), to enter into the joy of his eternal reality. That is the real meaning of the Creed.

The Creed 277

For speaking in open opposition to Adolf Hitler and the Nazi Regime, Alfred Delp was arrested and condemned to die.

The Creed and the Christian Life

Nevertheless, we may be a little suspicious of a formula like the Creed that we just repeat word-for-word. Our own age tends to prize originality and creativity. As we saw in the case of Steve Jobs's commencement speech at Stanford, the refusal to conform to tradition is often thought to be a mark of authenticity and self-realization, while acceptance of tradition seems to involve staleness, repression, or even hypocrisy. When the traditions that one is challenging are false or corrupt, this can be true. Many admirable examples come to mind: figures from the Civil Rights Movement like Rosa Parks, resisters of the Nazis like Fr. Alfred Delp, witnesses to radical discipleship like St. Francis of Assisi—even Jesus himself. But none of these individuals revolted against tradition simply because it was tradition. Their goal was not self-expression for its own sake, but truth and goodness.

If Christianity is true—if there really is a God who has revealed himself supremely in the person of Jesus Christ and has entrusted his saving truth to the Church—then, far from being a recipe for stunted inauthenticity, the teachings enshrined in the Creed are necessary to make us truly free. Jesus himself taught, "If you continue in my word,"—that is, in his teaching—"you are truly my disciples, and you will know the truth, and the truth will make you free" (Jn 8:31–32). Because it tells of the God who is all life, truth, and goodness, the Creed's antiquity cannot render it stale. It is always fresh, always new. By telling the truth about who we are as God's beloved creatures called into the fullness of his own Trinitarian life, the Creed orients us to a human flourishing that exceeds our imagination. It might be worth adding that, in light of many trends in the contemporary world, it is hard to imagine many things more non-conformist or countercultural than professing the Creed. St. Augustine once said that we should dress ourselves in the Creed each day, like clothing, and that this clothing will guard us against shame and adversity. By reminding us of the truths of our faith, the Creed frees us for true authenticity and creativity.

This does not happen without a cost. If the purpose of the Creed is not simply to communicate information about God but to proclaim, in Aquinas's words, "the way to that happiness" which is life with God, then it is evident that the Creed makes a claim on us that goes beyond mental assent to its teaching. The Creed asks of us what St. Paul calls "the obedience of faith" (Rom 1:5; 16:26). The Church has explained that this "obedience" means that "man commits his whole self freely to God" (*Dei Verbum*, 5). It is true that the Creed reminds us of who God is, not only as he can be known through philosophy, but as he has mercifully revealed himself in the history of his people Israel and, above all, in the sending of his Son and his Spirit. But it is equally true that the Creed reminds us of who we ourselves are. The Christian singer-songwriter Rich Mullins (1955–1997) once set the Apostles' Creed to music. Amid his sung recitation of the articles of faith, Mullins inserted this refrain: "I did not make it; no, it is making me." If we have been baptized into the life of the Trinity, then the Creed's profession of faith in the Triune God and in his plan for our salvation in Christ expresses the proper framework for our lives as disciples of Jesus. In the same sermon in which St. Augustine compared the Creed to clothing, he also exhorted his congregation to "treat your creed as your own personal mirror. Observe yourself there, if you believe all the things you confess to believing, and rejoice every day in your faith."

Memorizing the Creed and frequently calling it to mind can, slowly but surely, radically change our entire experience of ourselves, of others, and of the world. We might associate memorization with dry, unthinking, rote repetition. But when we understand and connect with what we memorize, it can profoundly shape our way of being in the world. Take a moment to consider the many things you have memorized already: song lyrics, movie lines, memes, and so on. Now think about how these things

St. Augustine loved to emphasize the importance of memorizing the Creed so that it could be called to mind regularly. We should keep it firm in our hearts, he said, by reciting it in bed, during our daily business, and over our meals. But he also reassured his congregants that they must not become anxious about getting the words slightly wrong. The Church is a family, and the priests who teach the faith are more concerned that we learn the meaning of the faith than that we never make a mistake in reciting the Creed. "Don't worry," St. Augustine said, "we are your fathers, we aren't carrying the canes and switches of schoolteachers. If any of you get the words wrong, at least don't get the faith wrong."

affect your experience of life. Certain songs evoke powerful emotions and memories—they are, people sometimes say, the "soundtrack of our lives." We lace our conversation with lines from favorite films or television shows. We adapt memes to express our opinion of a situation or issue. The things we memorize work as the lens through which we see the world, the glue that forms and strengthens our bonds with others, and—to use St. Augustine's image—the mirror in which we see ourselves. No wonder we refer to memorization as learning "by heart." This is why it is so important to stock the shelves of our minds and hearts with words and phrases that tell us the truth and that will shape our thoughts in accord, not merely with what is funny or cool, but with what is true and good. St. Paul gives us this advice: "whatever is true, whatever is honorable, whatever is just, whatever is pure, whatever is lovely, whatever is gracious, if there is any excellence, if there is anything worthy of praise, think about these things" (Phil 4:8). Along with verses and passages from Sacred Scripture, the Creed is a great place to start.

Certain songs evoke powerful emotions and memories—they are, people sometimes say, the "soundtrack of our lives." Memorizing the Creed and frequently calling it to mind can, slowly but surely, radically change our entire experience of ourselves, of others, and of the world.

Consider how this doctrine can spread like ripples on a pond to every corner of your life.

To illustrate what it might look like to allow the Creed to infiltrate your life, let us take a closer look at the Nicene Creed's affirmation that Christ is "consubstantial with the Father." "Consubstantial" is not exactly a word most of us use on a regular basis, and to many it might seem inscrutable. It is easy enough to explain (though not to understand) its surface meaning: the Son is of the same "substance," or "being," as the Father. That is, he is God in the very same way the Father is God. He and the Father are not two Gods; they are the same God. We might think, "Okay, but so what? Is this just a mind-bender the Church gives us to keep us on our toes?" Far from it. Consider how this doctrine can spread like ripples on a pond to every corner of your life. Start with the stories we read in the Bible. Jesus did not show compassion from a distance. He touched a leper (Mk 1:41). He forgave sins (Mk 2:5). He ate with sinners and tax collectors (Mk 2:15–17). And in the end, he freely suffered and died for our salvation. When we say that Jesus is "consubstantial with the Father," we assert that the one who touches, heals, forgives, and suffers with and for us is not some underling whom God sent to do his dirty work. He himself is God and the perfect revelation of the Father (see Jn 14:9). The love and mercy we see in Christ are the love and mercy of the eternal and omnipotent God who made all things.

Next, think how this realization might affect your experience of the eucharist. Not long after reciting the Creed at a Sunday Mass, the Church teaches us that the bread and wine on the altar is going to become the Body and Blood of Christ. If Christ is "consubstantial with the Father," then what you are about to see in the priest's hands is not a symbol or a metaphor, but the infinite God giving himself to you as your food. Finally, consider what Christ's consubstantiality with the Father might mean for how you live your faith outside of Mass. If the God of the

The Creed is the truth of God, received by the Apostles from Christ and "handed on" across the generations. Only by finding our true identity in this "great cloud of witnesses" (Heb 12:1) will we discover the courage to acknowledge Jesus before men (Mt 10:32).

universe chose to stoop down and identify with us in our poverty and brokenness, then our corporal and spiritual works of mercy are not just the fulfillment of duties. Empowered by the grace of the Holy Spirit, they are points of contact with the love and mercy that God himself is. This illustration is just a small taste of what St. Augustine meant by holding up the Creed as our clothing, as our mirror.

As you put on the Creed day by day, as you peer into it to find out who you are called to be as a son or daughter of God, it is important to realize that you are not alone. That the Creed is not just a form of self-expression but a "symbol" of communal faith should remind each of us that we belong to a worldwide communion that spans many centuries. And that communion, the Catholic Church, is not just a club formed by individuals who happen to hold similar opinions about God. It is formed by the complete self-gift of Jesus on the cross (see CCC 766). This gift is what the Creed expresses. Its truth is not the product of human wisdom or human power. It is the truth of God, received by the Apostles from Christ and "handed on" across the generations. Only by finding our true identity in this "great cloud of witnesses" (Heb 12:1) will we discover the courage, like Victorinus all those centuries ago, to acknowledge Jesus before men (Mt 10:32). We will be able to make our own the words that follow the profession of faith in the baptismal liturgy: "This is our faith. This is the faith of the Church. We are proud to profess it, in Christ Jesus our Lord."

Review Questions

1. What is "apostolic succession"? Where does it come from, and how does it relate to the Creed?

2. In what way does the Creed exhibit the proper relationship between faith and reason?

3. How are the three parts, or "paragraphs," of the Creed organized? Why are they organized this way?

4. Why does the Creed refer to so few stories from the Bible?

5. What is the point of memorizing and repeating a Creed you did not compose?

6. To what extent is your self-understanding built upon the truths expressed in the Creed? Do you see yourself as a beloved son or daughter of the Father? How might learning and thinking about the Creed alter your self-image?

7. What does the Creed tell us, explicitly or implicitly, about the meaning of true happiness? How can it help us attain true happiness?

Put Out Into the Deep

When early Christian martyrs were pressured to renounce their faith—on pain of imprisonment, torture, and death—they often simply repeated, "I am a Christian." Faith in Jesus Christ was so deeply imprinted on their hearts that it was constitutive of their very identity. One especially poignant example can be read in the early third-century account "The Martyrdom of Saints Perpetua and Felicity," the text of which is widely available online.

References

Unless noted, quotations and selections from the Fathers of the Church (e.g. St. Augustine) are taken from the standard nineteenth-century series *Ante-Nicene Fathers* and *Nicene and Post-Nicene Fathers,* both available online at several sites.

Chapter 4

William Provine, "Evolution and the Foundation of Ethics", *MBL Science 3,* no. 1 (Winter 1988): 27–28.

David Barash, "God, Darwin and My College Biology Class", *New York Times,* September 27, 2014.

Chapter 6

St. Gregory of Nazianzus, *On God and Christ: The Five Theological Orations and Two Letters to Cledonius,* trans. Lionel Wickham (Crestwood, New York: St. Vladimir's Seminary Press, 2002).

Chapter 8

Message du Saint-Père Jean-Paul II aux Membres de l'Assemblée Plénière de l'Académie Pontificale des Sciences (October 22, 1996), available at vatican.va.

Charles Darwin, *On the Origin of Species,* 2nd edition (1860; New York: Oxford University Press, 2008).

Franklin M. Harold, *The Way of the Cell: Molecules, Organisms and the Order of Life* (New York: Oxford University Press, 2001).

Benjamin H. Good, et alia, "The Dynamics of Molecular Evolution over 60,000 Generations," *Nature* 551 (2 November 2017): 45–50.

Asa Gray, "What is Darwinism?," *The Nation* (May 28, 1874), reprinted in his *Darwiniana* (New York, 1889).

Chapter 9

The Confessions of Saint Augustine, trans. by John K. Ryan (New York, NY: Doubleday, 1960; repr., 2014).

Chapter 10

Origen, *Frag. On Deut.* 1:21. Translation from Stephen Benin, *The Footprints of God: Divine Accommodation in Jewish and Christian Thought* (Albany, NY: State University of New York, 1993).

Chapter 12

Translation of *2 Baruch* taken from James H. Charlesworth, *The Old Testament Pseudepigrapha,* Anchor Bible Reference Library, 2 vols. (New York: Doubleday, 1985), 1:631.

Chapter 13

The passage from "The Martyrdom of Polycarp" is selected from the complete text as found in Michael William Holmes, *The Apostolic Fathers: Greek Texts and English Translations* (Grand Rapids, MI: Baker Books, 1999), 227–241.

Chapter 15

Saint Augustine, *The Confessions,* trans. John K. Ryan (New York: Image, 2014 [orig. New York: Doubleday, 1960]), 146–147.

1 Clement 42.1–2, in *The Apostolic Fathers: Greek Texts and English Translations,* ed. and trans. Michael W. Holmes, 3rd ed. (Grand Rapids, MI: Baker Academic, 2007), 101.

Saint Augustine, *Sermon* 58.13, in *Sermons III (51-94) on the New Testament,* trans. Edmund Hill, ed. John E. Rotelle, The Works of Saint Augustine: A Translation for the 21st Century, Part 3, Volume 3 (Brooklyn: New City Press, 1991).

Saint Augustine, *Sermon* 213.11 and 215.1, in *Sermons III/6 (184-229Z) on the Liturgical Seasons,* trans. Edmund Hill, ed. John E. Rotelle, The Works of Saint Augustine: A Translation for the 21st Century, Part 3, Volume 6 (New Rochelle, NY: New City Press, 1993).

St. Thomas Aquinas, *Expositio in Symbolum Apostolorum,* prologue, trans. Joseph B. Collins, ed. Joseph Kenny, O.P. http://dhspriory.org/thomas/Creed.htm; accessed 2 May 2018.

Art and Photo References

Cover   *Ecce Homo* by Ciseri © Restored Traditions. Used by permission.

P. 2   Standing Man watching the ocean view Sunrise. © PKpix/shutterstock.com

P. 5   © Restored Traditions. Used by permission.

P. 6   ROME, ITALY - MARCH 11, 2016: The fresco of Christ the Redeemer in Glory with the Heavenly Host by Niccolo Circignani Il Pomarancio (1588) in main apse of church Basilica di Santi Giovanni e Paolo. © Renata Sedmakova/shutterstock.com

P. 7   Pray in the Morning, Woman praying with hands together on white background, Woman praying while holding Bible © NATNN/shutterstock.com

P. 8   Easy belay-descender device in the hands of a climber closeup. Climbing gear and equipment. Tilt-Shift effect. © Salienko Evgenii/shutterstock.com

P. 9   Blur image of picture library background. Library resources, including vast knowledge and sun light. © Thiranun Kunatum/shutterstock.com

P. 10   Historic statue of Cardinal John Henry Newman. Due to be beatified by the Pope - a route to sainthood - on Sunday 19th September, Cardinal Newman converted from Anglicanism to Catholicism. © BasPhoto/shutterstock.com

P. 11   Hiking trail up the hill to the church, the trail over the sea from Oia to Fira in Santorini, Greece © kavalenkava/shutterstock.com

P. 12   Soft focus on a hand of woman while praying for christian religion with blurred of her body background , Casual woman praying with her hands together over a closed Bible © NATNN/shutterstock.com

P. 13   © Restored Traditions. Used by permission.

P. 14   Two friends talking sitting in a couch in the living room with a window in the background at home © Antonio Guillem/shutterstock.com

P. 16   Cropped image of smiling brunette woman in eyeglasses reading book in park © Dean Drobot/shutterstock.com

P. 18   Close up of face of young Woman © shootingstarstudio/shutterstock.com

P. 21 (upper)   A large group of people walking. Blurred motion © Artens/shutterstock.com

P. 21 (lower)   Cinema, entertainment, leisure and people concept - couple watching movie in theater from back © Syda Productions/shutterstock.com

P. 22   Female athletes at starting line © sirtravelalot/shutterstock.com

P. 23   SAN BENEDETTO DEL TRONTO, ITALY. MAY 16, 2015. Portrait of Darth Vader costume replica with grab hand and his red sword. Lord Fener is a fictional character of Star Wars saga. Red backlight and smoke © Stefano Buttafoco/shutterstock.com

P. 24   Serious teen boy surrounded by darkness looking at himself in mirror with wooden frame © Jan H Andersen/shutterstock.com

P. 25   Greek Philosopher Aristotle Sculpture Isolated on Black Background © MidoSemsem/shutterstock.com

P. 27   Female student outdoors © ESB Professional/shutterstock.com

P. 28   Loving stylish couple near a retro car outdoors.Stylish Great Gatsby wedding © Roman Yuklyaevsky/shutterstock.com

P. 29   Painted Emotion series. Canvas of colorful swirls and negative space forming male, female profiles and bird profiles on the subject of relationship, art and love. © PinkCat/shutterstock.com

P. 30   Close up portrait of a teenage girl in a city street during a sunny day, looking away from the camera and smiling against the sky with sun rays filtering through her neck. © MJTH/shutterstock.com

P. 32   Elementary school kids sitting around teacher in a classroom. © Monkey Business Images/shutterstock.com

P. 33   Staff Serving Food In Homeless Shelter Kitchen. © Monkey Business Images/shutterstock.com

P. 34   Happy young African woman at river side thinking © Rido/shutterstock.com

P. 35   Closeup portrait of a praying young woman with closed eyes. © ptnphoto/shutterstock.com

P. 36   What's your story? The text is typed on paper with an old typewriter, a vintage inscription, a story of life. © gerasimov_foto_174/shutterstock.com

P. 37   Saint Augustine © Augustine Institute. All rights reserved.

P. 38   Students communicating at cafe after lesson. © Pressmaster/shutterstock.com

P. 40   Classmate Classroom Sharing International Friend Concept. © Rawpixel.com/shutterstock.com

P. 42   Man using modern mobile smartphone with brick buildings in the background. © guteksk7/shutterstock.com

P. 43   Wilted pot plant. © OhEngine/shutterstock.com

P. 44   Asian woman relaxing with coffee © wavebreakmedia/shutterstock.com

P. 46   Handsome businessman and auto service mechanic are discussing the work and shaking hands. Car repair and maintenance. © 4 PM production/shutterstock.com

P. 47   Hands open Blank catalog, magazines,book mock up on wood table. © jannoon028/shutterstock.com

P. 49   Depressed teenage boy laying down on a couch with his smart phone. © mooremedia/shutterstock.com

P. 50   Jane Austen. Public Domain.

P. 52   Young couple in love walking in the autumn park holding hands looking in the sunset. © Rock and Wasp/shutterstock.com

P. 54   The final pizza in a white dish with a spoonful of concepts is very delicious. © The Five Aggregates/shutterstock.com

P. 55   School of Athens by Raphael. Public Domain.

P. 56   Crucifix made of marble with blue sky in background. France, Provence Region. © Paolo Gallo/shutterstock.com

P. 58   Spiral galaxy, illustration of Milky Way. © Alex Mit/shutterstock.com

P. 60   Group of Chimpanzee (Pan troglodytes) on mangrove branches. Mother-chimpanzee sits and holds on hands of the cub. Chimpanzees (chimps), (Pan troglodytes troglodytes). Congo. Africa. © Sergey Uryadnikov/shutterstock.com

P. 61   Human body by X-rays. 3d render. © Dim Dimich/shutterstock.com

P. 63   Couple smoking a no smoking sign. © paul prescott/shutterstock.com

P. 64   Sad female teenager sitting on park bench. © Axel Bueckert/shutterstock.com

P. 66   Landscape with Milky Way. Night sky with stars and silhouette of a standing happy man on the mountain. © Denis Belitsky/shutterstock.com

P. 67   VATICAN CITY, VATICAN - 27 APRIL 2005: Pope Benedict XVI greets the faithful as he arrives to lead his first general audience in St. Peter's Square at the Vatican. © Alessia Pierdomenico/shutterstock.com

P. 69	First-person view a man sitting on wooden bench in the park. © Kostenko Maxim/shutterstock.com
P. 70	Two happy teen girls looking in mirror. © MPH Photos/shutterstock.com
P. 71	ROME - MAY 01: Giant banner of pope John Paul's portrait in the streets of Rome during his ceremony of beatification on May 1 2011 at St Peter's square at Vatican city in Rome Italy. © ChameleonsEye/shutterstock.com
P. 72	A young black businessman is standing by a mirror and looking at the reflection / Looking at Mirror. © Alexander Image/shutterstock.com
P. 73	Panoramic photo of girl's face in sunglasses. © Sergey Mironov/shutterstock.com
P. 74	Twin sisters thinking and looking each other over ocher background. © Luis Molinero/shutterstock.com
P. 76	Focused millennial african american student in glasses making notes writing down information from book in cafe preparing for test or exam, young serious black man studying or working in coffee house. © fizkes/shutterstock.com
P. 79	Glass of milk, a carton of milk on wooden table. © BigBigbb1/shutterstock.com
P. 80	A mix of fresh Orange and green apple background. © Syibli Fakih/shutterstock.com
P. 82	Triangle pattern. Seamless vector background. Blue, gray, white triangles. © lovender/shutterstock.com
P. 84	Closeup of horse's eye © Carmina McConnell/shutterstock.com
	Leopard fur skin © Sarah Cheriton-Jones/shutterstock.com
	Colorful macaw feathers © studiojumpee/shutterstock.com
	Spiral snail shell © aga7ta/shutterstock.com
	Colorful reptile skin © Eric Isselee/shutterstock.com
	Golden eagle talons © Alex Jackson/shutterstock.com
	Lord Derby's Parakeet (Psittacula derbiana) © David Dohnal/shutterstock.com
	Dog's tail © Watunyu Wichakriengkai/shutterstock.com
P. 85	Young woman's eyes looking up. © B-D-S Piotr Marcinski/shutterstock.com
P. 86	Beautiful spring landscape. © majeczka/shutterstock.com
P. 88	Seamless vector geometric pattern. Colorful abstract mosaic backgrounds. © OLga Shishova/shutterstock.com
P. 89	Pencil's sketch of the cyborg. © Kutlayev Dmitry/shutterstock.com
P. 90	Magnetic resonance image (MRI) of the brain. © Triff/shutterstock.com
P. 91 (left)	Man's eye © billionphotos/shutterstock.com
P. 91 (right)	Siberian Husky blue eyes © Ivanova N/shutterstock.com
P.92	Light head. © Max4e Photo/shutterstock.com
P. 93	Future planning, Close up of woman hands making frame gesture with sunrise on mountain, Female capturing the sunrise, sunlight outdoor. © oatawa/shutterstock.com
P. 94	© Restored Traditions. Used by permission.
P. 96	Sunset over a mountain valley. © Yuriy Kulik/shutterstock.com
P. 99	Close up of a furniture maker chiselling a chair joint. © Fergus Coyle/shutterstock.com
P. 100	Large chandeliers on the chains. © Kolbakova Olga/shutterstock.com
P. 101	3d illustration of wagon of freight train with containers on the sky background. © Egorov Artem/shutterstock.com
P. 103	Mangrove above and below water surface, half and half, with fish and a jellyfish underwater, Caribbean sea. © Damsea/shutterstock.com
P. 104	WASHINGTON, DC, USA - FEBRUARY 2, 2005: President George W. Bush delivering his State of the Union speech before a joint session of Congress. © Rob Crandall/shutterstock.com
P. 105 (left)	Mountain Bluebird perched against a natural green background in Yellowstone National Park, Wyoming / Montana / Idaho songbird blue bird western eastern mountain. © Tom Reichner/shutterstock.com
P. 105 (right)	Birthday cake with cream chocolate drips on a white background. © Aksana Yasiuchenia/shutterstock.com
P. 106	Freight train with cargo containers. Against Sunrise. 3d rendering. © Pavel Chagochkin/shutterstock.com
P. 108	Friends. © Vasek Rak/shutterstock.com
P. 109	Horse with a foal on the meadow. © Chere/shutterstock.com
P. 112	Young attractive woman sitting and checking pictures after yoga photo session on her smartphone, enjoying and posting good shots, using filter application for images, view over the shoulder, closeup. © fizkes/shutterstock.com
P. 114	Stylish young women with sunglasses talking and enjoying tasty coffee sitting on green grass outdoors. Back view of student together with attractive brunette friend telling news each other during break. © GaudiLab/shutterstock.com
P. 118	Macbeth and Banquo meeting the witches on the heath by Chasseriau. Public Domain.
P. 119	The sleepwalking Lady Macbeth by Fuseli. Public Domain.
P. 121	MINNEAPOLIS - JUNE 29: A Minnesota Atheist carries a placard at the Twin Cities Gay Pride Parade on June 29, 2014, in Minneapolis. © miker/shutterstock.com
P. 124	Moses comes down from the mountain with the tablets of Law - Picture from The Holy Scriptures, Old and New Testaments books collection published in 1885, Stuttgart-Germany. Drawings by Gustave Dore. © Nicku/shutterstock.com
P. 125	VATICAN CITY, VATICAN - 25 APRIL 2004: Pope John Paul II blesses the pilgrims during the weekly general audience in Saint Peter's Square at the Vatican. © Alessia Pierdomenico/shutterstock.com
P. 126	Parents and kids having a lunch together in the garden. © Monkey Business Images/shutterstock.com
P. 127	New York City,NY - April 22, 2018 : The 9/11 Memorial Pool in a gloomy day in New York City,NY on April 22, 2018. © ben bryant/shutterstock.com
P. 128	The wooden cross necklace on man's neck. © Skylines/shutterstock.com
P. 130	Hands working on pottery wheel. © Rock and Wasp/shutterstock.com
P. 132	© Restored Traditions. Used by permission.

P. 134	Flood damage from Hurricane Katrina. © David Burkholder/shutterstock.com
P. 135	In the beginning … © Alistair Scott/shutterstock.com
P. 136	The Eagle Nebulaas Pillars of Creation. This image shows the pillars as seen in visible light, capturing the multi-coloured glow of gas clouds, Elements of this image are furnished by NASA. © Egyptian Studio/shutterstock.com
P. 138	Birds of different feathers flocking together. A metaphor for diversity. © SAJE/shutterstock.com
P. 139	The imprint of the ancient trilobites in a stone. 500 million Year old Trilobite. Trilobites meaning three lobes are a fossil group of extinct marine arachnomorph arthropods, form the class Trilobita. © Merlin74/shutterstock.com
P. 140	Grizzly Bear (Ursus arctos) - Frosty Grass. © NaturesMomentsuk/shutterstock.com
P. 141	E coli Bacteria close up. © fusebulb/shutterstock.com
P. 142	Forest panorama with sunshine. © Guenter Albers/shutterstock.com
P. 144	The Expulsion of Adam and Eve from Paradise, 1791, by Benjamin West, by Anglo-American painting, oil on canvas. Archangel Michael expels Adam and Eve, who wear coats of skins' from Eden. © Everett - Art/shutterstock.com
P. 145	Parthenon Temple © anyaivanova/shutterstock.com
P. 148	The Korean people, December 3, 2016, Seoul, Candlelight protests, Peacefully marching, Wanting to impeach President Park. © Rapture700/shutterstock.com
P. 151	Moses and the Burning Bush by Bouts © Restored Traditions. Used by permission.
P. 152	Distraught Confused And Anxious Teen Girl. © toonbst/shutterstock.com
P. 154	Theos (God) written at the beginning of John's Gospel © Swellphotography/shutterstock.com
P. 155	ATHENS, GREECE - FEBRUARY 6 2016: Little marble busts of ancient Greek authors on a white shelf. © Francesco Cantone/shutterstock.com
P. 156	The opening of St Luke's Gospel in the Lindisfarne Gospels. Public Domain.
P. 158	CREMONA, ITALY - MAY 24, 2016: The frescco of scene form Prophet Jonah in the vault in Chiesa di San Sigismondo by Giulio Campi (1564–1567). © Renata Sedmakova/shutterstock.com
P. 159	http://www.christianiconography.info/sicily/sarcophagusJonah.html
P. 160	Ancient Rome from facade of old building in Rome, Italy. © Goran Bogicevic/shutterstock.com
P. 161	Group of people in circle reading bibles © Andrey_Popov/shutterstock.com
P. 162	Nuestro Señor atado a la columna by Fernandez. https://commons.wikimedia.org/wiki/File:Cristo_atado_a_la_columna_20131225.jpg
P. 163	Easter. Illustration - fresco in Byzantine style depicting the scene of the Jesus Christ's resurrection. © Julia Raketic/shutterstock.com
P. 165	Statue of Liberty with blurred New York City background. © cpaulfell/shutterstock.com
P. 166	Public Domain.
P. 168	MADRID - SEP 13: People from the audience in a show at Dcode Festival on September 13, 2014 in Madrid, Spain. © Christian Bertrand/shutterstock.com
P. 171	Torah on the stone. © Polyanska Lyubov/shutterstock.com
P. 172	Jesus Christ-Hagia Sophia © Lukas Uher/shutterstock.com
P. 173	The Moses from Michelangelo, in the Church of San Pietro in Vincoli in Rome, Italy, March-24-2018. © Stefano_Valeri/shutterstock.com
P. 174	Man jeans and sneaker shoes walking on the road sunset light. © Lesterman/shutterstock.com
P. 175	© Restored Traditions. Used by permission.
P. 177	Christ and the Woman Taken in Adultery by Brueghel © Restored Traditions. Used by permission.
P. 178	Stained glass window depicting Moses showing the Stone Tablets with the Ten Commandments. This window is located in Saint James's Church in Stockholm, capital of Sweden. It was fabricated in 1893. © jorisvo/shutterstock.com
P. 179	Lion - egyptian basrelief and hieroglyphs in Karnak temple, Luxor, Egypt. © Chris102/shutterstock.com
P. 181	Silhouette of father and son holding hands at sunset. © NadyaEugene/shutterstock.com
P. 183	Young man praying to God during sunset by the sea. © Dream Perfection/shutterstock.com
P. 184	Skinny arms and hands of a very old woman lying in a bed. © Nielskliim/shutterstock.com
P. 186	Close up of African father and daughter hugging. © Blend Images/shutterstock.com
P. 187	Freedom travel man bible peace good inspire in morning. Christian prayer stand worship God in easter day concept vision to success financial, motivated energy self confident, reborn wellbeing summer. © Art Stocker/shutterstock.com
P. 188	© Restored Traditions. Used by permission.
P. 190	Silhouette of Jesus Christ crucifix on cross over sunset and blue sky. © Poh Smith/shutterstock.com
P. 192 (left)	Public Domain.
P. 192 (right)	Public Domain.
P. 194	© Restored Traditions. Used by permission.
P. 196	© Restored Traditions. Used by permission.
P. 197	Open pages of bible isolated on white background. © Lane V. Erickson/shutterstock.com
P. 198	Celtic trinity knot. © Lane V. TotemArt/shutterstock.com
P. 200	Crucifixion of Jesus Christ by Murillo © Restored Traditions. Used by permission.
P. 201	Statue of Saint Peter in Vatican. © josefkubes/shutterstock.com
P. 202	A man making a confession to the cross. © Creative Images/shutterstock.com
P. 203	Christ washing St. Peter's feet by Boccaccino © Restored Traditions. Used by permission.
P. 205	Sister Friendship. © Rawpixel/shutterstock.com
P. 207	Silhouette of christian raising hands while praying to the Jesus. © Creative Images/shutterstock.com
P. 208	Cross on sunset background . © winui/shutterstock.com

P. 210	Mosaic of the institution of the Eucharist at the last supper by Jesus. © Adam Jan Figel/shutterstock.com
P. 212	Groom and bride in church with priest performing eucharist. © IVASHstudio/shutterstock.com
P. 213	Public Domain.
P .214	Moses and Jews Gathering the Manna in the Desert by Mattia Bortoloni (1749 - 1751). © Renata Sedmakova/shutterstock.com
P. 215	View of the promised land as seen from Mount Nebo in Jordan. © CCinar/shutterstock.com
P. 217	Ancient mosaic inside the Church of the Multiplication of the Loaves and the Fishes, Tabgha, Israel . © Mihai-Bogdan Lazar/shutterstock.com
P. 219	Last Supper in Missale Romanum by unknown artist © Renata Sedmakova/shutterstock.com
P. 220	He wept over it by Simonet. Public Domain.
P. 222	Sacrament of communion, eucharist symbol © Sebastian Duda/shutterstock.com
P. 223	Jesus Discourses with His Disciples by Tissot. © Restored Traditions. Used by permission.
P. 224	Stained glass depicting Jesus holding a lamb. © CURAphotography/shutterstock.com
P. 225	Holy eucharist. © MarioA/shutterstock.com
P. 226	In church Monasterio de la Cartuja with St. Bruno and glory of Eucharist by Palomino (early 18. cent.) © Renata Sedmakova /shutterstock.com
P. 228	Priests enter San Firenze Church holding a high cross. © Francesco Cantone/shutterstock.com
P. 230	Polycarp before the Roman Proconsul - Illustration © whitemay/iStock.com
P. 232	© Restored Traditions. Used by permission.
P. 234	© Restored Traditions. Used by permission.
P. 235	© Restored Traditions. Used by permission.
P. 237	© Restored Traditions. Used by permission.
P. 238	Feeding the poor. © addkm/shutterstock.com
P. 240	Crucifix, Jesus on the cross in church © thanasus/shutterstock.com
P. 241	Holy communion. © Cavee/shutterstock.com
P. 242	© Restored Traditions. Used by permission.
P. 243	Public Domain.
P. 244	© Restored Traditions. Used by permission.
P. 246	Teen girl reading the Bible outdoors at sunset time. © photo.ua/shutterstock.com
P. 249	Public Domain.
P. 252	© Restored Traditions. Used by permission.
P. 253	Used with permission by the photographer Dnalor_01, Wikimedia Commons, and the license CC-by-SA3.0
P. 255	Public Domain.
P. 256	© Augustine Institute. Used by permission.
P. 258	This image was originally posted to Flickr, was uploaded to computers by using Flickrbot on 3 April, 2010, by Gun Powder MA.
P. 259	London, British Library, MS Cotton Nero D IV, f. 137v. http://www.bl.uk/manuscripts/FullDisplay.aspx?ref=Cotton_MS_Nero_D_IV
P.260	Woman reading and praying over Bible © Jantanee Runpranomkom/shutterstock.com
P. 262	Public Domain.
P. 264	Woman standing in church. © Rawpixel/shutterstock.com
P. 266	Constantine Basilica in Trier, Germany © Vytautas Kielaitis/shutterstock.com
P. 268	Hebrew plaque with the first words of the Shema prayer © Spiroview Inc/shutterstock.com
P. 269	Pope Francis greets the pilgrims during his weekly general audience in St Peter's square © Giulio napolitano/shutterstock.com
P. 270	Public Domain.
P. 271	Public Domain.
P. 272	Exile of Athanasius of St. Alexandria. © Sergey Kohl/shutterstock.com
P. 273	Teenage girl with cross on forehead in observance of Ash Wednesday © littlenySTOCK/shutterstock.com
P. 275	Icon depicting the First Council of Nicaea. Public Domain.
P. 276	Public Domain.
P. 277	A girl praying in church © No-Te Eksarunchai/shutterstock.com
P. 278	https://lordalton.files.wordpress.com/2016/12/alfred-delp-on-trial.jpg?w=676
P. 280	Young African man listening and dancing to music with earphones © Damir Khabirov/shutterstock.com
P. 281	Ripples on water surface. © Dudarev Mikhail/shutterstock.com
P. 282	Oil painting of Jesus Christ and his disciples on a meadow © Comaniciu Dan/shutterstock.com

Images in this book marked "Public Domain" consist of content the Augustine Institute believes are in the public domain in most territories. Content marked "Public Domain" indicates that the Augustine Institute is unaware of any current copyright restrictions on the Content either because: (i) the term of copyright has expired in most countries or: (ii) no evidence has been found that copyright restrictions apply.

The Augustine Institute has made every reasonable effort to locate, contact and acknowledge rights holders and to correctly apply terms and conditions to Content. In the event that any Content infringes your rights or the rights of any third parties, or Content is not properly identified or acknowledged we would like to hear from you so we may make any necessary alterations. In this event contact: WhyBelieve@AugustineInstitute.org